Da   Due

Music in New York during the American Revolution

MLA Index and Bibliography Series, Number 24
Robert Michael Fling, Editor

Overleaf

Page from Rivington's *Gazette* showing
"A List of Musick sold by James Rivington"

Music in New York During the American Revolution: An Inventory of Musical References in *Rivington's New York Gazette*

By Gillian B. Anderson

With the editorial assistance of Neil Ratliff

MLA Index and Bibliography Series
Number 24

Boston
Music Library Association, Inc.

Library of Congress Cataloging-in-Publication Data

Anderson, Gillian B., 1943-
   Music in New York during the American Revolution.

   (MLA index and bibliography series ; 24)
   Bibliography: p.
   1. Music--New York (N.Y.)--18th century--History and
criticism--Periodicals--Indexes. 2. Rivington's New-York
gazette, and universal advertiser--Indexes. I. Ratliff,
Neil. II. Title. III. Series.
ML200.8.N5A7   1987   780'.9747'1   87-7840
ISBN   0-914954-33-4

MLA Index and Bibliography Series Number 24

ISBN: 0-914954-33-4
ISSN: 0094-6478

Music Library Association, Inc.
P.O. Box 487
Canton, MA   02021

11-9-8?

CONTENTS

PREFACE

While collecting song texts for my book *Freedom's voice in poetry and song*, I noticed a large number of references to music in Rivington's *Gazette*, a New York newspaper published between 1773 and 1783. I made a mental note that I should return to Rivington's paper when I had more time, and I copied down some of the larger advertisements of musical works for sale. In retrospect, I realize that even from this first cursory look, I had received an impression about the nature of Anglo-American musical life in the eighteenth century. Subsequently, I used some of the works listed in Rivington in performances by the Colonial Singers and Players, and some of the information in my performing edition of Francis Hopkinson's *The Temple of Minerva*. Clearly, if I had found the information useful for performance and scholarship, others might also, so I returned to Rivington's paper in 1977 and collected every musical reference I could find. I submitted the raw data to the Music Library Association Publications Committee with the questions, "Would you be interested in publishing this?" and "How should I organize it?" I would like to express my thanks to the members of that Publications Committee, particularly to John Tanno, Linda Solow Blotner and Lenore Coral, who received the original inchoate version of this inventory a decade ago. Patiently, they began to educate me in the intricacies of indexing, but the process of education reached an intense level when Neil Ratliff was assigned the task of bringing this work to its final form. I am grateful to Neil, not just for his patience and his ability to convey often complex concepts simply (so I could use them thereafter in the inventory), but especially for his gift as an editor of prose. I also wish to thank Daniel Preston for his help concerning the history of New York, and my husband, Gordon Wood Anderson, who has heard entirely too much about this whole subject but whose insight, forthrightness, and editorial abilities are so great that they begged to be used. Finally, I would like to thank Michael Fling, whose superb technical and editorial assistance brought our work to a handsome looking, more nearly perfect, and slimmer end.

Gillian B. Anderson
Washington, DC
June, 1987

INTRODUCTION

The present work presents documentation for almost a decade of musical life in New York City. It is an inventory of all references to music, musicians, musical instruments, and musical events found in James Rivington's New York newspaper between 1773 and 1783. It supplements the documentation provided by other scholars, and thus it should be useful to historians interested in musical instruments, dance and theater, as well as social history, English and American music.[1] It should also be useful to compilers of family history. Popular music composer Frank Zappa, for example, used this inventory to discover that music by a relative, Francesco Zappa, had been advertised for sale in New York in 1779 and 1780. In addition, the inventory helps us to construct a hypothetical picture of the eighteenth-century musical patterns in relation to which all of New York's subsequent musical life must have developed.

---

1. The inventory supplements the information reported by Oscar Sonneck, *Early concert-life in America, 1731-1800* (Leipzig: Breitkopf & Härtel, 1907). (A number of Rivington's advertisements were not available to Sonneck, but he found similar information in *The New York Mercury*); Rita Sussman Gottesman, *The arts and crafts in New York, 1726-1799*, 2 vols. (New York: The New York Historical Society, 1938, 1954). (This work contains excerpts from a number of other New York newspapers which apparently were directed at different political and social groups. Thus, their information was sometimes quite different from that found in Rivington. See references to drum makers Daniel and Philip Pelton, organ and spinnet maker John Sheybli, fife and drum maker David Woolhaupter and music teachers John S. Slaiffer and Mr. Webster, Vol. 1, pp.366-67, and Vol. 2, pp.369-71); Kenneth Scott, *Rivington's New York newspaper: Excerpts from a Loyalist press, 1773-1783* (New York: The New York Historical Society, 1973). (For genealogical purposes this publication selectively indexed Rivington's newspaper for names of New York residents. Thus, advertisements for commodities like music and musical instruments are not indexed, whereas performers and salesmen are.) Gillian B. Anderson, *Freedom's voice in poetry and song*, Part I: *An inventory of political and patriotic lyrics in colonial American newspapers, 1773-1783*, Part II: *Songbook* (Wilmington, DE: Scholarly Resources, 1977); Kenneth Silverman, *A cultural history of the American Revolution: Painting, music, literature, and the theatre in the colonies and the United States from the Treaty of Paris to the inauguration of George Washington, 1763-1789* (New York: Thomas Y. Crowell Co., 1976); Ora Frishberg Saloman, "Victor Pelissier, composer in federal New York and Philadelphia," *The Pennsylvania magazine of history and biography* 102 (1978): 93-102; George G. Raddin, Jr., "The music of New York City, 1797-1804," *The New York Historical Society quarterly* 38/4 (October 1954): 478-99; Virginia Larkin Redway, *Music directory of early New York City* (New York: The New York Public Library, 1941).

Today, New York City is one of the largest metropolitan areas in the world and one of the three major entertainment centers in the United States. During the American Revolution, however, its population was dwarfed by that of London, and exceeded by that of Philadelphia.[2] Although the number and variety of New York's musical activities were comparable to those of Boston and Philadelphia, its musical institutions had not yet produced a native American composer.[3]

New York's progress from a town smaller and musically less prominent than Philadelphia to its current international status was caused by a fascinating confluence of historical events, social attitudes and musical traditions. In the eighteenth century the single most important event was the British occupation of the city during the American Revolution. From 1776 to 1783 the traditional trade patterns which had focused on Philadelphia were rerouted to New York. The disruption went on for long enough to change these patterns irrevocably. Philadelphia never recovered, and by 1790 New York's population had surpassed that of Philadelphia.[4] Throughout the next two-hundred years wave upon wave of immigrants altered the character of the population, bringing new customs and traditions.

These and many other factors affected New York's musical life. Yet most traditions, once established, are durable, conservative, and resistant to change. A natural disaster, catastrophe, or far-reaching technological development might destroy a city's economic base and eventually its traditions. Barring such a cataclysm, we would expect eighteenth-century musical traditions to grow and alter, as they clearly did in New York, but also to contain a continuous thread. What musical patterns were set by the eighteenth-century English and Dutch residents of New York? It is for an answer to this question that we turn to Rivington's *Gazette*.

From April 1773 to November 1775, Rivington's weekly paper was called *Rivington's New-York gazetteer*. After a 22-month hiatus it resumed publication under the titles *Rivington's New-York gazette* (October 1777), *Rivington's New-York loyal gazette* (October-December 1777), *Royal gazette* (December 1777-November 1783), and finally *Rivington's New-York gazette, and universal advertiser* (November-December 1783). Henceforth, it will be referred to as Rivington's *Gazette*.[5]

---

2. New York had 21,000 to 28,000 people, London 600,000 to 1,000,000, Philadelphia 23,700 in 1773.

3. Congregational singing schools and radical Whigs had nurtured William Billings in Boston. The University of Pennsylvania, Christ Church and the Franklin/Bache family circle had nurtured Francis Hopkinson in Philadelphia. As I have heard Richard Crawford point out in an unpublished paper delivered at the Baltimore meeting of the Sonneck Society, March 1980, most of the other native-born American composers, at least in the parish church tradition, were the products of small towns.

4. 49,401 as compared to 28,522 according to census reports.

5. Rivington's *Gazette* is available in microform from Readex Microprint Corporation in its series *Early American newspapers*.

James Rivington (1724-1802) was an English book dealer and printer who came to America in 1760. In 1773 he began publishing his weekly newspaper, and his print shop soon became the "crossroads of New York's social and cultural life."[6] Among other things the paper was a convenient vehicle for the advertisement of his own merchandise, which included music, musical instruments, and their accessories. He was one of a number of colonial bookdealers and printers who found it profitable "to keep on hand a large variety of imported music."[7] Eventually he sided with those loyal to the British, although there is evidence that he served the American rebels as a paid double agent. In 1775 his press was destroyed by the rebels, and he went back to England. Fifteen months later he returned to New York, where, subsidized by the British government, he resumed the publication of his newspaper. The evacuation of the British armed forces in 1783 left Rivington exposed to the hostility of their opponents, and he ceased publication at the end of 1783.

From 1773 to 1783 the profile of musical life reflected in Rivington's *Gazette* resembled that of other predominantly English-speaking provincial towns in the British Empire.[8] Music played a part in most aspects of life and served all classes of society. Native composers (English or American) were active primarily in the theater and parish churches. Concert music, either public or private, was dominated by Italian and German composers.

The *Gazette* reflected a wide range of musical activities. For example, there were reports of dancing assemblies and concerts organized by and for the black residents of New York City (19 January 1782; p.2, col.1). One advertisement promised the performance of "God save the King" every hour on the hour at the racetrack (11 November 1780; p.2, col.3). There were notices from instrument repairmen, instrument builders, dancing masters, music teachers, tavern owners, concert managers, theater managers and slave owners. They advertised musical services for hire, musical events, and even the musical accomplishments of escaped slaves. Almost every weekly issue contained the printed lyric of a song. One help-wanted advertisement requested the services of an entire woodwind octet for performance aboard the *General Pattison*, a private warship (14 April 1779; p.2, col.4).

---

6. Silverman, *A cultural history of the American Revolution*, p.372. For additional information see Leroy Hewlett, "James Rivington, royalist printer, publisher, and bookseller of the American Revolution, 1724-1802" (PhD dissertation, University of Michigan, 1958); and Catherine Snell Crary, "The Tory and the spy: The double life of James Rivington," *William and Mary quarterly*, 3rd series, 16 (January 1959): 61-72.

7. Silverman, *A cultural history of the American Revolution*, p.184

8. David Johnson, *Music and society in lowland Scotland in the eighteenth century* (London: Oxford University Press, 1972); T.J. Walsh, *Opera in Dublin, 1705-1797: The social scene* (Dublin: Allaen Figgis, 1973); Stanley Sadie, "Concert life in eighteenth-century England," *Proceedings of the Royal Musical Association* 85 (1958-59): 17-30; Michael Tilmouth, "The beginnings of provincial concert life," *Music in eighteenth-century England: Essays in memory of Charles Cudworth*, ed. by Christopher Hogwood and Richard Luckett (Cambridge: Cambridge University Press, 1983).

In addition to covering musically newsworthy events and to including notices and advertisements paid for by others, Rivington published a number of his own advertisements. In two or three columns of tiny type across half the twelve-inch page and down its eighteen-inch length, he offered to sell a full selection of music, musical instruments and musical accessories (see Frontispiece). Rarely did he identify the first names of composers or use the actual titles of publications.[9] Often the advertisement was in a sort of shorthand, for example, "OVERTURES Abel's Bach's Richter's 3d sett. . . ." Often the same advertisement appeared a number of times, but never did it contain updated information ("sold out" would have been useful).

Statistics tell a more detailed story about the range and variety of items advertised or reported in the newspaper. Exclusive of instrumental tutors and songs,[10] works by over 170 composers were listed for sale or announced for performance--often more than once. Of these works 324 were specified by name and 74 were referred to simply as "works". Seventy-one anonymous works also were listed or announced.[11] Sixty-three operas, pantomimes or

---

9. Full names have been supplied in the inventory. The Rivington titles have been supplied, followed by the presumed actual titles of the works they refer to. As the identification process involved considerable guesswork, all the supplied information must be regarded as tentative. It follows that all conclusions based on the data must be regarded similarly.

10. Tutors for most musical instruments were offered for sale but rarely were specific titles mentioned. Although a number of songs or tunes were named in the paper, more often the advertisements read "Great number of single songs adapted to the various humours and affections of the mind" (4 October 1777; p.4, col.2) or "Set to music, a vast variety of modern songs" (22 November 1777; p.2, col.4).

11. ANONYMOUS WORKS: Abbot of Canterbury, or Wilkes's wriggle; Ailen a roon; American robin; Away to the copse; The banks of the Dee; Black sloven; Bucks have at ye all; The bullfinch; The butterfly; By the gayly circling glass; The captive; A collection of Scotch songs; A collection of Scots songs; The convivial songster; The cut-purse; Derry down; The devil to pay; Doodle-doo; Elegant extracts; The entered apprentices song; Essex Orpheus; The Free Masons pocket book; Free Mason's song; God save the King; God save the King with variations; The golden pippin; Gramachree Molly; Hey! my kitten, my kitten; Hob in the wall [sic]; Hymns and songs sung at the Magdalen for guitar; If 'tis joy to wound a lover; If you can caper as well as you can modulate; Jockey to the fair; The ladle; The lark's shrill notes; Lillies of France; The London songster; Lovely nymph with variations; Lumps of pudding; A Mason's anthem; Medley for the light infantry; Midas; The minstrel; The mock doctor; The muses mirror; New golden pippin; New merry companion; Nottingham ale; O mother dear Jerusalem; Over the hills and far away; The roundelay; St. Cecilia's songs; Saw you my father; Shakespeare's ode; Smile Britannia; Songs naval and military; The songster's companion; There's nae luck about the house; Through the wood laddie; To thee oh! gentle sleep; 12 Canzonetts; Twelve lessons for the guitar; Twelve new songs and a cantata

plays with incidental music were either offered for sale or performed-- twelve by composer Charles Dibdin alone. Thirty-three songs were advertised or performed. Ninety-one song lyrics or poems were printed, and the names of twenty-eight tunes to which the lyrics were to be sung were mentioned.[12] Perhaps most surprising, thirty-three musical instruments, their accessories, and instruction books were advertised for sale between 1773 and 1783. Thirty-two notices advertised individual concerts or concert series. Thirty-seven notices advertised balls, dances, minuets, or dancing in general. Five notices appeared offering the sale or performance of catches and glees. Nine mentioned bands, and eight advertised collections of "Scotch" songs. Only twelve notices concerned the sale or performance of sacred music.

Almost all the music was contemporary (only twelve of the composers were born before 1700!; see Summary of Musical Works Cited on page xxii). Many of the pieces advertised in Rivington's *Gazette* were being advertised in publishers' catalogues in London during the same period.[13] Forty-three of the same works appear in Thomas Jefferson's music catalogue of 1783,[14] but surprisingly, none of the works appears among the publications in Francis Hopkinson's estate which is located in the University of Pennsylvania Rare Book Library.

Music for small ensembles predominated, probably because there was a larger market for such works, and, on the whole, the chamber music was geared toward players with beginning and intermediate skills. However, the proportionally higher percentage of advanced compositions in the Jefferson and Hopkinson music libraries proves that more sophisticated kinds of performance skills did exist. In Rivington's *Gazette* there was more chamber music by Italian and German composers than by native English composers, although the

---

for guitar; 24 country dances; 24 Italian and Spanish minuets; Vicar of Bray; Vocal music or songster's companion; The watry god; Watt's hymns; Would you have a young virgin of fifteen years; Yankee doodle.

12. Bagpipe, barrel-organ, bassoon, bugle horns, clarinet, classado, cornet, drum, English or common flute, fiddle, tenor fiddle, fife, flute, French horn, German flute, glassado, guitar, harp, harpsichord, hautboy, hunting horn, organ, pastorale, piano forte or forte piano, spinnet, sticcado, sticcado pastorale, tabors and pipes, trumpet, violin, tenor violin, violoncello and Welsh harp.

13. For example, 196 of the same pieces were advertised by Longman and Broderip in 1779; 151 by John Welcker; 67 by Peter Welcker in 1772(?); 46 by Longman, Lukey and Co. in 1772; 17 by Longman and Co. in 1769; 41 pieces by Samuel, Ann, and Peter Thompson in 1781; 42 pieces by the same firm in an undated catalogue; 21 by Elizabeth Randall in 1782(?). Citations for these publishers' catalogues, with Library of Congress call numbers, are included in the Bibliography.

14. Helen Cripe, *Thomas Jefferson and music* (Charlottesville: University Press of Virginia, 1974), pp.97-104.

theater music of the latter predominated over the former.[15]   Only three
American and six French composers' works were advertised or mentioned.[16]

In sum, the musical activities reflected in Rivington's *Gazette* more or less
conformed to the pattern of any provincial town in England.   This conformity
raises the question of how the British occupation (1776-1783) affected the
musical profile reflected in Rivington's *Gazette*.   Clearly, music making
continued unabated in spite of the American Revolution.   Students continued to
learn how to play new instruments.   Customers continued to buy instructional
pieces and to purchase and play chamber music.

---

15. The statistics from Rivington's *Gazette* are as follows:

	Italian	German	English	French	American	Unknown	Totals
Unspecified	2	4	5	1	0	14	26
Chamber Music	50	84	16	5	0	34	189
Teaching Pieces	15	6	6	0	0	8	35
Theater Music	1	0	53	1	2?*	0	57
Guitar Music	1	3	12	0	0	8	24
Sacred Music	0	2	5	0	2	0	9

These figures are extracted from the Summary of Musical Works Cited, p.xxii.
*Francis Hopkinson's "Oratorial Entertainment" and its Loyalist parody.

16. Of the 174 composers, I was unable to identify 59 (34%).   Thus, any
conclusions based on the following data should be made tentatively.   Of the
115 composers that were identified, the statistical breakdown is as follows:

Irish, English, Scottish:	42
Dutch, German, Austrian, Bohemian:	35
French:	6
Italian:	32
American (Amos Bull, Francis Hopkinson, James Lyon)**:	3
Foreigners who worked in London:	34
Born before 1700 (Corelli, Croft, Geminiani, Greene, Handel, Hasse,:	12

Leveridge, MacGibbon, D. Purcell, Quantz, Giuseppe Sammartini,
Tartini)

**James Lyon's *Urania* was advertised (16 December 1773; p.3, col.4); Amos
Bull advertised a singing school (24 November 1774; p.1, col.3); the words to
Hopkinson's "In memory of James Bremner" and *The Temple of Minerva* were
printed (28 February 1781; p.3, col.3, and 5 January 1782; p.2, col.1,
respectively).   "In memory of James Bremner" appeared only in Rivington's
Gazette.   This is rather surprising because, along with Hopkinson's *Temple of
Minerva*, Rivington published an offensive, scatalogical parody.   The music for
the Bremner memorial piece only existed in manuscript, a version of which has
just shown up in an eighteenth-century American manuscript which is still in
private hands.

Rivington advertised more large chamber music pieces after 1776 than before,[17] and he advertised bassoons, clarinets, harps, trumpets, violas and Welsh harps only after 1776. Many composers' works were advertised for the first time only during the British occupation (for example, Haydn, Jommelli, Daniel Purcell, Quantz). Other composers' works were advertised before and during the occupation (for example, T.A. Arne, C.P.E. and J.C. Bach, Boccherini, Dibdin, Geminiani, Giardini, Giordani, Hook, Martini, Stamitz). Few were advertised only before (for example, Lord Kelly and Piccinni). We can never know what might have happened had the British not occupied New York, nor can we know how many of the same composers' works would have been advertised after 1776 had the Revolution not occurred. We can say that during the British occupation public concert and theater life was at least as strong as, if not stronger than, it had been before 1776. This situation was not true in the other colonial cities at the same time.[18] One might hypothesize that the tastes of British General Henry Clinton (ca.1738-1795), the presence of British military bandsmen, and the stability brought by the occupying forces were partly responsible. General Clinton's "principal activity, to judge by his account books, was not military but musical."[19]

> During the occupation of Boston in 1775, he [Clinton] gave concerts in which he performed on the violin, one of several fiddles and bass viols he seems to have carried with him. In New York he maintained an amateur orchestra of violin, cello, and flute, and spent almost £50 on sheet music alone. He employed the printer James Rivington to bind some 27 volumes of concerti, quartets, and symphonies by Bach, Haydn, Boccherini, and others.[20]

Clinton may have brought skilled musicians with him. They in turn may have created a larger market for more demanding works that was reflected in Rivington's advertisements.

---

17. One symphony and one concerto were performed or advertised before the occupation; four symphonies, sixteen concertos and seven overtures during the occupation.

18. Music making continued in other cities but not at the level attained before the war. Francis Hopkinson in Philadelphia performed several times at the home of the French Ambassador, the Chevalier de la Luzerne. See Gillian B. Anderson, "'The Temple of Minerva' and Francis Hopkinson: A reappraisal of America's first poet-composer," *Proceedings of the American Philosophical Society* 120/3 (June 1976): 166-77. In Boston, William Billings actually may have had more opportunities to perform publicly because of the war and his alliance with the radical Whigs Samuel Cooper and Samuel Adams, but the overall quantity and variety of musical activities in Boston were probably fewer than before the war. Gillian B. Anderson, "Eighteenth-century evaluations of William Billings: A reappraisal," *Quarterly journal of the Library of Congress* 35/1 (January 1978): 48-58.

19. William B. Wilcox, *Portrait of a General: Sir Henry Clinton in the War of Independence* (New York, 1964), p.61, quoted in Silverman, *A cultural history of the American Revolution*, p.371.

20. Silverman, *Ibid.*

Fifty-three of the composers whose names have been included in this inventory were listed only once in Rivington's *Gazette*. They appeared in one very large advertisement, published twenty times in 1779 and 1780. Fifty-three composers out of 174 is a large percentage (30%), and it should remind us that the information in the *Gazette* is statistically a very small sampling. The paper only came out once a week (twice a week toward the end of the war). It was four pages long. The town had no more than 28,000 people. Since the presence of a single advertisement significantly changes the musical profile reflected in the newspaper, we should be hesitant about making any hard and fast conclusions based on this information alone. In addition, I may have missed a number of musical references, for peering at tiny eighteenth-century type for extended periods can induce a form of mental trance.[21]

The information in Rivington's *Gazette* may reflect only the fact of the British occupation and also may be a statistically insufficient sampling from which to generalize, but in Rivington's *Gazette* we find a wealth of musical minutiae which has just been summarized. Information in other newspapers (patriot and loyalist) and in other types of material (broadsides, prefaces to printed music books, literary and musical manuscripts) no doubt would fill out the picture. However, the musical life reflected in the *Gazette* appears to be continuous with that in other cities of the English-speaking part of the Empire. Foreign composers dominated the chamber music world (in America the English soon functioned as foreigners). Native-born composers dominated the country or parish church. Native-born English composers dominated the theater. In England a small number of native-born composers received a cultivated musical education and composed professionally for the cathedral and the court. In England there was also Italian opera. There is no evidence of such professional-level training in New York in Rivington's *Gazette*, and Italian opera was limited to Piccinni's *La buona figliuola* (22 November 1777; p.1, col.4).

Composers were trained and nurtured by institutions in a number of provincial cities of America as well as Britain, but not in New York City. In fact, until well past the American Revolution, New York produced no native-born composer. This circumstance may not be important because all the provincial composers were composing clearly within the English musical

---

21. Recently, while looking for a frontispiece for this inventory, I serendipitously found the following advertisement which I had missed:

The Printer being employed at the desire of many gentlemen, in compiling a collection of navy, military and constitutional songs, and being in want of the following, begs the favor of any gentlemen, possessed of the words to oblige him as soon as possible, with copies of them: Genius of England, Sing all ye muses, H. Purcell. Grog is the liquor of life, Harry Greene. The soldier who danger and death doth despise. Hot stuff. Col. Hale, 47th. (20 January 1779; p.3, col.1).

Undoubtedly, I missed others as well.

traditions,[22] and there were precious few of them anyway. However, as elsewhere in the Empire, New York's institutions might have been expected to cultivate the compositional gifts of at least one talented native-born musician in a century--unless there were attitudes which worked against it.

Since the 1740s, New York's Trinity Church had employed an English organist. It had a strong tradition of supporting music, and in 1753, in order to improve the church choir, William Tuckey undertook the musical education of the children in the Charity School which was closely associated with Trinity Church.[23] Yet, unlike the Congregational singing schools in New England, no composer appears to have been nurtured by the musical training of children at the Charity School. Nor did such training appear to produce an organist with the skills of a Francis Hopkinson, who played at Christ Church in Philadelphia. Similarly, unlike the University of Pennsylvania, Princeton, or Yale, King's College (now Columbia University) appears to have played no part in nurturing the skills of a budding composer.

In England some members of the aristocracy had such an antipathy toward music that they felt it should only be the province of foreigners and the lower class. Their feeling was that sane, upstanding Englishmen did not indulge in such frivolity. (Genteel members of society, particularly the female ones, were not supposed to sing in public either, even in church).[24] Clearly, however, other genteel amateurs spent many years learning how to play musical instruments and supporting the market for chamber music. This interest waned in the mid-1780s.

> Various social changes had a general adverse effect on classical music all over Britain at this time. The aristocracy rather suddenly became less willing to spend years and years learning to play instruments thoroughly, and town-life extended further and further into the small hours, making concert-going seem rather a tame way of spending the evening.[25]

---

22. Nicholas Temperley has suggested that Billings, while perhaps the most gifted composer in the eighteenth-century Anglo-American psalmody tradition, was writing fuging tunes that were actually closer to the English than American model. Nicholas Temperley and Charles Manns, *Fuging tunes in the eighteenth century* (Detroit: Information Coordinators, 1983).

23. Sonneck, *Early concert life in America*, pp.160-61. Arthur Messiter, *A history of the choir and music of Trinity Church, New York, from its organization to the year 1897* (New York: Edwin S. Gorham, 1906). The teaching of psalmody to the children of the Charity School was advertised in Rivington's *Gazette* (25 October 1783; p.3, col.2).

24. Anderson, "Eighteenth-century evaluations of William Billings."

25. Johnson, *Music and society in lowland Scotland in the eighteenth century*, pp.40-41.

Oscar Sonneck noticed a parallel stagnation in the interest taken in concerts in the United States.[26] During the British occupation of New York, however, the interest in chamber music was still very strong, at least among Rivington's subscribers.

Perhaps New York's gentility had some negative attitudes about financially supporting the training of composers. Had the city's inhabitants been mainly English, one might have said that the city picked up only the English predilection for musical imports without also acquiring their support for the training of native-born composers in the theater or parish church. The truth is we do not know why New York went without a native-born composer for over one-hundred years.

In the eighteenth century the concept of the "new world" carried with it an expectation that something new would happen here--in all fields of endeavour.[27] As an idea, this expectation had an intellectual reality. Some of the European settlers of America expected to establish the promised land in the wilderness. Because they expected it, to a certain extent, something promising did happen--from *Sacred Harp* singing to a new form of government to the American dream. But the settlers also brought to the new world many of their old attitudes, habits and customs, and musical life in New York City during the American Revolution is a perfect example. Unlike the old world, however, or even other provincial cities in the new world, New York did not have institutions--churches, schools, theaters--which trained native-born composers. Probably, because of its old-world traditions, the Anglo-Saxon community in America did not produce a uniquely American music until the nineteenth century, and then it happened first in country churches, just as one might have predicted based on the profile of eighteenth-century English musical life.

Based on the profile in Rivington's *Gazette*, however, not many of us would have predicted that in the twentieth century some uniquely American music would dominate the popular musical life of the rest of the world. Nor could we have expected that accomplished American art music composers would eventually populate the American landscape. Nor could we have known that most of the art music performed in this country in the twentieth century would be by dead composers (long dead composers at that). These developments must have been the result of the growth and alteration of the English musical tradition after 1783.

---

26. Sonneck, *Early concert life in America*, p.325.
27. The following books contain detailed discussions of the concept of the new world and the expectations that arose from it. Daniel J. Boorstin, *The Americans: The colonial experience* (New York: Random House, 1958); Howard Mumford Jones, *O strange new world: American culture, the formative years* (New York: Viking Press, 1964); Henry Nash Smith, *Virgin land: The American West as symbol and myth* (New York: Vintage Books, 1950); George Rogers Taylor, *The Turner Thesis concerning the role of the frontier in American history*, rev. ed. (Boston: D.C. Heath and Co., 1956); John Winthrop, "A model of Christian charity," *The American Puritans: Their prose and poetry*, ed. by Perry Miller (Garden City, NY: Doubleday Anchor Books, 1956), p.78-83.

Still, English musical life seems to have left an indelible impression on the American tradition and to have influenced subsequent developments. In New York, however, the full range of eighteenth-century English habits and attitudes toward music was not present. The preference for imports ruled to the exclusion of everything else, and this preference perhaps is the continuous thread that ties the eighteenth-, nineteenth-, and twentieth-century musical traditions of New York together. Ironically, the relish for and gathering together in New York of musical traditions from all over the world may have created the opportunity for the development of the "something uniquely new" that had been hoped for in the new world.

New York was well on its way to becoming the largest city in this country after the American Revolution. Its musical traditions seem to have made it both extremely open to the efforts of foreign composers and performers and resistant to the training of native-born composers. If the information in Rivington's *Gazette* is not too distorted by the influence of the British occupying forces and by James Rivington's Loyalist sympathies, it supports this statement.

In this introduction, I have described and summarized the types of information presented in the inventory of music, musicians, musical instruments and musical events in Rivington's *Gazette*. I have compared Rivington's New York musical life to that in other colonial and provincial English cities and in London. I have speculated about how and why New York's portrait seems to resemble and differ from the musical picture in those other places. The speculation has been fun, but the truth is that the sampling is entirely too small to be conclusive. Much more information is needed before we can decide whether New York's traditions really differed from those of other places, and, if they did, why. In the meantime, this inventory will be of use to a wide range of people, from scholars in search of information about itinerant musicians, to performers who might wish to perform music from New York's Revolutionary War past.

SUMMARY OF MUSICAL WORKS CITED

C = Chamber, solo or orchestral music
E = Teaching pieces (Lessons, duets for same instruments)
G = Guitar music
S = Sacred music
T = Theater music
W = Unspecified, generic "works"

Dates of Advertisement	Composer	Nationality (* = worked in England)	Number of Works	Type of Music
79-80	Abel, Carl Freidrich (1723-1787)	German*	3	CW
79-80	Agazzi, Gaetano		1	C
79-80	Agus, Giuseppe (ca.1725-ca.1800)	Italian*	2	CW
73;77	Alcock, John, Doctor (1715-1806)	English	2	EG
73;79	Alcock, John, the Younger (1740-1791)	English	2	CG
79-80	Alexander, B.		3	CW
73-4;77;80	Arne, Michael (ca.1740-1786)	English	4	T
73;77-83	Arne, Thomas Augustine (1710-1778)	English	16	GT
73;77;82	Arnold, Samuel (1740-1802)	English	3	GT
79-80	Aspelmayer, Franz (1728-1786)	Austrian	1	C
79-80	Avolio, J.		1	E
73-4;77;79-80	Bach, Carl Philipp Emanuel (1714-1788)	German*	5	CE
73-4;77;80;82	Bach, Johann Christian (1735-1782)	German*	19	CEW
79-80	Balentine		1	G
79-80	Barbella, Emanuele (1718-1777)	Italian	2	CW
77;79-80	Barthélémon, François Hippolyte (1741-1808)	French*	2	TC
79	Bartleman, James		1	W
73;77;79-80	Bates, William (ca.1750-ca.1780)	English	2	ET
83	Battishill, Jonathan (1738-1801)	English	1	T
73	Bem, Venceslav		1	C
79	Benzon		1	W
79-80	Bischoff, I.C.		1	C
77;79-80	Blanc		1	E
73	Blanck, Nicholas		1	C
73;77;79-80	Boccherini, Luigi (1743-1805)	Italian	4	CEW
77	Borghese, Antonio D.R. (fl. late 18th cent.)	French (*maybe)	1	C
82	Borghi, Luigi (?1745-ca.1806)	Italian*	1	C
77	Buhler		1	C
83	Camidge, John (1734-1803)	English	1	E
73-4;77;79-80	Campioni, Carlo Antonio (1720-1788)	Italian	11	CEW
79-80	Canaletti, Giovanni Battista		1	C
73;79-80	Cappelletti, Anthonio		1	C
80	Carolina, Signora		1	
82	Carter, Charles Thomas (ca.1735-1804)	Irish*	1	T

Dates of Advertisement	Composer	Nationality (* = worked in England)	Number of Works	Type of Music
79-80	Carter		1	G
79	Chalon, John		1	W
79-80	Chiesa, Melchior (fl.1758-1799)	Italian	2	CW
79-80	Cirri, Giovanni Battista (1724-1808)	Italian*	4	CW
73;79-80	Citracini		2	G
79-80	Cocchi, Gioacchino (ca.1720-1788)	Italian*	1	C
77	Corelli, Arcangelo (1653-1713)	Italian	1	W
79	Cramer, Wilhelm (1746-1799)	German*	1	W
73	Croft, William (1678-1727)	English	1	S
82	Davaux, Jean Baptiste (1742-1822)	French	1	C
77	Davis, Thomas (fl.mid-18th cent.)	English	1	E
79-80	Dezède, Nicolas Alexandre (ca.1740-1792)	French	1	C
73-4;77-9	Dibdin, Charles (1745-1814)	English	14	GT
79-80	Ditters von Dittersdorf, Carl (1739-1799)	Austrian	2	CW
79-80	Drezty		1	C
79	Dupin		1	W
79	Dusty		1	W
77	Eichner, Ernst (1740-1777)	German	1	C
73	Esher		1	C
79-80	Esser, Michel (1737-ca.1795)	German*	1	C
79	Filtz, Anton (1733-1760)	German	1	W
79-80;82	Fischer, Johann Christian (1733-1800)	German*	14	CW
73;77;79-80	Fisher, John Abraham (1744-1806)	English	5	CEGT
73;77	Florio, Pietro Grassi (ca.1740-1795)	Italian*	3	EW
77	Foote		1	C
77	Ford, Miss		1	E
77;79-80	Galeotti, Salvatore or Stefano	Italian*	2	C
79-80	Galuppi, Baldassare (1706-1785)	Italian*	1	C
73;79-80;83	Garth, John (ca.1722-ca.1810)	English	4	CSW
79	Gazardi		1	W
73;77-81	Geminiani, Francesco (1687-1762)	Italian*	4	E
77;79-80	Gerard, James		1	C
79-80	Gerlin		1	G
73;77;79-80	Giardini, Felice (1716-1796)	Italian*	6	CEW
73;77;79-80	Giordani, Tommaso (ca.1733-1806)	Italian*	14	CEW
79	Girandini		1	W
73;77	Graf, Christian Ernst (1723-1804)	German	2	CW
79-80	Graf, Friedrich Hartmann (1727-1795)	German	2	C
79-80	Grassi, Florio		1	C
83	Greene, Maurice (1696-1755)	English	1	S
79-80	Groneman, Johann Albert (ca.1710-1778)	German	1	C
79-80	Guerini, Francesco (fl.1740-1770)	Italian*	2	CW
73;77	Händel, Georg Friedrich (1685-1759)	German*	3	SW
79-80	Hasse, Johann Adolph (1699-1783)	German	1	C
77	Hawdon, Matthias (d.1787)	English	1	C
73	Haxby, R.		1	C
77;79-80;82	Haydn, Franz Joseph (1732-1809)	Austrian	8	CW

Dates of Advertisement	Composer	Nationality (* = worked in England)	Number of Works	Type of Music
79-80	Hayes, Philip (1708-1777 or 1738-1797)	English	1	C
79	Haysard		1	W
77	Heyden		1	W
79	Hickes, George		1	C
73	Holyoak		1	E
79	Honaur, Leontzi (ca.1735-?)	French	1	W
73;79;83	Hook, James (1747-1827)	English	6	TW
81-2	Hopkinson, Francis (1737-1791)	American	3	T
79	Huchall		1	W
77;79-80	Humble, Maximilian		6	CEW
77	Jackson, William (1730-1803)	English	1	C
79-80	Jommelli, Niccolo (1714-1774)	Italian	2	CW
73;77;79-80	Just, Johann August (ca.1750-1791)	German (*maybe)	9	CEW
77;79-80;82	Kammel, Anton (1730-1787)	Bohemian*	8	CEW
73	Kelly, Lord (1732-1781)	Scottish	1	C
79	Kelway, Joseph (ca.1702-1782)	English	1	W
73;77;79-80	Kerntl, C.F.		2	CE
79-80	Klöffler, Johann Friedrich (1725-1790)	German	2	CE
79-80	Kreusser, Georg Anton (1746-1810)	German	1	C
73	A Lady		1	E
80;82	Leveridge, Richard (ca.1670-1758)	English	1	T
77;79-80	Lidarti, Christiano Giuseppe (1730-1793)	Austrian/Italian	1	C
79-80	Lidel, Andreas (d.before 1789)	Austrian*	1	C
77;79-80	Linley, Thomas, the Elder (1733-1795)	English	3	T
73	Lyon, James (1735-1794)	American	1	S
74;77	MacGibbon, William (ca.1690-1756)	Scottish	2	CW
73	Magherini		1	C
79-80;82	Mahon, John (ca.1749-1834)	Irish	3	CW
73;79-80	Maldere, Pierre van (1729-1768)	Dutch	2	C
77;79-80	Mancinelli, Domenico (d.1802)	Italian*	5	CEW
79-80	Meneze		2	G
73	Milgrove		1	G
73;77	Miller, Edward (1735-1807)	English	1	C
73	Myslivecek, Josef (1737-1781)	Bohemian	1	C
79	Nair		1	W
79-80	Nardini, Pietro (1722-1793)	Italian	1	E
82	Nardino		1	C
73;77;79-80	Noferi, Giovanni Battista (fl.1750-1781)	Italian*	5	CEGW
79-80	Nottorne		1	C
79-80	Nussen, Frederick		2	CW
80	Oswald, James (1711-1769)	Scottish	1	T
73	Parry, John (ca.1710-1782)	Welsh	1	C
73	Pasquali, Nicolò (ca.1718-1757)	Italian*	2	E
73	Patoni, Giovanni Battista		1	C
79	Peck, James (fl.18th-early 19th cent.)	English	1	W
79	Pergolesi, Giovanni Battista (1710-1736)	Italian	1	W
79-80	Pesch, Carl August		1	C

Dates of Advertisement	Composer	Nationality (* = worked in England)	Number of Works	Type of Music
79-80	Philidor, François André Danican (1726-1795)	French	1	C
73	Piccinni, Niccolò (1728-1800)	Italian	1	T
77;79-80	Pla, José		4	CW
79-80	Pugnani, Giulio Gaetano (1731-1798)	Italian	2	CW
80;83	Purcell, Daniel (ca.1663-1717)	English	1	T
79	Quantz, Johann Joachim (1697-1773)	German	1	W
79-80	Rambach, F. Xaver Max		2	EW
73;77	Reid, John (1721-1807)	Scottish	2	CW
79-80	Reinards, William		1	E
79-80	Retzel, August Johann		2	CW
79	Rhodit		1	W
79-80	Ricci, Francesco Pasquale (1732-1817)	Italian*	3	C
79-80	Richter, Franz Xaver (1709-1789)	Bohemian	3	CW
79-80	Rodil, Antonio		1	C
79	Rush, George (fl.1760-1780)	English	1	W
79-80	Sabbatini, Luigi Antonio (1732-1809)	Italian	1	E
73	Sammartini, Giovanni Battista (1700/01-1775)	Italian	1	C
79-80	Sammartini, Giuseppe (1693-1751)	Italian*	1	C
77;79-80	Schumann, Friedrich Theodor (fl.1760-1780)	German*	3	CG
73;77;79-80	Schwindl, Friedrich (1737-1786)	Dutch	7	CEW
79	Sharp, Francis		1	W
79-80	Shield, William (1748-1829)	English	3	T
79-80	Sirmen, Maddalena Laura (1735-1785)	Italian	1	C
79-80	Smethergell, William (fl.18th cent.)	English	2	CW
79	Smith		1	W
79-80	Soderini		2	CW
73;79-80	Stamitz, Karl or Johann Wenzel Anton	Bohemian	5	CE
79	Stuart, A.		2	
73-4;77	Tacet, Joseph		4	CW
74	Tans'ur, William (1700-1783)	English	1	S
73;77	Tartini, Giuseppe (1692-1770)	Italian	1	C
77	Taylor, Raynor (1747-1825)	English	1	E
73;77;79-80	Thackray, Thomas (fl.1770-1780)	English	4	G
77	Thumoth, Burk (fl.1739-1750)	Irish	1	C
79;82	Toeschi, Carlo Giuseppi (1731-1788)	German/Italian	3	CW
83	Travers, John (ca.1703-1758)	English	1	T
79-80	Vento, Mattia (1735-1776)	Italian*	2	CW
82-3	Vernon, Joseph (ca.1739-1782)	English	2	T
82	Wanhall, Jan Baptiste (1739-1813)	Bohemian	1	C
79	Warren, Edmund Thomas (ca.1730-1794)	English	1	W
77	Weideman, Charles Frederick (d.1782)	German*	1	W
79-80	Weiss, Carl (ca.1735-1795)	Swiss*	2	CW
77;79-80	Wendling, Johann Baptist (1723-1797)	German*	1	C
74	Williams, Aaron (1731-1776)	English	1	S
79-80	Zappa, Francesco (fl.1763-1788)	Italian	1	C
79	Zapper		1	W
	Total		401	

NOTES TO THE USER

The references in this inventory were taken from advertisements, public notices, literary and news columns. The advertisements listed goods for sale or wanted, and services wanted or available. The public notices announced concerts, dancing assemblies, and theatrical performances. The literary columns contained song lyrics, and New York's musical events were included in the news columns.

In many cases the inventory entries are brief, e.g., "German flutes, to be sold." However, in a number of instances, excerpts from the newspaper copy are quoted more fully. For example:

Biferi, Nicholas, 1739-?.

_____   Music Master from Naples, "informs the young ladies, that he teaches vocal music from the harpsichord, after the best Italian method, at his house on Golden-Hill-Street, formerly occupied by Mr. Crimshire, Attorney at Law, on Tuesdays, Thursdays and Saturdays, in the afternoon, from two o'clock till eight in the evening, on the moderate terms of one pound - his currency for twelve lessons, and ten shillings entrance. --- Those gentlemen and ladies desirous to be attended at home, to pay one pound seventeen shillings. Mr. Biferi enables his pupils in a very short time, to play on the harpsichord, either pieces, sonatas, thorough bass, &c. He also teaches and composes vocal and instrumental music in all its branches. N.B. A very good spinnet to be disposed of, in exceeding good condition, and at a moderate price."
(1 Dec 74) 3/4; (8 Dec 74) 4/1.

The entire advertisement (which was not available to Sonneck) is quoted in the inventory because it contains so much interesting information that a summary could not have done it justice. Full quotations also should benefit those who might not have access to Rivington's original.

In many of the entries, additional information has been supplied in order to make the original references more useful. For example, identified first names and dates of composers have been added. Alternate spellings of names as used in the *Gazette* have been added in parentheses, and cross-references from variant forms of a name are included when necessary. The presumed actual titles of works and their bibliographical citations have been added if they could be identified. Thus, Rivington's advertisement (which appeared 20 times) reads "Overtures . . . Abel's Opera 4 and 14." The inventory entry is constructed as follows:

ABEL, Carl Friedrich, 1723-1787.

_____. Overtures, Opera 4 and 14, to be sold.
   RISM A60: *Six overtures in eight parts for two violins, two hoboys, two French horns, one tenor with a thorough bass for the harpsichord or violoncello . . . Opera 4.* London: Printed for the author . . . by R. Bremner, ca.1780.
   RISM A75: *Six overtures in eight parts; with a thorough bass for the harpsichord, Opera XIV. . . .* London: R. Bremner, for the author, 1778.
   (20-23 Oct 79) 3/3; (3-10 Nov 79) 4/2; (17-20 Nov 79) 4/2; (24 Nov 79) 3/2; (27 Nov - 1 Dec 79) 4/2; (22 Dec 79 - 12 Jan 80) 4/3; (15 Jan 80) 2/4; (26 Jan 80) 3/3; (5 Feb 80) 3/4.

By the use of the words "to be sold" it is understood that this was an advertisement for music available at Rivington's shop (other advertisers are always identified). The RISM citations A60 and A75 are educated guesses that the references in Rivington are possibly to those editions. When there is a choice, the edition closest in date to the advertisement is cited. The supplied titles and dates generally were transcribed first from Edith Schnapper's *The British union-catalog of early music printed before 1801.* Later in the preparation of this inventory the RISM numbers were added.[28] Discrepancies between the two sources have not been resolved. The final element in the inventory citation gives the specific issues in which the advertisement appeared--dates followed by page and column numbers.

   Cross-references are copiously supplied. As an example, see the entry for Mr. Biferi previously quoted. In the inventory there are cross-references to this entry from *Vocal music teachers, Harpsichord teachers,* and *Spinnets.* There are a number of instances, however, when it was more desirable to supply full citations in more than one entry. This obviously obviates cross-references for these entries. Cross-references have been supplied for names and words that appear in Rivington's *Gazette* but that are archaic, alternately spelled, or erroneous. The last names of composers whose works are advertised in the *Gazette* are in upper case; other names are in lower case. A number of cross-references have been constructed for general categories such as concertos, songs, operas, pantomimes, etc. Titles of theatrical works are shown in italics. Quotation marks have been used to distinguish the first lines of song texts from tune names and song lyric titles. The word "lyric" is defined as a text "suitable for being set to music and sung."[29] Eighteenth-century spelling has been retained, but every attempt at clarity has been made in the use of punctuation and capitalization.

---

   28. A word about the RISM entries. Since, in the eighteenth century, the words "concerto" and "symphony" were often used interchangeably, RISM entries for, say, a concerto might be listed by Rivington as a symphony. Since there is no possibility of proving these are the same work, such RISM entries are not included in this inventory.
   29. *Webster's third new international dictionary of the English language unabridged* (Springfield, MA: G.&C. Merriam Co., 1961).

Although the arrangement of this inventory is basically alphabetical, some modifications have been necessary. Most notable, entries under "Concert" are sub-arranged in chronological sequence, and "Assemblies" are sub-arranged by place (i.e. the hall or tavern) and then further sorted chronologically.

Entries for musical instruments are arranged in the following sequence:

- Instruments, to be sold.
- Accessories, to be sold.
- Music, to be sold.
- Performers.
- Tutors or instructors, to be sold.

Composers' compositions which were advertised only in the generic form of "works" are listed before specific titles.

Often, a number of advertisements which read "horns to be sold" or "a pair of horns to be sold" or even "sets of strings to be sold" or "strings to be sold" have been combined in this inventory. The minor differences in wording are usually added in parentheses or in quotes after the entry.

Some of the musical instruments, such as the clarichord and sticcado pastorale, may seem like misprints, but they are not. The term clarichord is an obsolete word for clavichord. The sticcado pastorale was a "crystallophone popular in England during the late-eighteenth century, manufactured there ca.1775, similar to the xylophone but with glass bars."[30]

---

30. Sibyl Marcuse, *Musical instruments: A comprehensive dictionary* (New York: W.W. Norton & Co., 1975).

ABBREVIATIONS

BMC   - British Museum, Department of Printed Books. *Catalogue of printed music published between 1487 and 1800 now in the British Museum.* Comp. by W. Barclay Squire. 2 vols. London: British Museum, 1912.

BUC   - *The British union-catalogue of early music printed before the year 1801.* Ed. by Edith B. Schnapper. 2 vols. London: Butterworths Scientific Publications, 1957.

DLC   - District of Columbia, Library of Congress.

LBM   - London, British Library.

LOW   - Irving Lowens, *A bibliography of songsters printed in America before 1821.* Worcester, MA: American Antiquarian Society, 1976.

RISM   - *Répertoire international des sources musicales / International inventory of musical sources.* Published by the International Musicological Society and the International Association of Music Libraries, Archives and Documentation Centres.

> *Einzeldrucke vor 1800.* Ed. Karlheinz Schlager. 9 vols. and supplements. Kassel: Bärenreiter, 1971-   . [RISM]
> *Écrits imprimés concernant la musique.* Ed. François Lesure. 2 vols. München: G. Henle Verlag, 1971. [RISM BVI]
> *Recueils imprimés XVIIIe siècle.* Ed. François Lesure. München: G. Henle Verlag, 1964. [RISM BII]

Abbott of Canterbury. *SEE* "On Calvert's plains new faction reigns."

ABEL, Carl Friedrich, 1723-1787.

_____. Works by, to be sold.
       (28 Aug 79) 2/2; (1 Sep 79) 2/4.
_____. Overtures, Opera 4 and 14, to be sold.
       RISM A6O: *Six overtures in eight parts for two violins, two hoboys, two French horns, one tenor with a thorough bass for the harpsichord or violoncello . . . Opera 4.* London: Printed for the author . . . by R. Bremner, ca.1780.
       RISM A75: *Six overtures, in eight parts; with a thorough base for* the harpsichord, Opera XIV. . . . *London: R. Bremner, for the author, 1778.*
       (20-23 Oct 79) 3/3; (3-10 Nov 79) 4/2; (17-20 Nov 79) 4/2; (24 Nov 79) 3/2; (27 Nov - 1 Dec 79) 4/2; (22 Dec 79 - 12 Jan 80) 4/3; (15 Jan 80) 2/4; (26 Jan 80) 3/3; (5 Feb 80) 3/4.
_____. Quartettos, Op. 8, to be sold.
       RISM A89: *Six quartettos for two violins, a tenor and violoncello obligati . . . Opera VIII.* London: R. Bremner, for the author, 1769.
       (20-23 Oct 79) 3/3; (3-10 Nov 79) 4/2; (17-20 Nov 79) 4/2; (24 Nov 79) 3/2; (27 Nov - 1 Dec 79) 4/2; (22 Dec 79 - 12 Jan 80) 4/3; (15 Jan 80) 2/4; (26 Jan 80) 3/3; (5 Feb 80) 3/4.

[Afro-American] balls, assemblies and concerts.
       (19 Jan 82) 2/1.

AGAZZI, Gaetano.

_____. Six sonatas for the violoncello, Op. 1, to be sold.
       RISM A392: *Six sonates à violoncelle et basse . . . Oeuvre première.* Amsterdam: S. Markordt, ca.1785.
       (20-23 Oct 79) 3/3; (3-10 Nov 79) 4/2; (17-20 Nov 79) 4/2; (24 Nov 79) 3/2; (27 Nov - 1 Dec 79) 4/2; (22 Dec 79 - 12 Jan 80) 4/3; (15 Jan 80) 2/4; (26 Jan 80) 3/3; (5 Feb 80) 3/4.

AGUS, Giuseppe, ca.1725-ca.1800. (AGUO; AUGUS)

_____. Works by, to be sold.
       (28 Aug 79) 2/2; (1 Sep 79) 2/4.
_____. Nottornos, to be sold.
       RISM A458: *Six notturnos for two violins and a violoncello obligato . . . Opera IV.* London: Welcker, 1770.

(20 Oct 79) 3/3; (23 Oct 79) 3/3; (3 Nov 79) 4/2; (6 Nov 79) 4/2;
(10 Nov 79) 4/2; (17 Nov 79) 4/2; (20 Nov 79) 4/2; (24 Nov 79)
3/2; (27 Nov 79) 4/2; (1 Dec 79) 4/2; (22 Dec 79) 4/3; (25 Dec 79)
4/3; (29 Dec 79) 4/3; (1 Jan 80) 4/3; (5 Jan 80) 4/3; (8 Jan 80)
4/3; (12 Jan 80) 4/3; (15 Jan 80) 2/4; (26 Jan 80) 3/3; (5 Feb 80)
3/4.

Ailen a roon. Sung by Miss Storer.
(24 Jun 73) 3/4; (22 Jul 73) 3/2.

ALCOCK, John, Doctor in Music, 1715-1806.

_____. Divertiments and songs for the guitar, to be sold.
RISM A771: *Twelve divertimentis for the guitar, harpsichord or piano forte . . . Book 2d.* London: John Rutherford, ca.1775.
(14 Oct 73) 1/4; (11 Nov 73) Supplement, 1/1.
_____. Keyboard lessons, to be sold.
RISM A773: *A favorite lesson for the harpsichord or forte piano.* London: G. Gardom, ca.1775.
(14 Oct 73) 1/4; (11 Nov 73) Supplement, 1/1; (22 Nov 77) 1/3-4.

ALCOCK, John, the Younger, 1740-1791.

_____. Divertiments and songs for the guitar, to be sold.
RISM A788: *Twelve songs for the guittar, etc.* London: C. and S. Thompson, ca.1770.
(14 Oct 73) 1/4; (11 Nov 73) Supplement, 1/1.
_____. Two duets for two bassoons and a violoncello, to be sold.
RISM A790: *A favorite duett for two bassoons or violoncello's, etc.* London: Richard Bride, 1775.
(20 Oct 79) 3/3; (23 Oct 79) 3/3; (3 Nov 79) 4/2; (6 Nov 79) 4/2;
(10 Nov 79) 4/2; (17 Nov 79) 4/2; (20 Nov 79) 4/2; (24 Nov 79)
3/2; (27 Nov 79) 4/2; (1 Dec 79) 4/2; (22 Dec 79) 4/3; (25 Dec 79)
4/3; (29 Dec 79) 4/3; (1 Jan 80) 4/3; (5 Jan 80) 4/3; (8 Jan 80)
4/3; (12 Jan 80) 4/3; (15 Jan 80) 2/4; (26 Jan 80) 3/3; (5 Feb 80)
3/4.

ALEXANDER, B.

_____. Works by, to be sold.
(28 Aug 79) 2/2; (1 Sep 79) 2/4.
_____. Concertos, to be sold.
(20-23 Oct 79) 3/3; (3-10 Nov 79) 4/2; (17-20 Nov 79) 4/2; (24
Nov 79) 3/2; (27 Nov - 1 Dec 79) 4/2; (22 Dec 79 - 12 Jan 80)
4/3; (15 Jan 80) 2/4; (26 Jan 80) 3/3; (5 Feb 80) 3/4.
_____. Sonatas for two German flutes or violins, to be sold.
(20-23 Oct 79) 3/3; (3-10 Nov 79) 4/2; (17-20 Nov 79) 4/2; (24
Nov 79) 3/2; (27 Nov - 1 Dec 79) 4/2; (22 Dec 79 - 12 Jan 80)
4/3; (15 Jan 80) 2/4; (26 Jan 80) 3/3; (5 Feb 80) 3/4.

"All Hail! Britannia hail!" To the tune of Smile Britannia. Song lyric printed.
>   (2 May 81) 2/3.

Allemande to be taught by W. Birchall Tetley.
>   (3 Nov 74) 3/4; (10 Nov 74) 4/4.
>   For fuller reference, *SEE* Tetley, W. Birchall.

Allemande. *SEE ALSO* Dancing.

"Ame du héros, et du sâge." *SEE* "Life of the hero, as well as of the sage."

The American robin, a collection of new songs. Just published and to be sold
>   by Hodge and Shober, at the newest printing-office, in Maiden-Lane,
>   near the head of the Fly-Market.
>   (23 Dec 73) 3/4; (13 Jan 74) Supplement, 1/4.

Amiel, Brigade General. In charge of subscription assemblies.
>   (22 Jan 83) 3/3.

"And so, you've been courting the muses, my boy." Song lyric printed.
>   (2 Jan 79) 3/3.

Anthem, a Mason's. *SEE* Wools, Mr.

Anthem for any grand funeral. *SEE* Church-music.

Anthem 133d Psalm. *SEE* Church-music.

Anthem to be sung at the time of any charitable contribution. *SEE* Church-
>   music.

Anthem. *SEE ALSO* CROFT, William.

The apprentice with a song, a farce, to be performed on Monday.
>   (9 May 78) 3/4.

"Arise! arise! your voices raise." *SEE* HOPKINSON, Francis.

ARNE, Michael, ca.1740-1786.

_____. *Cymon.* English opera, harpsichord/vocal edition, to be sold.
>   RISM A1436: *Cymon. A dramatic romance, etc.* London: John
>   Johnston, 1767.
>   (30 Sep 73) 3/4; (7 Oct 73) 4/3; (14 Oct 73) 1/4, Supplement, 1/3;
>   (11 Nov 73) Supplement, 1/1; (4 Oct 77) 4/2; (25 Oct 77) 4/4.
_____. *Cymon*, airs in, for guitar, to be sold.
>   (14 Oct 73) 1/4; (11 Nov 73) Supplement, 1/1.
_____. *Cymon* will be acted on January 7 at Hull's Long Room.
>   (6 Jan 74) 3/4.

_____. *The fathers, or goodnatured man.* The favourite song in, to be sold.
    RISM A1467: *While the sweet blushing spring. The favorite song in the new comedy of The fathers, etc.* London: Longman and Broderip, 1778.
    (19 Feb 80) 1/4.

_____. *The maid of the mill. SEE* ARNOLD, Samuel.

_____. Thro' the wood, laddie. *SEE* Scotch songs.

ARNE, Thomas Augustine, 1710-1778.

_____. *Artaxerxes.* English opera, keyboard/vocal edition, to be sold.
    RISM A1616: *Artaxerxes. An English opera, as it is performed at the Theatre Royal. . . .* London: John Johnston, 1762.
    (4 Oct 77) 4/2; (25 Oct 77) 4/4; (28 Aug 79) 2/2; (1 Sep 79) 2/4.

_____. *Artaxerxes.* "The soldier tired." Song sung by Miss Hallam in concert.
    RISM A1695: *The soldier tir'd, sung by Mrs. Brent in Artaxerxes.* London, ca.1775
    (6 May 73) 3/3.

_____. *Artaxerxes.* "The soldier tir'd of war's alarms." Performed in the theatre.
    RISM A1695: See entry above.
    (6 Feb 82) 2/4; (9 Feb 82) 2/3; (20 Feb 82) 2/4; (23 Feb 82) 3/3.

_____. *Artaxerxes.* "Soldier tir'd of wars alarms." Sung by Mrs. Hyde, to be performed.
    RISM A1695: See entry above.
    (27 Apr 82) 3/3.
    For fuller reference *SEE* Concert (27 Apr 82).

_____. *The beggar's opera.* English opera, to be sold. [An adaptation by Arne of the 1728 ballad opera on text by John Gay and music arranged by John Christopher Pepusch]
    BUC I, p.96; RISM A1740: *The beggar's opera, as it is performed at both theatres, with the additional alterations by Dr. Arne for the voice, harpsichord and violin, the basses entirely new.* London: Thomas Straight &c Skillern, ca.1775.
    (4 Oct 77) 4/2; (25 Oct 77) 4/4; (6 Jun 81) 3/4.

_____. *The beggar's opera.* English opera, performed.
    BUC I, p.96: See entry above.
    (20 May 73) 3/3.

_____. *Comus.* Miss Hallam singing a song as the character Sabrina in *Comus*.
    RISM A1755: *The songs, duetto and trio in the masque of Comus . . . .* London: Jas. and Jno. Simpson, ca.1770.
    (17 Jun 73) 3/3.

_____. *Comus.* "Sweet Echo." A song sung by Miss Hallam in the masque, *Comus*.
    RISM A1778: *Sweet echo. Sung by Miss Catley.* Dublin, ca.1770.
    (17 Jun 73) 3/3.

_____. *Elfrida.* English opera, harpischord/vocal edition, to be sold.
    RISM A1805: *The songs duets and chorusses in the tragedy of Elfrida . . . with the overture adapted for the harpsi^d.* London: John Johnston . . . and Longman, Lukey and Co., 1772.
    (4 Oct 77) 4/2; (25 Oct 77) 4/4; (22 Nov 77) 1/3-4.

_____. The girdle, a favorite cantata sung by Mr. Arrowsmith at Vauxhall, to be sold.
> (18 Oct 83) 2/2.

_____. "If fortune would smile, and I cannot complain." A moral song by Dr. Arne, song lyric printed.
> (17 Mar 74) 3/1.

_____. *The king and the miller of Mansfield*, in which will be introduced a song on Monday June 7, 1778.
> RISM A1886: *How happy a state does ye miller posses. A song in The miller of Mansfield.* London, ca.1737.
> (3 Jun 78) 2/4; (10 Jun 78) 4/4.

_____. *King Arther*, Dibden's [sic?]. English opera, keyboard/vocal edition, to be sold.
> BUC II, p.862: *The songs airs duets & chorusses in the masque of King Arthur, as perform'd at the Theatre Royal in Drury Lane composed by Purcel & Dr. Arne.* London: John Johnston, ca.1770.
> (14 Oct 73) 1/4; (11 Nov 73) Supplement, 1/1.

_____. *Lady's frolick.* English opera, keyboard/vocal edition, to be sold.
> BUC II, p.587: *The ladies' frolick. A comic opera. . . . by Mr. Bates and Dr. Arne.* London: Longman, Lukey & Co., 1770.
> (14 Oct 73) 1/4; (11 Nov 73) Supplement, 1/1; (22 Nov 77) 1/3-4.

_____. *Ladies frolick.* Airs in, for guitar, to be sold.
> BUC II, p.587: *The ladies' frolick, a comic opera being the airs, simphonies, overture, duets, & vaudevilles with the words . . . for one, and two guittars.* London: Longman, Lukey & Co., 1770.
> (14 Oct 73) 1/4; (11 Nov 73) Supplement, 1/1.

_____. *Love in a village.* English opera, harpsichord/vocal edition, to be sold.
> RISM A1857: *Love in a village. A comic opera. . . . The music by Handel, Boyce, Arne, Howard, Baildon, Festing, Geminiani, Galuppi, Giardini, Paradies, Agus, Abos. For the harpsichord, voice, German flute, or violin.* London: I. Walsh, 1763.
> (30 Sep 73) 3/4; (7 Oct 73) 4/3; (14 Oct 73) Supplement, 1/3, 1/4; (11 Nov 73) Supplement, 1/1; (4 Oct 77) 4/2; (25 Oct 77) 4/4; (28 Aug 79) 2/2; (1 Sep 79) 2/4.

_____. *Love in a village.* Airs in, set for guitar, to be sold.
> BUC II, p.631: *The airs with all the symphonies in the comic opera of Love in a village correctly transposed for the guittar.* London: David Rutherford, ca.1765.
> (14 Oct 73) 1/4; (11 Nov 73) Supplement, 1/1; (20-23 Oct 79) 3/3; (3-10 Nov 79) 4/2; (17-20 Nov 79) 4/2; (24 Nov 79) 3/2; (27 Nov - 1 Dec 79) 4/2; (22 Dec 79 - 12 Jan 80) 4/3; (15 Jan 80) 2/4; (26 Jan 80) 3/3; (5 Feb 80) 3/4.

_____. *Love in a village.* A comic opera, performance.
> (6 May 73) 3/3; (15 Oct 83) 2/4; (22 Oct 83) 3/2.

_____. *Love in a village.* Copy wanted for the theatre.
> (6 Feb 82) 2/4.

_____. *Miss in her teens.* Farce to be performed in the theatre.
> BUC I, p.45: *Miss in her teens. A ballad. Sung by Miss Jameson at Vauxhall.* London: J. Bland, ca.1780.

BUC I, p.45: No ice so hard, so cold as I. IN: *Thalia. A collection of six songs . . . by . . . Dr. Arne, etc.* No. 2. ca.1767.
(6 Aug 82) 3/2.

_____. A moral song. SEE his "If fortune would smile."

_____. Rule Britannia. SEE "As bending o'er the azure tide "; "When Britain, by divine command"; "When rival nations first descried."

_____. The syren. A songbook to be sold.
RISM A2005: *The syren. A new collection of favorite songs sung by Mrs. Farrell at the Theatre Royal, Covent Garden and at Ranelagh* . . . London: Longman and Broderip, 1777.
(7 Jun 83) 3/3; (11 June 83) 1/1; (14 Jun 83) 1/1.

_____. *Thomas and Sally: or, the sailor's return.* A farce to be performed in the theatre.
RISM A1924: *Thomas and Sally, or the sailor's return, a dramatic pastoral, with the overture in score, songs, dialogues, duettos and dance-tunes, etc.* London: Printed for the author, 1761.
(6 Sep 83) 3/4; (20 Sep 83) 2/4.

_____. *The way to keep him.* Misses [sic] Hallam singing a song as the character, Widow Belmore.
RISM A1969: *Ye fair marri'd dames. A song, sung by Mrs. Cibber in The way to keep him, etc.* London, ca.1765.
(22 Apr 73) 3/2.

_____. "When Britain on her sea-girt shore." The wooden walls of England, by Henry Green and Dr. Arne. Song lyric printed.
RISM BII, p.87-88: The wooden walls of England. "When Britain on her sea girt shore." IN: *Amusement for the ladies* . . . Vol. II. London: Longman and Broderip, 179-, p.65-71.
(8 Jul 80) 2/2.

ARNOLD, Samuel, 1740-1802.

_____. *Maid of the mill.* English opera, harpsichord/vocal edition, to be sold.
RISM A2286: [Attributed to Samuel Arnold.] *The maid of the mill. A comic opera . . . for the voice, harpsichord, or violin.* London: R. Bremner, 1765.
(30 Sep 73) 3/4; (7 Oct 73) 4/3; (14 Oct 73) 1/4; (14 Oct 73) Supplement, 1/3; (11 Nov 73) Supplement, 1/1; (4 Oct 77) 4/2; (25 Oct 77) 4/4; (22 Nov 77) 1/3-4.

_____. *The portrait.* English opera, keyboard/vocal edition, to be sold.
BUC I, p.53: *The portrait, a burletta, etc.* [An adaptation from the French, by G. Colman] London: Welcker, 1770.
(14 Oct 73) 1/4; (11 Nov 73) Supplement, 1/1; (22 Nov 77) 1/3-4.

_____. "Tho' the fate of battle on to-morrow wait." The original music French, accompaniement by Dr. Arnold. The tobacco box; or, the soldiers pledge of love. Song lyric printed.
BMC II, p.576: *Tho' the fate of battle on to-morrow wait. The tobacco box or soldier's pledge of love. A favorite dialogue.* London: Longman & Broderip, ca.1785.
(23 Nov 82) 3/1.

_____. 24 lessons. For guitar, to be sold.
(14 Oct 73) 1/4; (11 Nov 73) Supplement, 1/1.

Arrowsmith, Mr. Sings The girdle at Vauxhall. *SEE* ARNE, Thomas
      Augustine. The girdle.

Artaxerxes. *SEE* ARNE, Thomas Augustine.

"As bending o'er the azure tide." To the tunes of The watry god and Rule
      Britannia. Song lyric printed.
          (16 Oct 82) 3/3.

"As for his religion he could mix." Song lyric printed.
          (4 Oct 80) 3/3.

"As his worm eaten volumes old time tumbled o'er." Song lyric printed.
          (26 Jun 80) 3/3.

"As Spain's proud monarch sat in state." Song lyric printed.
          (4 Dec 82) 3/1.

"As tyrant power and slavish fear." The Sacrifice. To the tune of How much
      superior beauty awes. Song lyric printed.
          (2 Jan 79) 3/2.

Asket Heath. *SEE* Sport.

ASPELMAYER, Franz, 1728-1786. (ASPELMAYR; ASPLMAYR)

_____. Duetts for violin and violoncello, to be sold.
      (20-23 Oct 79) 3/3; (3-20 Nov 79) 4/2; (24 Nov 79) 3/2; (27 Nov
      79 -1 Dec 79) 4/2; (22 Dec 79 - 12 Jan 80) 4/3; (15 Jan 80) 2/4;
      (26 Jan 80) 3/3; (5 Feb 80) 3/4.

Assembly.

_____. The New-York assembly. Advertised for March 26.
      (26 Mar 83) 3/2.
_____. Subscription assembly. Cancelled because of Ash Wednesday.
      (1 Mar 83) 3/4.
_____. Subscription assembly. Fifth one advertised for March 10.
      (8 Mar 83) 1/2.

Assembly. At Loosley's, Brooklyn Hall.

_____. Subscription assembly. At Loosley's Brooklyne-Hall. Advertised to
      begin February 6 and every Thursday thereafter.
      (1 Feb 83) 3/4.
_____. Subscription assembly. Loosley's, Brooklyne Hall on February 27.
      (19 Feb 83) 3/3; (26 Feb 83) 3/4.
_____. Subscription assembly. Brooklyne-Hall assembly, advertised for March
      13.
      (12 Mar 83) 3/3.

_____. Subscription assembly. Advertised for March 27 at Brooklyn Hall.
(26 Mar 83) 3/2.

Assembly. At Roubalet's.

_____. Subscription assembly. Advertisement for the first one on January 13
at Roubalet's Tavern.
(8 Jan 83) 3/2; (11 Jan 83) 3/1.
_____. Subscription assembly. Advertised for January 27 at Roubalet's.
(25 Jan 83) 3/4.
_____. Subscription assembly. To be held at Roubalet's on January 27.
Brigade General Amiel.
(22 Jan 83) 3/3.

Assembly. *SEE ALSO* [Afro-american] balls, assemblies and concerts;
Dancing assembly.

The Association, &c held at Philadelphia, September 1. Versified and adapted
to music, by Bob Jingle, Esq. [pseudonym of Francis Hopkinson?], Poet
Laureat to the Congress.
(8 Dec 73) 1/4; (15 Dec 74) 4/3; (29 Dec 74) 2/3; (9 Feb 75) 3/4.

AUGUS. *SEE* AGUS, Giuseppe.

AVOLIO, J.

_____. Duetts for violins, to be sold.
(20-23 Oct 79) 3/3; (3-10 Nov 79) 4/2; (17-20 Nov 79) 4/2; (24
Nov 79) 3/2; (27 Nov - 1 Dec 79) 4/2; (22 Dec 79 - 12 Jan 80)
4/3; (15 Jan 80) 2/4; (26 Jan 80) 3/3; (5 Feb 80) 3/4.

Away to the copse. *SEE* A medley for the light infantry.

BACCHERINI. *SEE* BOCCHERINI, Luigi.

BACH, Carl Philipp Emanuel, 1714-1788.

_____. Concertos, Opera 3 and 8, to be sold.
RISM B47: *Concertos for the harpsicord, or organ. With accompanyments for violins . . . Op. 3ª.* London: John Walsh, n.d.
(20-23 Oct 79) 3/3; (3-10 Nov 79) 4/2; (17-20 Nov 79) 4/2; (24
Nov 79) 3/2; (27 Nov - 1 Dec 79) 4/2; (22 Dec 79 - 12 Jan 80)
4/3; (15 Jan 80) 2/4; (26 Jan 80) 3/3; (5 Feb 80) 3/4.
_____. Concertos, three keyboard, 2d set, to be sold.
RISM B48: *A second sett of three concertos for the organ or
harpsicord with instrumental parts, etc.* London: Longman, Lukey &
Co., ca.1775.
(22 Nov 77) 1/3-4.

_____. Concerto, favourite keyboard, to be sold.
   RISM B100: *A favourite concerto for the harpsichord, or piano forte*. London: Longman, Lukey & Co., ca.1770.
   (22 Nov 77) 1/3-4.

_____. Duetts for two German flutes, to be sold.
   RISM B98: *Zwölff zwey-und drey-stimmige kleine Stücke für die Flöte oder Violin und das Clavier*. Hamburg: Friedrich Schönemann, 1770.
   (20-23 Oct 79) 3/3; (3-10 Nov 79) 4/2; (17-20 Nov 79) 4/2; (24 Nov 79) 3/2; (27 Nov - 1 Dec 79) 4/2; (22 Dec 79 - 12 Jan 80) 4/3; (15 Jan 80) 2/4; (26 Jan 80) 3/3; (5 Feb 80) 3/4.

_____. Sonatas, harpsichord, to be sold.
   RISM B82: *Six sonatas for the piano forte or harpsicord*. London: Longman, Lukey & Co., ca.1775.
   (21 Apr 74) 3/4; (5 May 74) 3/2.

_____. Sonatas, keyboard, to be sold.
   RISM B82: See entry above.
   (14 Oct 73) 1/4; (11 Nov 73) Supplement, 1/1.

_____. Six sonatas, keyboard, to be sold.
   RISM B82: See entry above.
   (22 Nov 77) 1/3-4.

BACH, Johann Christian, 1735-1782.

_____. Works, to be sold.
   (30 Sep 73) 3/4; (7 Oct 73) 4/3; (14 Oct 73) Supplement, 1/3; (4 Oct 77) 4/2; (25 Oct 77) 4/4; (28 Aug 79) 2/2; (1 Sep 79) 2/4.

_____. Concertos, Opera 3 and 8, to be sold.
   (20-23 Oct 79) 3/3; (3-10 Nov 79) 4/2; (17-20 Nov 79) 4/2; (24 Nov 79) 3/2; (27 Nov - 1 Dec 79) 4/2; (22 Dec 79 - 12 Jan 80) 4/3; (15 Jan 80) 2/4; (26 Jan 80) 3/3; (5 Feb 80) 3/4.

_____. Concertos, Op. 7, to be sold.
   RISM B278: *Sei concerti per il cembalo o piano e forte con due violini e violoncello d'accompagnamento . . . Op. VII. . . .* London: Welcker, ca.1770.
   RISM B281: *A second sett of six concertos for the harpsichord or piano forte with accompanyments for two violins & a violoncello . . . Opera VII*. London: Welcker, ca.1775.
   (20-23 Oct 79) 3/3; (3-10 Nov 79) 4/2; (17-20 Nov 79) 4/2; (24 Nov 79) 3/2; (27 Nov - 1 Dec 79) 4/2; (22 Dec 79 - 12 Jan 80) 4/3; (15 Jan 80) 2/4; (26 Jan 80) 3/3; (5 Feb 80) 3/4.

_____. Concerto, keyboard, third set, Opera 13, to be sold.
   RISM B282: *A third sett of six concertos for the harpsichord, or piano forte, with accompaniments for two violins and a bass, two hautboys and two French horns ad libitum. Opera XIII*. London: John Welcker, 1777.
   (22 Nov 77) 1/3-4.

_____. Concerto, favourite keyboard, to be sold.
   RISM B289: *A favorite concerto for the harpsichord, or piano-forte, etc*. London: Longman, Lukey & Co., 1777.
   (22 Nov 77) 1/3-4.

_____. Concerto, favourite keyboard. *SEE ALSO* BACH, Carl Phillip Emanuel.
_____. Duetts for two German flutes, to be sold.
  RISM B98: See entry under BACH, Carl Philipp Emanuel.
_____. Six duets for two violins, to be sold.
  RISM B378: *Six duetts for two violins.* London: Longman, Lukey & Co., ca.1775.
  (22 Nov 77) 1/3-4.
_____. Quartettos, Opera 9, to be sold.
  RISM B309: *Six quatuor à deux violons, ou une flutte, un violon, taille, et basse . . . Oeuvre IX.* La Haye: A. Stechway, ca.1780.
  (20-23 Oct 79) 3/3; (3-10 Nov 79) 4/2; (17-20 Nov 79) 4/2; (24 Nov 79) 3/2; (27 Nov - 1 Dec 79) 4/2; (22 Dec 79 - 12 Jan 80) 4/3; (15 Jan 80) 2/4; (26 Jan 80) 3/3; (5 Feb 80) 3/4.
_____. 6 quartettos for German flute, to be sold.
  RISM B308: *Six quartettos for a German flute, violin, tenor and violoncello . . . Opera VIII.* London: Welcker, ca.1770.
  (14 Oct 73) 1/4; (11 Nov 73) Supplement, 1/1.
_____. Six quartettos for two violins, a German flute, violin, taille and bass, to be sold.
  RISM B309: See entry above, Quartettos, Opera 9.
  (22 Nov 77) 1/3-4.
_____. Quintetto for flauto, to be performed.
  RISM B301: *Six quintettos for a flute, hautboy, violin, tenor, and bass . . . [Op. 11].* London: John Welcker.
  (27 Apr 82) 3/3.
  For fuller reference, *SEE* Concert (27 Apr 82).
_____. 6 simphonies for violin, to be sold
  RISM B224: *Six simphonies à deux violons, deux hautbois, deux cors de chasse, alto viola et basse, . . . Oeuvre III.* London: Printed for the author, ca.1765.
  RISM B225: *Six simphonies à deux violons, alto viola et basse, deux hautbois et cors de chasse . . . Oeuvre troisième.* Amsterdam: J.J. Hummel, ca.1765.
  RISM B236: *Six simphonies à 8 instrum. deux violons, taille, & basse, deux hautbois, et deux cors de chasses . . . Oeuvre huitième.* Amsterdam: S. Markordt, ca.1775.
  (14 Oct 73) 1/4; (11 Nov 73) Supplement, 1/1.
_____. Sinfonie, to be performed.
  (27 Apr 82) 3/3.
  For fuller reference, *SEE* Concert (27 Apr 82).
_____. Six sonatas for keyboard, Opera 10, to be sold.
  RISM B333: *Six sonatas for the harpsichord or piano forte: with an accompagnament [sic] for a violin, . . . Opera X.* London: Welcker, 1773.
  (22 Nov 77) 1/3-4.
_____. Four sonatas for two German flutes or violins, to be sold.
  RISM B362: *Four sonatas and two duets . . . [for violin or flute] Opera 18.* London: Welcker.
  (20-23 Oct 79) 3/3; (3-10 Nov 79) 4/2; (17-20 Nov 79) 4/2; (24 Nov 79) 3/2; (27 Nov - 1 Dec 79) 4/2; (22 Dec 79 - 12 Jan 80) 4/3; (15 Jan 80) 2/4; (26 Jan 80) 3/3; (5 Feb 80) 3/4.

_____. Sonatas for guitar, to be sold.
> RISM B380: *A sonata for the guitar with an accompaniment for a violin, etc.* London: Longman, Lukey & Co., ca.1775.
> (14 Oct 73) 1/4; (11 Nov 73) Supplement, 1/1.

_____. Sonatas, keyboard, to be sold.
> RISM B382: *Six sonates pour le clavecin ou le piano forte . . . Oeuvre V.* London: Welcker, ca.1768.
> (14 Oct 73) 1/4; (11 Nov 73) Supplement, 1/1.

Bagpipe. Tutors and instructors, to be sold.

_____. New instruction for playing on the bagpipe.
> (8 Sep 79) 2/4; (2 Oct 79) 2/3; (9 Oct 79) 3/4.

Bagpipe. Accessories, to be sold.

_____. Reeds with and without cases.
> (14 Oct 73) 1/4; (11 Nov 73) Supplement, 1/1.

BALENTINE. (VALENTINE?)

_____. Twenty-six duets for guitar, to be sold.
> (20-23 Oct 79) 3/3; (3-10 Nov 79) 4/2; (17-20 Nov 79) 4/2; (24 Nov 79) 3/2; (27 Nov - 1 Dec 79) 4/2; (22 Dec 79 - 12 Jan 80) 4/3; (15 Jan 80) 2/4; (26 Jan 80) 3/3; (5 Feb 80) 3/4.

Ball.

_____. Ball for the ladies and gentlemen to be held January 7 after performance of *Cymon* and *Padlock.*
> (5 Jan 74) 3/4.

_____. Ball after a concert to be held May 26, 1774.
> (19 May 74) 3/3; (26 May 74) 2/4.

_____. Ball to follow a concert for Mr. Biferi.
> (23 Feb 75) 3/2; (2 Mar 75) 2/3; (9 Mar 75) 2/4; (16 Mar 75) 1/2; (23 Mar 75) 3/3.

_____. Ball following concert on April 27.
> (20 Apr 75) 3/3.

_____. Ball given by the Friendly Brethren of St. Patrick on Friday last.
> (22 Mar 80) 2/4; (25 Mar 80) 4/1.

_____. The Garrison Anniversary Coronation Ball. Advertised.
> (18 Sep 79) 3/2; (22 Sep 79) 3/3.

_____. Jamaica Accession Ball. To be held October 25, 1779. "A grand band of musick will be wanted. Musicians are desired to deliver in their proposals at the Queen's-Head Jamaica."
> (25 Sep 79) 2/3.

Ball. *SEE ALSO* [Afro-American] balls, assemblies and concerts.

Ballad farce. *SEE* BATES, William. *Flora.*

Band.

_____. Band of martial music to attend celebration of Prince of Wales's birthday at Loosley's tavern.
(9 Aug 80) 3/3; (12 Aug 80) 2/2.

_____. Band of music at the White Conduit House September 16, 1780.
(16 Sep 80) 2/4.

_____. Band of Music, benefit for, at Mr. Hull's Assembly Room on April 27.
(20 Apr 75) 3/3.

_____. Band of music to play every Saturday night at White Conduit House. *SEE* White Conduit House.

_____. Band of musick marched in funeral procession for Michael Cressop deceased.
(26 Oct 75) 4/1.

_____. Band of musick wanted for Jamaica Accession Ball.
(25 Sep 79) 2/3.

_____. Band of musick to attend races on Asket Heath on November 13, 1780. *SEE* Sport.

_____. Band wanted for the *General Pattison*, private ship of war.
(14 Apr 79) 2/4; (21 Apr 79) 4/3.

Band director wanted for a regiment. *SEE* Musicians. Wanted for a regiment.

Band music. *SEE* DREZTY; GIORDANI, Tommaso.

The banks of the Dee. *SEE* Scotch songs.

BARBELLA, Emanuele, 1718-1777. (BARBELLO)

_____. Works by, to be sold.
(28 Aug 79) 2/2; (1 Sep 79) 2/4.

_____. Trios, to be sold.
RISM B883: *Six trios for two violins and a violoncello . . . dedicated to Sir William Hamilton.* London: Welcker, 1772.
(20-23 Oct 79) 3/3; (3-10 Nov 79) 4/2; (17-20 Nov 79) 4/2; (24 Nov 79) 3/2; (27 Nov - 1 Dec 79) 4/2; (22 Dec 79 - 12 Jan 80) 4/3; (15 Jan 80) 2/4; (26 Jan 80) 3/3; (5 Feb 80) 3/4.

Barrel organs tuned and repaired. William Pearson, clock and watch-maker.
(14 Apr 74) 1/1; (21 Apr 74) 4/4.

Barrel organs. *SEE ALSO* Organ.

BARTHÉLÉMON, François Hippolyte, 1741-1808.

_____. Concertos, to be sold.
RISM B1107: *Six concertos for three violins, a tenor & violoncello to which may be added ad libitum two repiano [sic] violins & a thorough bass for the harpsichord . . . Opera IIId.* London: Welcker, ca.1775.

(20-23 Oct 79) 3/3; (3-10 Nov 79) 4/2; (17-20 Nov 79) 4/2; (24 Nov 79) 3/2; (27 Nov - 1 Dec 79) 4/2; (22 Dec 79 - 12 Jan 80) 4/3; (15 Jan 80) 2/4; (26 Jan 80) 3/3; (5 Feb 80) 3/4.

_____. *The maid of the oaks.* English opera, harpsichord/vocal edition, to be sold.

RISM B1084: *The maid of the oaks, etc.* London: Longman, Lukey and Co. . . . & J. Johnson, 1774.

(4 Oct 77) 4/2; (25 Oct 77) 4/4; (22 Nov 77) 1/3-4.

BARTLEMAN, James.

_____. Works by, to be sold.

(28 Aug 79) 2/2; (1 Sep 79) 2/4.

Bassoon. Instruments, to be sold.

_____. Bassoon of an excellent and well approved tone, formerly the property of the famous Scammadine, who was acknowledged to be the first performer in the universe.

(19 Aug 78) 4/3; (22 Aug 78) 1/1; (26 Aug 78) 4/2.

_____. Bassoons, two.

(28 Oct 78) 2/3; (31 Oct 78) 4/1; (4 Nov 78) 1/4; (7 Nov 78) 4/3; (11 Nov 78) 1/4.

_____. Bassoons, a pair truly excellent. Made in Europe.

(18-22 Dec 79) 4/1; (29 Dec 79) 2/3.

_____. Bassoons.

(23-26 Dec 78) 3/4; (26 Dec 78 - 9 Jan 79) 1/1; (28 Aug 79) 2/2; (1 Sep 79) 2/4; (29 Sep 79) 2/3; (2-7 Oct 79) 3/4; (13 Oct 79) Supplement, 1/1; (3 Nov 79) Supplement, 2/1; (10-17 Nov 79) 4/4;, (20-24 Nov 79) 1/4; (3 May 80) 3/3-4; (27 May 80) 3/3; (17 Jun 80) 4/2; (8 Jul 80) 3/4; (23 Dec 80) 3/4; (27 Dec 80) 4/3; (30 Dec 80) 4/3; (3 Jan 81) 4/3; (6 Jan 81) 2/2; (26 Sep 81) 4/1; (29 Sep 81) 4/2; (6-31 Oct 81) 4/2; (27 Oct 81) 3/4; (3-7 Nov 81) 4/4; (10-21 Nov 81) 4/2; (24 Nov 81) 4/4; (5 Dec 81 - 5 Jan 82) 4/4; (9 Jan 82) 3/3; (16 Jan 82) 1/2; (19 Jan 82) 4/4; (23 Jan - 23 Feb 82) 4/2; (23-27 Mar 82) 4/2; (13 Apr 82) 3/4; (24 Apr - 1 May 82) 1/3; (4-29 May 82) 1/1; (1 Jun 82) 1/3; (5 Jun 82) 1/2; (8 Jun 82) 1/1; (12-22 Jun 82) 4/1; (22 Jun - 13 Jul 82) 4/4; (17 Jul 82) 1/1; (20-31 Jul 82) 4/1; (3-17 Aug 82) 4/3; (21 Aug - 4 Sep 82) 4/1.

Bassoon. Accessories, to be sold.

_____. Reeds.

(30 Sep 73) 3/4; (7 Oct 73) 4/3; (14 Oct 73) Supplement, 1/3; (21 Apr 74) 3/4; (5 May 74) 3/2; (22 Nov 77) 1/3-4; (25 Jul 78) 3/1.

_____. Reeds of different kinds to be sold by Valentine Nutter.

(23 Dec 80) 2/4; (30 Dec 80) 3/3.

_____. Reeds with and without cases.
(14 Oct 73) 1/4; (11 Nov 73) Supplement, 1/1; (4 Oct 77) 4/2; (25 Oct 77) 4/4; (3 May 80) 3/3-4; (27 May 80) 3/3; (17 Jun 80) 4/2; (8 Jul 80) 3/4; (23 Dec 80) 3/4; (27 Dec 80) 4/3; (30 Dec 80) 4/3; (3 Jan 81) 4/3; (6 Jan 81) 2/2.

Bassoon music. *SEE* ALCOCK, John, the Younger; BUHLER; DREZTY.

Bassoon performers. *SEE* Musicians. Wanted. . . .

Bassoon tutors or instructors, to be sold.
(14 Oct 73) 1/4; (11 Nov 73) Supplement, 1/1; (4 Oct 77) 4/2; (25 Oct 77) 4/4.

BATES, William, ca.1750-ca.1780

_____. Duetts for German flute, to be sold.
RISM B1274: *Twelve duets for two German flutes, or violins. Compos'd in a familiar style . . . Book 3d, etc.* London: Longman, Lukey & Co., ca.1770.
(14 Oct 73) 1/4; (11 Nov 73) Supplement, 1/1.
_____. Six duets for two violins and German flutes, to be sold.
RISM B1274: See entry above.
(22 Nov 77) 1/3-4.
_____. Duetts for violins and German flutes, to be sold.
RISM 1274: See entry above.
(20-23 Oct 79) 3/3; (3-10 Nov 79) 4/2; (17-20 Nov 79) 4/2; (24 Nov 79) 3/2; (27 Nov - 1 Dec 79) 4/2; (22 Dec 79 - 12 Jan 80) 4/3; (15 Jan 80) 2/4; (26 Jan 80) 3/3; (5 Feb 80) 3/4.
_____. *[Flora, or] Hob in the well.* English opera, keyboard/vocal edition, to be sold.
RISM B1244: *Flora, or Hob in the well! . . . The overture, duet and principal songs, etc.* London: Longman, Lukey & Co., ca.1775.
(14 Oct 73) 1/4; (11 Nov 73) Supplement, 1/1.
_____. *[Flora, or] Hob in the well.* Machinery for necessitates postponement of performance to April 19.
(15 Apr 80) 2/4.
_____. *Flora, or Hob in the well.* In the Fair Scene will be introduced the favourite song of Lads and lasses.
(19 Apr 80) 3/1; (29 Apr 80) 2/4.
_____. *The ladies' frolick.* *SEE* ARNE, Thomas Augustine. *Lady's frolick.*

BATTISHILL, Jonathan, 1738-1801.

_____. *High life below stairs.* A farce to be performed in the theatre. A song and epilogue by Miss Wall.
RISM B1308: *Come here fellow servant. A new song. Sung by Mrs. Clive, in the farce of High life below stairs.* London, 1760.
(27 Sep 83) 3/4.

Beattie, James, 1735-1803.

_____. Essays on music, to be sold.
    RISM BIV[1], p.127: *Essays . . . on poetry and music, as they affect the mind; on laughter and ludicrous composition; on the utility of classical learning.* Third edition corrected. London: E. and C. Dilly; Edinburgh: W. Creech, 1779.
    (11 Aug 79) 2/2; (21 Aug 79) 3/4; (25 Aug 79) 2/2.

Beaux stratagem. SEE PURCELL, Daniel.

The beggar's opera. SEE ARNE, Thomas Augustine.

"Behold this badge the female test." Song lyric printed.
    (17 Mar 79) 3/1.

"Behold with what ardor to action they press." SEE A medley for the light infantry.

Bells cast by Richard Skellorn.
    (11 May 75) 2/4; (18 May 75) 4/1; (1 Jun 75) 4/3; (22 Jun 75) 4/4.

BEM, Venceslav.

_____. Quartettos for German flute, to be sold.
    (14 Oct 73) 1/4; (11 Nov 73) Supplement, 1/1.

Benedicit omnia opera Domini. *SEE* Church-music.

BENZON.

_____. Works by, to be sold.
    (28 Aug 79) 2/2; (1 Sep 79) 2/4.

BICKHOOFF. *SEE* BISCHOFF, I. C.

Biferi, Nicholas, 1739-?.

_____. Master of music from Naples "lately arrived from London . . . will teach vocal music, the harpsichord, to play pieces of music, and an easy method to learn composition, which he printed for the public at Paris; he composes all sorts of music, vocal and instrumental."
    (5 May 74) 3/2.
_____. Master of music from Naples, harpsichord player and composer. To perform in a concert for his benefit, May 26, 1774.
    (19 May 74) 3/3; (26 May 74) 2/4.
    For fuller reference, *SEE* Concert (19 May 74).
_____. Orchestral composition to be performed May 26, 1774 at concert.
    (19 May 74) 3/3; (26 May 74) 2/4.
    For fuller reference, *SEE* Concert (19 May 74).

_____. Musician of Naples, ". . . being determined to stay in this city, informs the public, that he now teaches singing after the Italian way, also the harpsichord, and the compositon of music. . . ."
(30 Jun 74) 2/4; (7 Jul 74) 4/3.

_____. Music Master from Naples, "informs the young ladies, that he teaches vocal music from the harpsichord, after the best Italian method, at his house on Golden-Hill-Street, formerly occupied by Mr. Crimshire, Attorney at Law, on Tuesdays, Thursdays and Saturdays, in the afternoon, from two o'clock till eight in the evening, on the moderate terms of one pound - his currency for twelve lessons, and ten shillings entrance. --- Those gentlemen and ladies desirous to be attended at home, to pay one pound seventeen shillings. Mr. Biferi enables his pupils in a very short time, to play on the harpsichord, either pieces, sonatas, thorough bass, &c. He also teaches and composes vocal and instrumental music in all its branches. N.B. A very good spinnet to be disposed of, in exceeding good condition, and at a moderate price."
(1 Dec 74) 3/4; (8 Dec 74) 4/1.

_____. Teacher of singing after the Italian manner. Advertisement.
(1 Dec 74) 3/4; (8 Dec 74) 4/1.

_____. Concert and ball for his benefit on March 23.
(23 Feb 75) 3/2; (2 Mar 75) 2/3; (9 Mar 75) 2/4; (16 Mar 75) 1/2; (23 Mar 75) 3/3.

BISCHOFF, I. C. [i.e. Johann Georg] (BICKHOOFF)

_____. Six sonatas for a violoncello and bass, to be sold.
RISM B2737: *Six sonates, à violoncello et basse . . . Oeuvre première.* Amsterdam: Joseph Schmitt.
(20-23 Oct 79) 3/3; (3-10 Nov 79) 4/2; (17-20 Nov 79) 4/2; (24 Nov 79) 3/2; (27 Nov - 1 Dec 79) 4/2; (22 Dec 79 - 12 Jan 80) 4/3; (15 Jan 80) 2/4; (26 Jan 80) 3/3; (5 Feb 80) 3/4.

Black sloven. *SEE* "For battle prepar'd in their country's just cause."

BLANC. (BLANE)

_____. Six duets for two flutes, to be sold.
BUC I, p.111: *Six duets for German flutes.* London: J. Longman & Co., 1768.
(22 Nov 77) 1/3-4.

_____. Duetts for German flutes, to be sold.
BUC I, p.111: See entry above.
(20-23 Oct 79) 3/3; (3-10 Nov 79) 4/2; (17-20 Nov 79) 4/2; (24 Nov 79) 3/2; (27 Nov - 1 Dec 79) 4/2; (22 Dec 79 - 12 Jan 80) 4/3; (15 Jan 80) 2/4; (26 Jan 80) 3/3; (5 Feb 80) 3/4.

BLANCK, Nicholas.

_____. Solos for German flute, to be sold.
    RISM B2838: *Six solos for the German flute . . . Opera terza.*
London: J. Johnston, 1770.
    (14 Oct 73) 1/4; (11 Nov 73) Supplement, 1/1.

BLANE. *SEE* BLANC.

Blessed is he that cometh. *SEE* Church-music.

Blubber Hall. *SEE* "Some muse assist me to relate."

BOCCHERINI, Luigi, 1743-1805. (BACCHERINI)

_____. Works by, to be sold.
    (28 Aug 79) 2/2; (1 Sep 79) 2/4.
_____. Duetts for two violins, to be sold.
    RISM B3050: *Four duetts for two violins, Op. X.* London: Long-
man, Lukey & Co., ca.1775.
    (14 Oct 73) 1/4; (11 Nov 73) Supplement, 1/1; (20-23 Oct 79) 3/3;
    (3-10 Nov 79) 4/2; (17-20 Nov 79) 4/2; (24 Nov 79) 3/2; (27 Nov
    - 1 Dec 79) 4/2; (22 Dec 79 - 12 Jan 80) 4/3; (15 Jan 80) 2/4; (26
    Jan 80) 3/3; (5 Feb 80) 3/4.
_____. 6 sonatas for keyboard, to be sold.
    RISM B3028: *Six sonatas for the harpsicord or pianoforte, with an
accompaniment for a violin or German flute . . . Opera 3.* London:
Longman, Lukey & Co., ca.1776.
    (14 Oct 73) 1/4; (11 Nov 73) Supplement, 1/1.
_____. Six sonatas for keyboard, Opera 3, to be sold.
    RISM B3028: See entry above.
    (22 Nov 77) 1/3-4.
_____. Six sonatas for a violoncello, to be sold.
    RISM B3015: *Six sonatas's pour le violoncelle.* London: R. Bremner,
1771.
    (20-23 Oct 79) 3/3; (3-10 Nov 79) 4/2; (17-20 Nov 79) 4/2; (24
    Nov 79) 3/2; (27 Nov - 1 Dec 79) 4/2; (22 Dec 79 - 12 Jan 80)
    4/3; (15 Jan 80) 2/4; (26 Jan 80) 3/3; (5 Feb 80) 3/4.

BORCHY. *SEE* BORGHI, Luigi.

BORGHESE, Antonio D. R.

_____. Six sonatas for keyboard, Opera 1, to be sold.
    RISM B3687: *Six sonatas for the piano forte or harpsichord, with an
accompanyment for a violin. Opera I.* London: Longman, Lukey and
Broderip, 1776.
    (22 Nov 77) 1/3-4.

BORGHI, Luigi, 1745?-ca.1806. (BORCHY)

____. Solo concerto for violino, to be performed.
> RISM B3703: *Six concertos for the violin, in nine parts . . . Opera 2^d^*. London: W. Napier, 1780?
>> (27 Apr 82) 3/3.
>> For fuller reference, *SEE* Concert (27 Apr 82).

Bows. *SEE* Fiddle; Giardini screw bows; Violin; Violin, tenor; Violoncello.

Bremner, James, d.1780. *SEE* HOPKINSON, Francis.

Bretagne. *SEE* Dancing. Taught by William Charles Hulett.

"Bright author of my present flame." *SEE* TRAVERS, John.

The British light infantry. *SEE* "For battle prepar'd in their country's just cause." *SEE ALSO* A medley for the light infantry.

Brooklyn Hall. *SEE* Assembly. At Loosley's; Loosley, Brooklyn Hall; Loosley's tavern.

Brown, Mr. [William Brown?] German flute player advertising two concerts to be held at Roubalet's Room.
> (2 Aug 83) 2/3; (13 Aug 83) 3/3.
> For fuller reference, *SEE* Concert (2 Aug 83).

The buck, or the Englishman in Paris. *SEE* Storer, Miss.

"Bucks have at ye all." *SEE Jane Shore* (play).

Bugle horns. 18 surrendered by British at Yorktown.
> (26 Dec 81) 2/2.

BUHLER.

____. Two concertos for a bassoon obligato, two violins, a tenor and a violoncello, to be sold.
> (22 Nov 77) 1/3-4.

Bull, Amos, 1726-1814. Teacher of psalmody. Advertisement for singing school to start by December 1, 1774. "The subscriber having for many years taught psalmody in several parts of New-England. . . ."
> (24 Nov 74) 1/3; (1 Dec 74) 4/1.

The bullfinch. A songbook, to be sold.
> (7 Jun 83) 3/3; (11-14 Jun 83) 1/1.

La buona figliuola. *SEE* PICCINNI, Niccolò.

Burial service. *SEE* Church-music.

Burney, Charles, 1726-1814.

_____. On musick, to be sold.
    RISM BVI[1], p.192: *The present state of music in France and
Italy; or, the journal of a tour through those countries, undertaken to
collect materials for a general history on music.* London: T. Becket
and Co., 1771.
    RISM BVI[1], p.192: *The present state of music in Germany, the
Netherlands, and United Provinces. Or, the journal of a tour through
those countries, undertaken to collect materials for a general history of
music.* London: T. Becket, J. Robinson, G. Robinson, 1773.
    (6 Jan 74) 3/2; (13 Jan 74) 4/1.

The butterfly. English opera, harpsichord/vocal edition, to be sold.
    (22 Nov 77) 1/3-4.

By the gayly circling glass. *SEE* A medley for the light infantry.

CAMIDGE, John, 1734-1803. (CAMMIDGE)

_____. Six lessons for keyboard, to be sold privately.
    RISM C563: *Six easy lessons for the harpsichord.* York: Thos.
Haxby for the author, 1764.
    RISM C564: *Six easy lessons for the harpsichord.* London: Welcker,
ca.1770.
    (4 Oct 83) 2/2.

The camp. SEE LINLEY, Thomas, the Elder.

CAMPIONI, Carlo Antonio, 1720-1788.

_____. Music, to be sold.
    (4 Oct 77) 4/2; (25 Oct 77) 4/4.
_____. Works by, to be sold.
    (28 Aug 79) 2/2; (1 Sep 79) 2/4.
_____. Duetts for German flute, to be sold.
    RISM C648: *VIII sonates à deux flûtes et une basse . . . Opera IV.*
London: R. Bremner, ca.1770.
    (14 Oct 73) 1/4; (11 Nov 73) Supplement, 1/1.
_____. Sonatos [sic] and trios, Operas 1-7, to be sold.
    RISM C630: *Six sonatas for two violins with a thorough bass for the
harpsichord or violoncello . . . Opera prima.* London: Wm. Randall, ca.
1770.
    RISM C635: *Six sonatas for two violins with a thorough bass for the
harpsicord or violoncello . . . Opera 2da.* London: Wm. Randall, ca.
1770.
    RISM C638: *Six sonatas for two violins with a thorough bass for the
harpsicord or violoncello . . . Opera III.* London: I. Walsh, 1759.

RISM C639: *Six sonatas for two violins with a thorough bass for the harpsicord or violoncello . . . Opera III.* London: Wm. Randall, ca. 1770.

RISM 642: *Six sonatas for two violins with a thorough bass for the harpsicord or violoncello . . . Opera IV.* London: I. Walsh, 1765.

RISM 655: *Six sonatas for two violins with a thorough bass for the harpsicord or violoncello . . . Opera quinta.* London: I. Walsh, 1760.

RISM 659: *Six sonatas for two violins with a thorough bass for the harpsicord or violoncello . . . Opera VI.* London: I. Walsh, 1765.

RISM 664: *Six sonates à deux violons & violoncello. . . . Opera VII.* London: Welcker, 1770.

BMC I, p.219: *Six sonatas or trio's [sic] for two violins or German flutes with the thorough bass for the harpsichord* [by Campioni and Charles Chabran]. London: C. and S. Thompson, 1764.

(21 Apr 74) 3/4; (5 May 74) 3/2.

_____. Six sonatas for violin and German flute, Opera 3 and 4, to be sold.
RISM C638: See entry above.
RISM C642: See entry above.
(22 Nov 77) 1/3-4.

_____. Sonatas for two German flutes or violins, Op. 7, to be sold.
RISM C664: See entry above, Sonatos [sic] and trios.
(20-23 Oct 79) 3/3; (3-10 Nov 79) 4/2; (17-20 Nov 79) 4/2; (24 Nov 79) 3/2; (27 Nov - 1 Dec 79) 4/2; (22 Dec 79 - 12 Jan 80) 4/3; (15 Jan 80) 2/4; (26 Jan 80) 3/3; (5 Feb 80) 3/4.

_____. Trio's [sic], to be sold.
BMC I, p.219: See entry above, *Six sonatas and trio's* [sic].
(30 Sep 73) 3/4; (7 Oct 73) 4/3; (14 Oct 73) Supplement, 1/3.

_____. Trios for violin, to be sold.
BMC I, p.219: See entry above, *Six sonatas and trio's* [sic].
(14 Oct 73) 1/4; (11 Nov 73) Supplement, 1/1.

CANALETTI, Giovanni Battista.

_____. Trios, to be sold.
RISM C777: *VI Trii per violini due e cetra.* London: Longman & Lukey & Co.
(20-23 Oct 79) 3/3; (3-10 Nov 79) 4/2; (17-20 Nov 79) 4/2; (24 Nov 79) 3/2; (27 Nov - 1 Dec 79) 4/2; (22 Dec 79 - 12 Jan 80) 4/3; (15 Jan 80) 2/4; (26 Jan 80) 3/3; (5 Feb 80) 3/4.

Cantata Domino. *SEE* Church-music.

Cantatas. *SEE* ARNE, Thomas Augustine. The girdle; The minstrell; A song book.

Canzonetts, to be sold.
BUC I, p.160: *Twelve canzonets for two voices composed by different authors.* London: P. Hodgson, 1770?
(22 Nov 77) 1/3-4.

CAPPELLETTI, Anthonio.

____. 12 sonatas for German flute, to be sold.
(14 Oct 73) 1/4; (11 Nov 73) Supplement, 1/3
____. Sonatas for two German flutes or violins, to be sold.
RISM C918: *Twelve sonatas for two violins and a violoncello or thorough bass for the harpsicord or organ, etc.* London: Longman, Lukey & Co., ca.1777.
(20-23 Oct 79) 3/3; (3-10 Nov 79) 4/2; (17-20 Nov 79) 4/2; (24 Nov 79) 3/2; (27 Nov - 1 Dec 79) 4/2; (22 Dec 79 - 12 Jan 80) 4/3; (15 Jan 80) 2/4; (26 Jan 80) 3/3; (5 Feb 80) 3/4.

The captive. English opera, harpsichord/vocal edition, to be sold.
BUC I, p.161: *The songs in the comic opera of The captive. . . . The words by the author of Love in a village and the music by the most eminent composers.* London: John Johnston, 1769.
(22 Nov 77) 1/3-4.

Cards in packs containing the figures and musick for a great number of cotillons and country dances, to be sold.
(4 Oct 77) 4/2; (25 Oct 77) 4/4.

CAROLINA, Signora.

____. "O wherefore, brother Jonathan." Set to music by Signora Carolina. Song lyric printed.
(27 Sep 80) 3/1.

CARTER, Charles Thomas, ca.1735-1804.

____. Tally ho. Favourite song to be sung between the play and farce in the theatre.
RISM C1342: *Tally Ho. A favourite hunting song. Sung by Mrs. Wrighten at Vauxhall, etc.* London, ca.1780.
(30 Mar 82) 3/3.

CARTER.

____. Carter's lessons and duetts for guitar, to be sold.
(20-23 Oct 79) 3/3; (3-10 Nov 79) 4/2; (17-20 Nov 79) 4/2; (24 Nov 79) 3/2; (27 Nov - 1 Dec 79) 4/2; (22 Dec 79 - 12 Jan 80) 4/3; (15 Jan 80) 2/4; (26 Jan 80) 3/3; (5 Feb 80) 3/4.

Catches and glees performed at the Catch Clubs in Great-Britain. With a vast variety of English songs, set for the violin, German flute, guitar etc., to be sold.
(19 Feb 80) 1/4.

Catches, glees, to be sold.
(22 Nov 77) 1/3-4; (20-23 Oct 79) 3/3; (3-10 Nov 79) 4/2; (17-20 Nov 79) 4/2; (24 Nov 79) 3/2; (27 Nov - 1 Dec 79) 4/2;

(22 Dec 79 - 12 Jan 80) 4/3; (15 Jan 80) 2/4; (26 Jan 80) 3/3; (5 Feb 80) 3/4.

Catches to be sung between play and entertainment in the theatre. *SEE Tamerlane.*

Catches. *SEE ALSO* A song book; Vocal music.

CHALON, John. (CHALENS)

_____. Works by, to be sold.
(28 Aug 79) 2/2; (1 Sep 79) 2/4.

Chamber organ. *SEE* Organ.

Chançons, to be sold. *SEE* The songster's companion.

CHIESA, Melchior, fl.1758-1799. (CHRESA)

_____. Works by, to be sold.
(28 Aug 79) 2/2; (1 Sep 79) 2/4.
_____. Trios, to be sold.
RISM C2047: *Sei trio per due violini e basso, etc.* London:
Welcker, ca.1775.
(20-23 Oct 79) 3/3; (3-10 Nov 79) 4/2; (17-20 Nov 79) 4/2; (24 Nov 79) 3/2; (27 Nov - 1 Dec 79) 4/2; (22 Dec 79 - 12 Jan 80) 4/3; (15 Jan 80) 2/4; (26 Jan 80) 3/3; (5 Feb 80) 3/4.

Chorus. *SEE* Church-music.

CHRESA. *SEE* CHIESA, Melchior.

Christie and Duncan. *SEE* Violin. Instruments, to be sold.

Chrononhotonthologos, the tragedy, and *Taste,* the comedy. Songs performed between the acts of.
(6 Jan 79) 3/4; (9 Jan 79) 1/1.

Church-music, "ready for engraving, and to be published by subscription, the following select pieces, consisting of a compleat sett of church service, viz. A Te Deum laudamus; Jubilate Deo; Benedicit omnia opera Domini; Cantate Domino; and Deus misereatur; a burial service, and an anthem for any grand funeral; a compleat and well adapted anthem to be sung at the time of any charitable contribution; a grand chorus, Hosanna to the Son of David, Blessed is [he] that cometh in the name of the Lord, &c proper to be sung at any meeting, or convention of the clergy, of any denomination; as also an anthem 133d Psalm, for any grand meeting of Free and Accepted Masons. . . . "
(24 Jun 77) 3/3.

CIRRI, Giovanni Battista, 1724-1808.

_____. Works by, to be sold.
   (28 Aug 79) 2/2; (1 Sep 79) 2/4.
_____. Duetts for violins and German flutes, Op. 12, to be sold.
   RISM C2525: *Six duetts for a violin and a violoncello . . . Opera
   XII*. London: Welcker, 1770.
   (20-23 Oct 79) 3/3; (3-10 Nov 79) 4/2; (17-20 Nov 79) 4/2; (24
   Nov 79) 3/2; (27 Nov - 1 Dec 79) 4/2; (22 Dec 79 - 12 Jan 80)
   4/3; (15 Jan 80) 2/4; (26 Jan 80) 3/3; (5 Feb 80) 3/4.
_____. Quartettos, to be sold.
   RISM C2504: *Six quartettos, four for a German-flute, 2 violins and
   a bass, and two for 2 violins, a violoncello obligato and a bass . . .
   Opera X*. London: Welcker, 1768.
   RISM C2505: *Six quartettos for two violins, a tenor and violoncello
   obligato . . . Opera XIII*. London: For the author, 1775.
   (20-23 Oct 79) 3/3; (3-10 Nov 79) 4/2; (17-20 Nov 79) 4/2; (24
   Nov 79) 3/2; (27 Nov - 1 Dec 79) 4/2; (22 Dec 79 - 12 Jan 80)
   4/3; (15 Jan 80) 2/4; (26 Jan 80) 3/3; (5 Feb 80) 3/4.
_____. Six sonatas, a violoncello solo e basso, Op. 3, to be sold.
   RISM C2517: *Sei sonate à violoncello solo e basso . . . Gravée par
   Mme. Leclair. Opera terza*. Paris: Chez l'Auteur, ca.1765.
   (20-23 Oct 79) 3/3; (3-10 Nov 79) 4/2; (17-20 Nov 79) 4/2; (24
   Nov 79) 3/2; (27 Nov - 1 Dec 79) 4/2; (22 Dec 79 - 12 Jan 80)
   4/3; (15 Jan 80) 2/4; (26 Jan 80) 3/3; (5 Feb 80) 3/4.

The citizen and all the songs. An excellent farce written by Mr. Murphy, to
   be performed next Thursday.
   (17 Jan 78) 2/4.

CITRACINI. (CITRALINI)

_____. Six divertimentos for guitar, to be sold.
   (14 Oct 73) 1/4; (11 Nov 73) Supplement, 1/1; (20-23 Oct 79) 3/3;
   (3-10 Nov 79) 4/2; (17-20 Nov 79) 4/2; (24 Nov 79) 3/2; (27 Nov
   - 1 Dec 79) 4/2; (22 Dec 79 - 12 Jan 80) 4/3; (15 Jan 80) 2/4; (26
   Jan 80) 3/3; (5 Feb 80) 3/4.

Clarichord (Claricord). Instruments, to be sold.

_____. Claricord, to be sold by Benjamin Davies.
   (2 Sep 74) 3/4.
_____. Clarichord having four stops, to be sold by David Phillips.
   (16 Dec 73) 3/2; (23 Dec 73) 4/2; (30 Dec 73) 4/4; (31 Mar 74)
   3/3; (7 Apr 74) 4/1.
_____. Clarichord, to be sold by James Griffiths.
   (15 Oct 83) 3/3.

Clarichords. Stringing, quilling and tuning by William Pearson, clock and
watch-maker.
(14 Apr 74) 1/1; (21 Apr 74) 4/4.
For fuller reference, *SEE* Pearson, William.

Clarinet. Instruments, to be sold.

_____. Clarinets, two.
(28 Oct 78) 2/3; (31 Oct 78) 4/1; (4 Nov 78) 1/4; (7 Nov 78) 4/3;
(11 Nov 78) 1/4.
_____. Clarinets, a pair.
(24 Apr 79) 2/2; (28 Apr 79) 2/1; (5 May 79) 4/4.
_____. Clarinets.
(28 Aug 79) 2/2; (1 Sep 79) 2/4; (3 May 80) 3/3-4; (27 May 80)
3/3; (17 Jun 80) 4/2; (8 Jul 80) 3/4; (23 Dec 80) 3/4; (27 Dec 80 -
3 Jan 81) 4/3; (6 Jan 81) 2/2; (26 Sep 81) 4/1; (29 Sep - 31 Oct
81) 4/2; (3-7 Nov 81) 4/4; (10-21 Nov 81) 4/2; (24 Nov 81) 4/4; (5
Dec 81 - 23 Feb 82) 4/1; (27 Feb 82) 4/3; (6-16 Mar 82) 1/2; (20
Mar 82) 4/2; (23-27 Mar 82) 4/2; (13 Apr 82) 3/4; (24 Apr - 1
May 82) 1/3; (4-29 May 82) 1/1; (1 Jun 82) 1/3; (5 Jun 82) 1/2; (8
Jun 82) 1/1; (12-22 Jun 82) 4/1; (26 Jun - 13 Jul 82) 4/4; (17 Jul
82) 1/1; (20-31 Jul 82) 4/1; (3-17 Aug 82) 4/3; (21 Aug - 4 Sep
82) 4/1; (11 Sep 82) 3/4; (14-21 Sep 82) 1/2; (19 Oct 82) 2/4; (23
Oct 82) 1/1.

Clarinet. Accessories, to be sold.

_____. Reeds and cases.
(3 May 80) 3/3-4; (27 May 80) 3/3; (17 Jun 80) 4/2; (8 Jul 80)
3/4; (23 Dec 80) 3/4; (27 Dec 80 - 4 Jan 81) 4/3; (6 Jan 81) 2/2.

Clarinet. Music, to be sold.

_____. Clarinet, works for.
(28 Aug 79) 2/2; (1 Sep 79) 2/4.

Clarinet. Music. *SEE ALSO* GIORDANI, Tommaso.

Clarinet and French horn music. *SEE* DREZTY; GALEOTTI, Salvatore *or*
Stefano; GIORDANI, Tommaso.

Clarinet. Performers.

_____. Clarinet players wanted for band on board the *General Pattison*,
private ship of war.
(14 Apr 79) 2/4; (21 Apr 79) 4/3.

Clarinet. Performers. *SEE ALSO* Musicians wanted for a regiment.

Clarinet. Tutors or instructors, to be sold.

_____. Clarinet tutors.
        (14 Oct 73) 1/4; (11 Nov 73) Supplement, 1/1; (25 Jul 78) 3/1; (8 Sep 79) 2/4; (2 Oct 79) 2/3; (9 Oct 79) 3/4.

Classados, to be sold.
        (28 Aug 79) 2/2; (1 Sep 79) 2/4.

Classados. *SEE ALSO* Glassado.

Clavichord. *SEE* Clarichord.

"The cloud is burst, behold a clearer sky!" Song lyric printed.
        (11 May 82) 3/1.

COCCHI, Gioacchino, ca.1720-1788. (COCCI)

_____. Quintettos, to be sold.
        (20-23 Oct 79) 3/3; (3-10 Nov 79) 4/2; (17-20 Nov 79) 4/2; (24 Nov 79) 3/2; (27 Nov - 1 Dec 79) 4/2; (22 Dec 79 - 12 Jan 80) 4/3; (15 Jan 80) 2/4; (26 Jan 80) 3/3; (5 Feb 80) 3/4.

A collection of ancient and modern Scotch songs. *SEE* Scotch songs.

A collection of Scots songs in two volumes. *SEE* Scotch songs.

"Come cheer up, my lads, let us haste to the main." To the tune of Hearts of oak. Song lyric printed.
        (27 Nov 79) Supplement, 1/2.

"Come, each death-doing dog who dare venture his neck." Hot stuff. To the tune of Lilies of France. Song lyric printed.
        (5 May 74) 2/3.

"Come let us rejoice." The seige of Savannah. To the tune of The free mason's song. Song lyric printed.
        (27 Nov 79) 3/3.

"Come let us run at once they cry." To the tune of O mother dear Jerusalem. Song lyric printed.
        (12 Feb 80) 2/1.

"Come, my boys, in jovial strain." Song lyric printed.
        (23 Jul 83) 2/1.

Common concert flutes. *SEE* English, or common, flute.

Comus. *SEE* ARNE, Thomas Augustine.

Concert (by date).

_____. Concert "of vocal and instrumental music, for the benefit of Mr. Zedtwitz, at Mr. Hull's assembly room. The concert to be conducted, and the first violin perform'd, by Mr. Zedtwitz, the other instrumental parts, by the gentleman [sic] of the Harmonic Society. In act the first, a solo by Mr. Zedtwitz, by particular desire. Vain is beauty's gawdy flowers, and The soldier tired, by Miss Hallam: In act the second, a singing by Miss Storer, a duet with Mr. Hulett's son 10 years old." Advertisement for concert to be performed on May 11, 1773.
    (6 May 73) 3/3.

_____. Subscription concert. Rehearsal for on Saturday, December 4.
    (2 Dec 73) 3/4.

_____. Subscription concert. First concert to be held on December 9 at Hull's Assembly Room.
    (2 Dec 73) 3/4.

_____. Subscription concert. First concert to be December 10, afterwards on Thursday evening every fortnight at Mr. Hull's Assembly Room.
    (9 Dec 73) 3/4.

_____. Subscription concert. "The subscribers are desired to be assured, that the first concert will be on Friday evening next, the 10th instant; and afterwards on Thursday evening every fortnight at Mr. Hull's Assembly Room."
    (16 Dec 73) 4/3

_____. Concert and ball, on Tuesday, the 4th of January 1774. At Mr. Hull's room. Tickets to be sold by Mr. Zedtwitz and Mr. Hulett. 5s. Concert to begin at six o'clock.
    (23 Dec 73) 3/4; (30 Dec 73) 4/1.

_____. Concert deferred until March 21.
    (17 Mar 74) 3/3.

_____. Subscription concert. Deferred first until April 24 then until April 28 and "allowed to be a public concert for the use of Signiora [sic] Mazzanti, Messrs. Zedwitz & Hulett: on which evening the gentlemen of the Harmonic Society have been pleased to promise their assistance; and Signiora Mazzanti will sing several English and Italian songs. After the concert proper music will be ready to wait upon such ladies and gentlemen as may choose to dance."
    (14 Apr 74) 3/3; (21 Apr 74) 3/2; (28 Apr 74) 2/2.

_____. Concert to be performed May 26, 1774 at Mr. Hull's Assembly Room ". . . for the benefit of Mr. Biferi and Mr. Sodi. The said concert will be divided into two acts, each act composed of four pieces. Mr. Biferi, master of music from Naples, will perform on the harpsichord a piece of music of his composition with the orchestra; in the second act he will perform a solo, accompanied with the violin. There will follow a ball, in which Mr. Sodi will dance the louvre [i.e. loure] and the minuet, with Miss Sodi, a young lady nine years of age; and Miss Sodi will dance a rigadoon with young Mr. Hulet. . . ."
    (19 May 74) 3/3; (26 May 74) 2/4.

_____. Concert and ball to be performed at Mr. Hull's Tavern on March 23, for the benefit of Mr. Biferi.

(23 Feb 75) 3/2; (2 Mar 75) 2/3; (9 Mar 75) 2/4; (16 Mar 75) 1/2;
(23 Mar 75) 3/3.

_____. Concert by Mr. Zedtwitz and Mr. Hulett at Mr. Hull's Assembly
Room on April 4th.
(30 Mar 75) 2/3.

_____. Concert for the benefit of a band of music, to be held at Mr. Hull's
Assembly Room on April 27. To be followed by a ball.
(20 Apr 75) 3/3.

_____. Concert of music, January 24 at the Coffee-House.
(24 Jan 78) 2/3.

_____. "Some gentlemen being desirous of having musical parties this winter,
have entered into a subscription of two guineas each for to have a
concert twice a week, and to commence as soon as there are twelve
subscribers that are performers. The particulars to be had at Mr.
Rivington's, where the subscription is to be paid. As soon as the
subscription is filled Mr. Rivington will call a meeting of the
subscribers to settle in what manner the monies arising from said
subscription shall be appropriated."
(25 Nov 78) 3/2; (28 Nov 78) 4/2.

_____. Concert to be performed in the evening, September 10. "The best
entertainments will be provided for ladies and gentlemen, by John
Mackenzie" at the White Conduit House.
(9 Sep 80) 2/4.

_____. "The public are desired to take notice that there will be neither play
nor concert, during the ensuing week, but that they will be renewed
the week following." In the theatre.
(6 Apr 81) 3/1.

_____. Subscription concert. At Roubalet's. The first concert to be on
January 19 and on every Wednesday evening following. To be two
acts.
(16 Jan 82) 3/4; (19 Jan 82) 2/4.

_____. Subscription concert. At Roubalet's. To be on January 23, 1782.
(23 Jan 82) 2/1.

_____. Subscription concert. Announcement about how non-subscribers can get
tickets.
(6 Mar 82) 3/3.

_____. Concert for refugees. Tickets to be made available.
(24 Apr 82) 3/4.

_____. Concert ". . . of vocal and instrumental musick for the benefit of two
distressed refugee families . . . to be performed April 27, 1782. Act I.
Sinfonie of Toeschi, Quartetto of Davaux, for violino, song by Mrs.
Hyde, Soldier tir'd of wars alarms. Violino, Solo Concerto of Borchy.
Quintetto of C. Bach for flauto. Sinfonie of Stamitz. Act II. Sinfonie
of Haydn. Quartetto of Kammell, for violino. Song by Mrs. Hyde,
The lark's shrill notes. Hoboy solo concerto by C. Fischer. Quartetto
of Vanhall, for flauto. Sinfonie of Haydn Act III. Sinfonie of Bach.
Quartetto of Davaux, for violino. Song by Mrs. Hyde, If 'tis joy to
wound a lover. Clarenetto solo of Mahoy. Quartetto of Toeschi, for
flauto. Sinfonie of Mardino. . . ."
(27 Apr 82) 3/3.

_____. Subscription concert. Postponed and 18th and final performance announced.
    (8 May 82) 3/3.

_____. Subscription concert. At Roubalet's. "The 17th will be on Monday, May 13th."
    (11 May 82) 3/3.

_____. Subscription concert. First one advertised to begin at Roubalet's Tavern on November 30, 1782.
    (30 Nov 82) 3/4.

_____. Subscription concert. Advertisement for weekly concert. Postponed to January 16th.
    (15 Jan 83) 3/2.

_____. Subscription concert. Advertisement for, on January 25 at Roubalet's.
    (22 Jan 83) 3/3.

_____. Subscription concert. Next one advertised for February 1 at Roubalet's. No dance after the concert.
    (29 Jan 83) 3/4.

_____. Subscription concert. At Roubalet's on February 1, 1783.
    (1 Feb 83) 3/4.

_____. Concert. To be performed June 9, 1783 "for the benefit of Signor Gaetano Franceschini. . . ."
    (4 Jun 83) 3/2; (7 Jun 83) 4/2.

_____. "Mr. [William?] Brown, who has exhibited on the German flute, in most parts of Europe, and is allowed by the first judges, to be a most capital performer on that instrument, proposes, during his stay in this city, to give two concerts by subscription, at Roubalet's Room; viz. on Tuesday and Friday next, in case a sufficient number of subscribers give him encouragement. . . ."
    (2 Aug 83) 2/3.

_____. "Mr. [William?] Brown's second concert will be at Roubalet's, on Friday next, if he is honoured with a sufficient audience. . . ."
    (13 Aug 83) 3/3.

Concert. *SEE ALSO* [Afro-American] assemblies, balls and concerts.

Concerto spirituale. "To be performed on Saturday, March 25th. Of three acts, each act will consist of an overture, song, solo, song, trio, song, symphony. The whole to conclude with the grand chorus of the *Messiah*. The orchestra will be on stage, which will be properly decorated on this occasion."
    (22 Mar 80) 3/3; (25 Mar 80) 3/4.

Concertos. *SEE* ALEXANDER, B.; BACH, Carl Philipp Emanuel; BACH, Johann Christian; BARTHÉLÉMON, François Hippolyte; BORGHI, Luigi; BUHLER; DITTERS VON DITTERSDORF, Carl; ESSER, Michael; FISCHER, Johann Christian; GIARDINI, Felice; GIORDANI, Tommaso; HAWDON, Matthias; HAYES, Philip; JUST, Johann August; KLÖFFLER, Johann Friedrich; KREUSSER, Georg Anton; MAHON, John; MALDERE, Pierre van; PLA, José; RETZEL, August Johann; RICCI, Francesco Pasquale; RICHTER, Franz Xaver; SCHWINDL, Friedrich; SMETHERGELL, William; STAMITZ.

Contra dances and other easy baggatelles for young adepts on the German
flute, fiddle, guittar, hautboy, &c.
(20-23 Oct 79) 3/3; (3 Nov 79) 4/2; (3 Nov 79) Supplement, 2/1;
(6-10 Nov 79) 4/2; (17-24 Nov 79) 4/2; (24 Nov 79) 3/2;
(27 Nov - 1 Dec 79) 4/2; (22 Dec 79 - 12 Jan 80) 4/3; (15 Jan 80)
2/4; (26 Jan 80) 3/3; (5 Feb 80) 3/4.

The convivial songster. Songbook, to be sold.
BUC I, p.213: *The convivial songster, being a select collection of
the best songs in the English language . . . with the music prefixed to
each song.* London: John Fielding, 1782.
(7 Jun 83) 3/3; (11-14 Jun 83) 1/1.

CORELLI, Arcangelo, 1653-1713.

_____. Music, to be sold.
(4 Oct 77) 4/2; (25 Oct 77) 4/4.

Cornet players, surrendered at Yorktown to General Washington by the British.
(26 Dec 81) 1/4.

Cotillon. *SEE* Cards in packs; Dance books; Dancing.

Cottillion, to be taught by W. Birchall Tetley.
(3 Nov 74) 3/4; (10 Nov 74) 4/4.
For fuller reference, *SEE* Tetley, W. Birchall.

Cottillion. *SEE ALSO* Dancing; Dancing school.

"Could I the abundance of my sorrow show." Song lyric printed.
(12 Jan 75) 2/3.

Country dance. Conclusion to *The mayor of Garrat.*
(6 May 73) 3/3.

Country dance. Concluding theatrical entertainment.
(1 Jul 73) 3/3.

Country dance books, to be sold.
(29 Dec 81) 3/4; (2-5 Jan 82) 4/4; (9 Jan 82) 4/3.

Country dance books. *SEE ALSO* Dance books.

Country dances. Tabor and pipes for, to be sold.
(22 Nov 77) 1/3-4.

Country dances, 24. Violin music, to be sold.
(14 Oct 73) 1/4; (11 Nov 73) Supplement, 1/1.

Country dances. *SEE ALSO* Cards in packs; Dance; Dances; Dancing;
Dancing school; English country dances; Minuets.

Cozani, Mrs., lately arrived from London. Advertisement for French boarding school for young ladies. "There will be masters for music, dancing and writing."
(28 Jul 74) 4/1.

CRAMER, Wilhelm, 1746-1799.

_____. Work by, to be sold.
(28 Aug 79) 2/2; (1 Sep 79) 2/4.

CROFT, William, 1678-1727.

_____. Anthems mentioned in advertisement for an American church music imprint costing two guineas.
(24 Jun 73) 3/3.

The cut-purse. *SEE* "The old English cause knocks at every man's door."

Cymon. *SEE* ARNE, Michael.

Damon and Phillida. *SEE* DIBDIN, Charles.

Dance.

_____. To follow public concert on April 28, 1774.
(14 Apr 74) 3/3; (21 Apr 74) 3/2; (28 Apr 74) 2/2.
_____. Not to be had after the concert.
(29 Jan 83) 3/4; (1 Feb 83) 3/4.

Dance. *SEE ALSO* Assembly; Ball; Country dance; English country dances; Pantomime.

Dance books. Minuet, country dance and cotillon, to be sold.
(4 Oct 77) 4/2; (25 Oct 77) 4/4.

Dances, cotillons and country. Figures and musick for, on packs of cards, to be sold.
(4 Oct 77) 4/2; (25 Oct 77) 4/4.

Dances, new. To be sold.
(21 Apr 74) 3/4; (5 May 74) 3/2; (28 Aug 79) 2/2; (1 Sep 79) 2/4.

Dancing.

_____. Taught by William Charles Hulett "according to the present taste, both in London and Paris. The louvre [i.e. loure], minuet, minuette Dauphine, rigadoon, Bretagne, the allemande, double minuet, minuet by eight, hornpipes, the cotillions, and English country dances. . . ."
(12 Jan 75) 3/4; (19 Jan 75) 4/2.

_____. Taught by William Birchall Tetley. "Teaches the old and new louvre [i.e. loure] , the various sorts of minuets, allemandes, cottillions, English country dances, single, double and tripple hornpipes, and other dances as they are now danced at London and Paris. . . ."
    (12 Jan 75) 3/4; (19 Jan 75) 4/2.

_____. Taught with French and fencing by Du Poke and De St. Pry. "Teaches French jigs, hornpipes, cotillons, German dances, and French country dances of all kinds. . . ."
    (23 Mar 75) 3/4; (30 Mar 75) 4/3.

Dancing. *SEE ALSO* Assembly; Ball; Country dances; Dancing school; English country dances; Pantomime.

Dancing Assembly.
    (17 Jan 78) 2/3; (14 Feb 78) 2/1; (14 Mar 78) 2/2; (24 Feb 79) 1/1; (6 Mar 79) 3/3; (29 Mar 80) 3/2; (13 Dec 83) 4/3; (17 Dec 83) 3/4; (20 Dec 83) 2/3.

Dancing Assembly. Cancelled because of Passion Week.
    (13 Apr 75) 1/2.

Dancing in the theatre.
    (22 Apr 73) 3/2; (29 Apr - 13 May 73) 3/3; (3 Jun 73) 3/2; (10-17 Jun 73) 3/3; (1 Jul 73) 3/3; (8 Jul 73) 3/1; (22 Jul 73) 3/2.

Dancing in the theatre. *SEE ALSO* Old women ground young; Pantomime dance; Roussell, Mr.

Dancing school. To be taught by Martin Foy, starting September 20. "He teaches a minuet with proper graces in exact time, and in the newest taste; also cotillions, and a variety of country dances..."
    (18 Sep 79) 3/3; (25 Sep 79) 3/4; (2 Oct 79) 2/2; (6 Oct 79) 4/4.

Dancing school. *SEE ALSO* Biferi, Nicholas; Dancing.

Dancing teachers. *SEE* Mrs. Cozani; Du Poke; Foy, Martin; Hulett, William Charles; Sodi, Pietro; Tanner, J. and M.; Tetley, William Birchall.

DAVAUX, Jean Baptiste, 1742-1822.

_____. Quartetto for violino, to be performed.
    RISM D1158: *Six quartettos for two violins, a tenor, and violoncello . . . Opera IX.* London: W. Napier, 1780?
    (27 Apr 82) 3/3.
    For fuller reference, *SEE* Concert (27 Apr 82).

Davies, Benjamin. *SEE* Claricord; Guitar; Harpsichord; Music, to be sold; Music desks; Pens; Spinnet; Violin. Accessories.

DAVIS, Thomas, fl.mid-18th century.

_____. 20 airs for two German flutes or two violins, to be sold.
RISM D1236: *Twenty familiar English and Scotch airs for German flutes or two violins.* London: H. Waylett.
(22 Nov 77) 1/3-4.

Deblois, George. German flutes, music books, violins and violin strings, to be sold.
(18 Jul 78) 4/4; (22 Jul 78) 1/3.

Derry down. *SEE* "Our farce is now finish'd"; "Rouse, Britons! at length."

DES AIDES. *SEE* DEZÈDE, Nicolas Alexandre.

De St. Pry. *SEE* Dancing. Taught with French and fencing. . . .

The deserter. SEE DIBDIN, Charles.

DESSAIDES. *SEE* DEZÈDE, Nicolas Alexandre.

Deus misereatur. *SEE* Church-music.

The devil to pay, or the wives metamorphosed. With a song. A farce to be performed on Tuesday evening.
BUC I, p.270: *The devil to pay; or, the wives metamorphos'd. An opera. With the music prefix'd to each song.* London: J. Watts, 1731.
(2 May 78) 3/2.

DEZÈDE, Nicolas Alexandre, ca.1740-1792. (DES AIDES; DESSAIDES)

_____. Overtures, to be sold.
RISM D2159: *Ouverture de Blaise et Babet, à deux violons, viola et basse, deux hautbois, ou flûtes, fagotti, violoncello, et deux cors de chasse.* Amsterdam: Vve. Markordt & fils.
RISM D2215: *Ouverture des deux tuteurs, à deux violons, taille, et basse, deux hautbois, fagotte, & deux cors de chasse.* Berlin: Johann Julius Hummel.
RISM D2225: *La fête de la imquantaine. Ouverture . . . à grand orchestre telle que l'on joue au théâtre.* Paris: Jean Henri Naderman.
RISM D2243: *Julie. Overture. . . .* Amsterdam: S. Markordt.
(20-23 Oct 79) 3/3; (3-10 Nov 79) 4/2; (17-20 Nov 79) 4/2; (24 Nov 79) 3/2; (27 Nov - 1 Dec 79) 4/2; (22 Dec 79 - 12 Jan 80) 4/3; (15 Jan 80) 2/4; (26 Jan 80) 3/3; (5 Feb 80) 3/4.

DIBDIN, Charles, 1745-1814. (DIBDEN)

_____. *Damon and Phillida.* English opera, harpsichord/vocal edition, to be sold.

RISM D2357: *Damon and Phillida. A comic opera . . . for the voice, harpsichord or violin.* London: C. and S. Thompson, 1768.
   (22 Nov 77) 1/3-4.
_____. *Deserter.* English opera, to be sold.
   BUC II, p.685: *The overture songs &c in The deserteur. A musical drama . . . composed by Monsigny, Philidor & Dibdin. Adapted for the German flute.* London: John Johnston . . . and Longman, Lukey & Co., ca.1773.
   (4 Oct 77) 4/2; (25 Oct 77) 4/4.
_____. *Institution of the garter.* Guitar edition, to be sold.
   RISM D2437: *The overture, songs, duets, trios, choruses, marches, &c. in The institution of the garter . . . adapted with the words for the guitar.* London: Longman, Lukey & Co., 1771.
   (14 Oct 73) 1/4; (11 Nov 73) Supplement, 1/1.
_____. *Institution of the garter.* English opera, harpsichord/vocal edition, to be sold.
   RISM D2436: *The overture, songs, duets, trios, choruses, marches, &c in The institution of the garter, or Arthur's Round Table restored as perform'd at . . . Drury Lane . . . adapted for the harpsichord, voice, German-flute, & violin.* London: Longman, Lukey & Co., 1771.
   (14 Oct 73) 1/4; (11 Nov 73) Supplement, 1/1; (22 Nov 77) 1/3-4.
_____. *The jubilee.* English opera, harpsichord/vocal edition, to be sold.
   RISM D2444: *The overture, songs, airs, and chorusses, in The jubilee or Shakspear's garland . . . to which is added a cantata called Queen Mab or The fairies' jubilee.* London: J. Johnston, etc., 1770.
   (4 Oct 77) 4/2; (25 Oct 77) 4/4; (22 Nov 77) 1/3-4.
_____. *The jubille.* SEE his *The jubilee.*
_____. *King Arther.* SEE *Institution of the garter*; ARNE, Thomas Augustine. *King Arthur.*
_____. *Lionel and Clarissa.* English opera, harpsichord/vocal edition, to be sold.
   RISM D2479: *Lionel and Clarissa, or a school for fathers, a comic opera as perform'd at the Theatre-Royal. By the author of Love in a village. The music composed by eminent masters.* London: J. Johnston, ca.1770.
   (30 Sep 73) 3/4; (7 Oct 73) 4/3; (14 Oct 73) Supplement, 1/3; (14 Oct 73) 1/4, (11 Nov 73) Supplement, 1/1; (4 Oct 77) 4/2; (25 Oct 77) 4/4.
_____. *The padlock.* English opera, harpsichord/vocal edition, to be sold.
   RISM D2557: *The padlock, a comic opera . . . the words by the author of The maid of the mill, etc. . . .* London: J. Johnston, 1768.
   (30 Sep 73) 3/4; (7 Oct 73) 4/3; (14 Oct 73) Supplement, 1/3; (4 Oct 77) 4/2; (25 Oct 77) 4/4; (22 Nov 77) 1/3-4.
_____. *The padlock.* Airs in for guitar, to be sold.
   (14 Oct 73) 1/4; (11 Nov 73) Supplement, 1/1.
_____. *The padlock.* Will be acted on January 7 at Hull's Long Room.
   (6 Jan 74) 3/4.
_____. *The pigmy revels.* English opera, harpsichord/vocal edition, to be sold.
   RISM D2578: *The comic tunes, songs and dances in the pantomime of The pigmy revels, etc.* London: Longman, Lukey & Co., 1773.
   (22 Nov 77) 1/3-4.

_____. *Poor Vulcan.* English opera, keyboard/vocal edition, to be sold.
  RISM D2580: *The overtures, songs, &c in Poor Vulcan, a comic opera . . . composed by C. Dibdin.* London: J. Johnston and W. Randall, 1778.
  (28 Aug 79) 2/2; (1 Sep 79) 2/4.

_____. *The Quaker.* English opera, keyboard/vocal edition, to be sold.
  RISM D2627: *The overture, songs, &c. in The Quaker, a comic opera . . . composed by C. Dibdin.* London: J. Johnston, 1777.
  (28 Aug 79) 2/2; (1 Sep 79) 2/4.

_____. *The recruiting serjeant.* English opera, harpsichord/vocal edition, to be sold.
  RISM D2666: *The recruiting serjeant. A new musical entertainment perform'd . . . at Ranelagh and at . . . Drury Lane, etc.* London: C. and S. Thompson, 1771.
  (22 Nov 77) 1/3-4.

_____. *The touchstone.* English opera, keyboard/vocal edition, to be sold.
  RISM D2722: *The overture, songs, duettos, chorusses, dances, comic-tunes, &c. in the new speaking pantomime called The touchstone composed by Charles Dibdin.* London: S. and A. Thompson, 1779.
  (28 Aug 79) 2/2; (1 Sep 79) 2/4.

_____. *The wedding ring.* English opera, harpsichord/vocal edition, to be sold.
  RISM D2844: *The songs, &c. in The wedding ring. A new comic opera . . . compos'd by C. Dibdin.* London: J. Johnston and Longman, Lukey & Co., 1773.
  (22 Nov 77) 1/3-4.

DITTERS VON DITTERSDORF, Carl, 1739-1799. (DITER; DITTER; DITTERS; Carlo).

_____. Works by, to be sold.
  (28 Aug 79) 2/2; (1 Sep 79) 2/4.
_____. Concertos, to be sold.
  (20-23 Oct 79) 3/3; (3-10 Nov 79) 4/2; (17-20 Nov 79) 4/2; (24 Nov 79) 3/2; (27 Nov - 1 Dec 79) 4/2; (22 Dec 79 - 12 Jan 80) 4/3; (15 Jan 80) 2/4; (26 Jan 80) 3/3; (5 Feb 80) 3/4.

Divertiments. *SEE* ALCOCK, John, Doctor in Music; ALCOCK, John, the Younger; CITRACINI; JUST, Johann August; MENEZE; TACET, Joseph; THACKRAY, Thomas.

Doctor Lucas. *SEE* "What did my phlogy, my phlogy."

Doodle-doo. *SEE* "The Frenchmen came upon the coast."

Dorcas, with the songs in character, to be performed.
  (20 Mar 82) 3/4; (23 Mar 82) 3/3.

"Down the burn Davy, love." *SEE* Scotch songs.

DREZTY.

_____. Grand military sonatas, for two clarinets, two horns, and a bassoon,
to be sold.
(20-23 Oct 79) 3/3; (3-10 Nov 79) 4/2; (17-20 Nov 79) 4/2; (24
Nov 79) 3/2; (27 Nov - 1 Dec 79) 4/2; (22 Dec 79 - 12 Jan 80)
4/3; (15 Jan 80) 2/4; (26 Jan 80) 3/3; (5 Feb 80) 3/4.

Drum. Works for, to be sold.
(28 Aug 79) 2/2; (1 Sep 79) 2/4.

Drum. Accessories, to be sold.

_____. Drum heads.
(6 Dec 77) 1/3; (13 Dec 77) 1/3; (20 Dec 77) 1/4; (8 Sep 79) 2/4;
(11 Sep 79) 2/4; (6 Oct 79) Supplement, 2/1; (9 Oct 79) Supplement,
1/2; (30 Oct 79) 2/4; (3 Nov 79) Supplement, 2/1; (10 Nov 79)
Supplement, 2; (17 Nov 79) Supplement, 2/1; (24 Nov 79) Supplement, 2/1; (27 Nov 79) Supplement, 2/1; (1 Dec 79) 2/1.
_____. Drum heads, with some fine vellum.
(25 Jul 78) 3/1.
_____. Excellent batter and snare drum heads, to be sold by Valentine Nutter.
(31 Mar 79) 2/4; (7 Apr 79) 3/4.
_____. Vellum drum heads, to be sold by Valentine Nutter.
(8 Sep 79) 2/3.

Drum captured in skirmish in Cambridge, Massachusetts.
(21 Jul 75) 3/2.

Drummer, the play of. Wanted for the theater.
(13 Mar 82) 2/3.

Drummers (164). Surrendered at Yorktown to General Washington by the
British.
(26 Dec 81) 1/3-4.

Drums and fifes marched in the funeral procession for Michael Cressop,
deceased. October 23.
(26 Oct 75) 4/1.

Drums (81), drum slings (18), drummers uniforms (17) surrendered at Yorktown
to General Washington by the British.
(26 Dec 81) 2/2-3.

The duenna. SEE LINLEY, Thomas, the Elder.

Duets, to be sold.
(21 Apr 74) 3/4; (5 May 74) 3/2; (29 Dec 81 - 23 Feb 82) 1/1;
(27 Feb 82) 4/3; (6-16 Mar 82) 1/2; (20 Mar 82) 4/2.

Duets for violins and German flutes, to be sold.
(22 Nov 77) 1/3-4.

Duets for violins and/or German flutes. *SEE* ALEXANDER, B.;
ASPELMAYER, Franz; AVOLIO, J.; BACH, Carl Philipp Emanuel;
BACH, Johann Christian; BATES, William; BLANC; BOCCHERINI,
Luigi; CAMPIONI, Carlo Antonio; CAPPELLETTI, Anthonio; CIRRI,
Giovanni Battista; DAVIS, Thomas; FISHER, John Abraham;
FLORIO, Pietro Grassi; GALEOTTI, Salvatore *or* Stefano; GARTH,
John; GERARD, James; GIARDINI, Felice; GRASSI, Florio;
GRONEMAN, John Albert; GUERINI, Francesco; HOLYOAK;
HUMBLE, Maximilian; JUST, Johann August; KAMMEL, Anton;
KERNTL, C.F.; KLÖFFLER, Johann Friedrich; LIDARTI,
Christiano Giuseppe; MANCINELLI, Domenico; NARDINI, Pietro;
NOFERI, Giovanni Battista; NOTTORNE; NUSSEN, Frederick;
PESCH, Carl August; PLA, José; RAMBACH, F. Xaver
Max; REINARDS, William; RODIL, Antonio; SABBATINI, Luigi
Antonio; SIRMEN, Maddalena Laura; STAMITZ, Karl Philipp *or*
Johann Wenzel Anton; TACET, Joseph; VENTO, Mattia; WENDLING,
Johann Baptist.

Duets. *SEE ALSO* The minstrell.

DUPIN.

_____. Works by, to be sold.
(28 Aug 79) 2/2; (1 Sep 79) 2/4.

Du Poke. French dancing teacher. Advertising a school to teach dance,
French and fencing.
(23 Mar 75) 3/4; (30 Mar 75) 4/2.
For fuller reference, *SEE* Dancing. Taught with French and fencing.

DUSTY.

_____. Works by, to be sold.
(28 Aug 79) 2/2; (1 Sep 79) 2/4.

The Earl of Essex. Mr. Wools to sing in.
(29 Apr 73) 3/3.

Edgar and Emmeline. Songs and dances incidental to, to be performed.
(22 Jul 73) 3/2.

EICHNER, Ernst, 1740-1777.

_____. Six sonatas for keyboard, to be sold.
RISM E566: *Six sonatas for the harpsichord or piano forte.* London:
R. Wornum, 1774.
(22 Nov 77) 1/3-4.

Elegant extracts, to be sold.
> BUC I, p.314: *Elegant extracts for the guittar, consisting of . . . songs . . . canzonets, rondos, airs with variations, allemands, dances, &c . . . by the most eminent masters.* London: J. Preston, ca.1785.
> (2 Jul 83) 4/1; (5 Jul 83) 4/1.

Elfrida. *SEE* ARNE, Thomas Augustine.

Ellen a roon. *SEE* Ailen a roon.

English country dances, to be taught by W. Birchall Tetley.
> (3 Nov 74) 3/4; (10 Nov 74) 4/4.
> For fuller reference, *SEE* Tetley, W. Birchall.

English country dances. *SEE ALSO* Country dance; Dancing.

English, or common, flute. Instruments, to be sold.

_____. Common flutes with cases or covers.
> (4 Oct 77) 4/2; (25 Oct 77) 4/4.

_____. English flutes.
> (29 Sep 79) 2/3; (2-9 Oct 79) 3/4; (13 Oct 79) Supplement, 1/1; (3 Nov 79) Supplement, 2/1; (10-17 Nov 79) 4/4; (20 Nov 79) 1/4; (24 Nov 79) 1/4; (3 May 80) 3/3-4; (27 May 80) 3/3; (17 Jun 80) 4/2; (8 Jul 80) 3/4.

_____. English flutes with cases or covers.
> (25 Oct 77) 4/4.

_____. English fourth concert flutes.
> (22 Nov 77) 1/3-4.

_____. English, or common flutes.
> (14 Oct 73) 1/4; (11 Nov 73) Supplement, 1/1.

_____. English, or common concert flutes.
> (22 Nov 77) 1/3-4.

_____. English second concert flutes.
> (22 Nov 77) 1/3-4.

_____. English third concert flutes.
> (22 Nov 77) 1/3-4.

_____. Porter's and other English and German flutes.
> (3 May 80) 3/3-4; (27 May 80) 3/3; (17 Jun 80) 4/2; (8 Jul 80) 3/4.

English, or common, flute. Tutors, to be sold.

_____. New instruction for playing on.
> (8 Sep 79) 2/4; (2 Oct 79) 2/3; (9 Oct 79) 3/4.

English hunting horns, to be sold.
> (23 Dec 80) 3/4; (27 Dec 80 - 3 Jan 81) 4/3; (6 Jan 81) 2/2.

English hunting horns. *SEE ALSO* Hunting horns.

English songs. Set for the violin, German flute, guitar, etc., to be sold.
(19 Feb 80) 1/4.

English songs. *SEE ALSO* The minstrell.

The entered apprentices song. Sung by Mr. Woolls.
(24 Jun 73) 3/4.

ERSKINE, Thomas Alexander, Sixth Earl of Kelly. *SEE* KELLY, Lord.

ESHER.

_____. Simphonies for keyboard, to be sold.
(14 Oct 73) 1/4; (11 Nov 73) Supplement, 1/1.

ESSER, Michel, 1737-ca.1795.

_____. Concertos, to be sold.
(20-23 Oct 79) 3/3; (3-10 Nov 79) 4/2; (17-20 Nov 79) 4/2; (24
Nov 79) 3/2; (27 Nov - 1 Dec 79) 4/2; (22 Dec 79 - 12 Jan 80)
4/3; (15 Jan 80) 2/4; (26 Jan 80) 3/3; (5 Feb 80) 3/4.

Essex Orpheus. For the violin, to be sold.
(14 Oct 73) 1/4; (11 Nov 73) Supplement, 1/1.

The fathers, or goodnatured man. SEE ARNE, Michael.

Fiddle. Instruments, to be sold.

_____. Fiddle. A very good one wanted.
(27 Jan 79) 3/4.
_____. Fiddle. To be sold by an officer going to England.
(30 Aug 80) 2/3; (2 Sep 80) 1/3; (6 Sep 80) 1/3.
_____. Fiddles. From seven dollars to nine guineas.
(29 Dec 81 - 23 Feb 82) 1/1; (27 Feb 82) 4/3; (6-16 Mar 82) 1/2;
(20 Mar 82) 4/2.
_____. Fiddles. Most excellent at £3:4:0 up to £14.
(30 Sep 73) 3/4; (7 Oct 73) 4/3; (14 Oct 73) Supplement, 1/3.
_____. Fiddles. Up to fourteen pounds a piece.
(9 Feb 75) 2/4.
_____. Fiddles.
(10 Jun 73) 3/2; (17 Jun 73) 4/2; (7 Apr 74) 3/1; (21 Apr 74) 3/4;
(5 May 74) 3/2; (21 Jul 75) 3/4; (22 Nov 77) 1/3-4; (29 Sep 79)
2/3; (2-9 Oct 79) 3/4; (13 Oct 79) Suppl., 1/1; (3 Nov 79) Suppl.,
2/1; (10-17 Nov 79) 4/4; (20 Nov 79) 1/4; (24 Nov 79) 1/4; (29
Dec 81) 3/4; (2-5 Jan 82) 4/4; (9-16 Jan 82) 4/3; (19 Jan 82) 1/2;
(23 Jan - 20 Mar 82) 4/4; (23 Mar - 6 Apr 82) 4/3; (10 Apr-1
May 82) 4/1; (4-8 May 82) 4/3; (11 May - 20 Jul 82) 4/2; (24-31
Jul 82) 4/4; (7-10 Aug 82) 4/2; (14-17 Aug 82) 4/1; (21 Aug 82)
4/3; (11 Sep 82) 3/4; (14-21 Sep 82) 1/2; (19 Oct 82) 2/4; (23 Oct
82) 1/1; (7 Jun 83) 3/3; (11-14 Jun 83) 1/1; (16 Aug 83) 3/4.

Fiddle. Accessories, to be sold.

_____. Fiddle bows. (Sticks)
(4 Oct 77) 4/2; (25 Oct 77) 4/4; (22 Nov 77) 1/3-4; (29 Sep 79) 2/3; (2-9 Oct 79) 3/4; (13 Oct 79) Supplement, 1/1; (3 Nov 79) Supplement, 2/1; (10-17 Nov 79) 4/4; (20 Nov 79) 1/4; (24 Nov 79) 1/4; (7 Jun 83) 3/3; (11-14 Jun 83) 1/1.

_____. Fiddle bridges.
(30 Sep 73) 3/4; (7 Oct 73) 4/3; (14 Oct 73) Supplement, 1/3; (14 Oct 73) 1/4; (11 Nov 73) Supplement, 1/1; (22 Nov 77) 1/3-4; (29 Sep 79) 2/3; (2-9 Oct 79) 3/4; (13 Oct 79) Supplement, 1/1; (3 Nov 79) Supplement, 2/1; (10-17 Nov 79) 4/4; (20-24 Nov 79) 1/4; (7 Jun 83) 3/3; (11-14 Jun 83) 1/1.

_____. Fiddle cases. (With locks and keys; flat cases of mahogany)
(30 Sep 73) 3/4; (7 Oct 73) 4/3; (14 Oct 73) Supplement, 1/3; (22 Nov 77) 1/3-4; (29 Sep 79) 2/3; (2-9 Oct 79) 3/4; (13 Oct 79) Supplement, 1/1; (3 Nov 79) Supplement, 2/1; (10-17 Nov 79) 4/4; (20-24 Nov 79) 1/4.

_____. Fiddle mutes.
(30 Sep 73) 3/4; (7 Oct 73) 4/3; (14 Oct 73) Supplement, 1/3; (22 Nov 77) 1/3-4; (29 Sep 79) 2/3; (2-9 Oct 79) 3/4; (13 Oct 79) Supplement, 1/1; (3 Nov 79) Supplement, 2/1; (10-17 Nov 79) 4/4; (20-24 Nov 79) 1/4; (23 Dec 80) 3/4; (27 Dec 80 - 3 Jan 81) 4/3; (6 Jan 81) 2/2; (7 Jun 83) 3/3; (11-14 Jun 83) 1/1.

_____. Fiddle pegs. (With and without screws)
(14 Oct 73) 1/4; (11 Nov 73) Supplement, 1/1; (4 Oct 77) 4/2; (25 Oct 77) 4/4; (22 Nov 77) 1/3-4; (29 Sep 79) 2/3; (2-9 Oct 79) 3/4; (13 Oct 79) Supplement, 1/1; (3 Nov 79) Supplement, 2/1; (10-17 Nov 79) 4/4; (20-24 Nov 79) 1/4; (23 Dec 80) 3/4; (27 Dec 80 - 3 Jan 81) 4/3; (6 Jan 81) 2/2

_____. Fiddle strings, a fine supply of fresh Roman.
(30 Sep 73) 3/4; (7 Oct 73) 4/3; (14 Oct 73) Supplement, 1/3.

_____. Fiddle strings, lst, 2nd, 3rd, and 4th, to be sold by Valentine Nutter.
(31 Mar 79) 2/4; (7 Apr 79) 3/4.

_____. Fiddle strings, fresh Italian.
(22 Nov 77) 1/3-4.

_____. Fiddle strings, silver bases by the dozen.
(29 Sep 79) 2/3; (2-9 Oct 79) 3/4; (13 Oct 79) Supplement, 1/1; (3 Nov 79) Supplement 2/1; (10-17 Nov 79) 4/4; (20-24 Nov 79) 1/4.

_____. Fiddle strings.
(21 Apr 74) 3/4; (5 May 74) 3/2; (9 Feb 75) 2/4; (21 Jul 75) 3/4; (4 Oct 77) 4/2; (25 Oct 77) 4/4; (28 Aug 79) 2/2; (1 Sep 79) 2/4; (29 Sep 79) 2/3; (2-9 Oct 79) 3/4; (13 Oct 79) Supplement, 1/1; (3 Nov 79) Supplement, 2/1; (10-17 Nov 79) 4/4; (20-24 Nov 79) 1/4; (3 May 80) 3/3-4; (27 May 80) 3/3; (17 Jun 80) 4/2; (8 Jul 80) 3/4; (23 Dec 80) 3/4; (27 Dec 80 - 3 Jan 81) 4/3; (6 Jan 81) 2/2; (29 Dec 81 - 23 Feb 82) 1/1; (27 Feb 82) 4/3; (6-16 Mar 82) 1/2; (20 Mar 82) 4/2; (7 Jun 83) 3/3; (11-14 Jun 83) 1/1.

Fiddle.   Music, to be sold.

_____.   Fiddle music.
> (30 Sep 73) 3/4; (7 Oct 73) 4/3; (14 Oct 73) Supplement, 1/3; (28 Aug 79) 2/2; (1 Sep 79) 2/4; (3 May 80) 3/3-4; (27 May 80) 3/3; (17 Jun 80) 4/2; (8 Jul 80) 3/4.

Fiddle.   Tutors, to be sold.

_____.   A new and excellent pocket book for the German flute and fiddle.
> (22 Nov 77) 1/3-4.

_____.   Fiddle, tutors for.
> (30 Sep 73) 3/4; (7 Oct 73) 4/3; (14 Oct 73) Supplement, 1/3; (21 Apr 74) 3/4; (5 May 74) 3/2; (4 Oct 77) 4/2; (25 Oct 77) 4/4; (22 Nov 77) 1/3-4.

Fiddle.   *SEE ALSO* Violin.

Fiddle, tenor.   Instruments, to be sold.

_____.   Fiddles, tenor.
> (29 Sep 79) 2/3; (2-9 Oct 79) 3/4; (13 Oct 79) Supplement, 1/1; (3 Nov 79) Supplement, 2/1; (10-17 Nov 79) 4/4; (20-24 Nov 79) 1/4; (7 Jun 83) 3/3; (11-14 Jun 83) 1/1.

Fiddle, tenor.   Accessories, to be sold.

_____.   Fiddles, tenor.   With spare bows.
> (7 Jun 83) 3/3; (11-14 Jun 83) 1/1.

_____.   Fiddle, tenor.   Strings.
> (28 Aug 79) 2/2; (1 Sep 79) 2/4; (29 Sep 79) 2/3; (2-9 Oct 79) 3/4;, (13 Oct 79) Supplement, 1/1; (3 Nov 79) Supplement, 2/1; (10-17 Nov 79) 4/4; (20-24 Nov 79) 1/4; (3 May 80) 3/3-4; (27 May 80) 3/3; (17 Jun 80) 4/2; (8 Jul 80) 3/4.

Fife.   Instruments, to be sold.

_____.   Fifes for 8s. each.
> (30 Sep 73) 3/4; (7 Oct 73) 4/3; (17 Oct 73) Supplement, 1/3.

_____.   Fifes. (Regimental; Single)
> (14 Oct 73) 1/4; (11 Nov 73) Supplement, 1/1; (21 Apr 74) 3/4; (5 May 74) 3/2; (14 Sep 75) 3/4; (21 Sep 75) 4/2; (28 Sep - 19 Oct 75) 4/4; (22 Nov 77) 1/3-4; (29 Sep 79) 2/3; (2-9 Oct 79) 3/4; (13 Oct 79) Supplement, 1/1; (3 Nov 79) Supplement, 2/1; (10-17 Nov 79) 4/4; (20-24 Nov 79) 1/4; (3 May 80) 3/3-4; (27 May 80) 3/3; (17 Jun 80) 4/2; (8 Jul 80) 3/4; (23 Dec 80) 3/4; (27 Dec 80 - 3 Jan 81) 4/3; (6 Jan 81) 2/2; (26 Sep 81) 4/1; (29 Sep 81) 4/2; (6-31 Oct 81) 4/2; (29 Dec 81 - 23 Feb 82) 1/1; (27 Feb 82) 4/3; (6-16 Mar 82) 1/2; (20 Mar 82) 4/2; (11 Sep 82) 3/4; (14-21 Sep 82) 1/2; (19 Oct 82) 2/4; (23 Oct 82) 1/1; (7 Jun 83) 3/3; (11-14 Jun 83) 1/1.

Fife. Accessories.

_____. Fife-cases (10) and fife-slings (7) surrendered by the British at
Yorktown.
(26 Dec 81) 2/2.

Fife. Music, to be sold.

_____. Fife Music.
(30 Sep 73) 3/4; (7 Oct 73) 4/3; (14 Oct 73) Supplement, 1/3; (28
Aug 79) 2/2; (1 Sep 79) 2/4.

Fife. Performers.

_____. Fifes and drums marched in funeral procession for Michael Cressop,
deceased.
(26 Oct 75) 4/1.
_____. Fifers wanted for His Majesty's 88th regiment in Jamaica. Salary
offerred for wife and child too.
(19 Dec 81) 2/4; (22 Dec 81) 2/3; (26-29 Dec 81) 1/2.
_____. Fifer, a good one wanted. "Such a person disposed to teach that
instrument, and enlist in a new regiment shall have fifteen guineas
over and above the usual bounty money. . . ."
(9 Mar 82) 3/3.
_____. Fife major and music master wanted for a regiment.
(20 Apr 82) 3/3; (24 Apr 82) 2/2; (27 Apr - 1 May 82) 1/3; (4
May 82) 1/2; (8-11 May 82) 4/3.
_____.   Fife played by escaped negro slave, James Jackson.
(12 Nov 83) 2/3.

Fife. Tutors or instructors, to be sold.

_____. Fife tutors.
(30 Sep 73) 3/4; (7 Oct 73) 4/3; (14 Oct 73) Supplement, 1/3; (14
Oct 73) 1/4; (11 Nov 73) Supplement, 1/1; (21 Apr 74) 3/4; (5 May
74) 3/2; (4 Oct 77) 4/2; (25 Oct 77) 4/4; (25 Jul 78) 3/1; (8 Sep
79) 2/4; (2 Oct 79) 2/3; (9 Oct 79) 3/4.

The fife and drum. *SEE* LEVERIDGE, Richard. *The recruiting officer.*

FILTZ, Anton, 1733-1760.

_____. Works by, to be sold.
(28 Aug 79) 2/2; (1 Sep 79) 2/4.

FISCHER, Johann Christian, 1733-1800.

_____. Works by, to be sold.
(28 Aug 79) 2/2; (1 Sep 79) 2/4.

_____. 1st, 2d and 3d concertos, to be sold.

    RISM F990: *A favourite concerto for the harpsichord.* London: Welcker.

    RISM F994: *A favourite concerto adapted for the harpsichord or piano forte.* London: The author.

    RISM F998: *A third concerto adapted for the harpsichord or piano forte.* London: Welcker.

    (20-23 Oct 79) 3/3; (3-10 Nov 79) 4/2; (17-20 Nov 79) 4/2; (24 Nov 79) 3/2; (27 Nov - 1 Dec 79) 4/2; (22 Dec 79 - 12 Jan 80) 4/3; (15 Jan 80) 2/4; (26 Jan 80) 3/3; (5 Feb 80) 3/4.

_____. Concertos for hautboys or German flute, to be sold.

    RISM F987: *A favourite concerto for the hoboy or German flute, with instrumental parts.* London: Welcker.

    RISM F992: *A second concerto for a hautboy, German flute, or violin, with accompanyments for two violins, two French horns, tenor and bass.* London: Welcker.

    RISM F997: *A third concerto for a hautboy, German flute, or violin, with accompanyments for two violins, two French horns, tenor and bass.* London: Welcker.

    RISM F999: *A concerto for a hautboy, German flute, or violin, with accompaniments for two violins, two French horns, tenor and bass . . . No. 4.* London: John Welcker.

    RISM F1001: *A concerto for a hautboy, German flute, or violin, with accompaniments for two violins, two French horns, tenor and bass . . . No. 5.* London: John Welcker.

    RISM F1003: *A concerto for a hautboy, German flute, or violin, with accompaniments for two violins, two French horns, tenor and bass . . . No. 6.* London: John Welcker.

    RISM F1005: *A seventh concerto with the favorite air "Gramachree Molly" for a hautboy or German flute, accompanied by two violins, two French horns, tenor and bass.* London: Longman & Broderip.

    RISM F1008: *An eighth concerto . . . for a hautboy or German flute, with accompanyments for two violins, two French horns, tenor and bass.* London: John Preston.

    RISM F1010: *Concerto IX for a hautboy or German flute or violin, with accompanyments for two violins, two French horns, tenor and bass.* London: The author.

    RISM F1011: *A concerto for a hautboy, German flute, or violin, with accompanyments for two violins, two French horns, tenor and bass.* London: The author.

    (20-23 Oct 79) 3/3; (3-10 Nov 79) 4/2; (17-20 Nov 79) 4/2; (24 Nov 79) 3/2; (27 Nov - 1 Dec 79) 4/2; (22 Dec 79 - 12 Jan 80) 4/3; (15 Jan 80) 2/4; (26 Jan 80) 3/3; (5 Feb 80) 3/4.

_____. Hoboy solo concerto, to be performed.

    RISM F987: See entry above.

    (27 Apr 82) 3/3.

    For fuller reference, *SEE* Concert (27 Apr 82).

FISHER, John Abraham, 1744-1806.

_____. Duet for violin, to be sold.
RISM F1075: *Six duettos for two violins.* London: Longman, Lukey & Co., ca.1773.
(14 Oct 73) 1/4; (11 Nov 73) Supplement, 1/1.

_____. Six duets for two violins, to be sold.
RISM F1075: See entry above.
(22 Nov 77) 1/3-4.

_____. Duetts for violins, to be sold.
RISM F1075: See entry above.
(20-23 Oct 79) 3/3; (3-10 Nov 79) 4/2; (17-20 Nov 79) 4/2; (24 Nov 79) 3/2; (27 Nov - 1 Dec 79) 4/2; (22 Dec 79 - 12 Jan 80) 4/3; (15 Jan 80) 2/4; (26 Jan 80) 3/3; (5 Feb 80) 3/4.

_____. Duetts for violins and German flutes, to be sold.
RISM F1075: See entry above.
(20-23 Oct 79) 3/3; (3-10 Nov 79) 4/2; (17-20 Nov 79) 4/2; (24 Nov 79) 3/2; (27 Nov - 1 Dec 79) 4/2; (22 Dec 79 - 12 Jan 80) 4/3; (15 Jan 80) 2/4; (26 Jan 80) 3/3; (5 Feb 80) 3/4.

_____. *Harlequin's gambols. SEE* his *The sylphs.*

_____. Simphonies for keyboard, to be sold
RISM F1071: *Six simphonys in eight parts for violins, hoboys, horns, tenor and bass.* London: Longman, Lukey & Co.
(14 Oct 73) 1/4; (11 Nov 73) Supplement, 1/1.

_____. *The sylphs.* English opera, harpsichord/vocal edition, to be sold.
RISM F1055: *The songs, chorusses, and comic-tunes in the entertainment of The sylphs (or Harlequin's gambols), etc.* London: Longman, Lukey & Co., 1774.
(4 Oct 77) 4/2; (25 Oct 77) 4/4; (22 Nov 77) 1/3-4.

_____. [*The sylphs*] Songs in *Harlequin's gambols*, set for guitar, to be sold.
(20-23 Oct 79) 3/3; (3-10 Nov 79) 4/2; (17-20 Nov 79) 4/2; 24 Nov 79) 3/2; (27 Nov - 1 Dec 79) 4/2; (22 Dec 79 - 12 Jan 80) 4/3; (15 Jan 80) 2/4; (26 Jan 80) 3/3; (5 Feb 80) 3/4.

The flitch of bacon. SEE SHIELD, William.

Flora, or Hob in the well. SEE BATES, William.

FLORIO, Pietro Grassi, ca.1740-1795.

_____. Works by, to be sold.
(30 Sep 73) 3/4; (7 Oct 73) 4/3; (14 Oct 73) Supplement, 1/3; (4 Oct 77) 4/2; (25 Oct 77) 4/4.

_____. Duetts for German flute, to be sold.
RISM F1195: *Six sonatas or duets for two German-flutes or two violins. Composed by Sigr. Florio Grassi. Opera prima.* London:. Maurice Whitaker, 1763.
RISM F1197: *Six sonatas for two German flutes . . . Opera II.* London: Messrs. Thompson, ca.1765.
(14 Oct 73) 1/4; (11 Nov 73) Supplement, 1/1.

FLORIO. *SEE ALSO* German flute. Tutors.

Florio's German flutes. *SEE* German flute.

Flute.

_____. To be sold at private sale.
(16 Aug 83) 3/4.
_____. Music, to be sold by Valentine Nutter.
(23 Dec 80) 2/4; (30 Dec 80) 3/3.

Flute. *SEE ALSO* English, or common, flute; German flute; Voice flutes.

Flutes, voice. *SEE* Voice flutes.

FOOTE.

_____. Foote's Prussian [sic] minuet for keyboard, to be sold.
RISM F1501: *Foote's Russian minuet, with variations for the harpsichord or piano forte.* N.p: n.p.
(22 Nov 77) 1/3-4.

"For battle prepar'd in their country's just cause." The British light infantry.
To the tune of Black sloven. Song lyric printed.
(30 Dec 78) 3/4.

FORD, Miss.

_____. Lessons and instructions for the guittar, to be sold.
(22 Nov 77) 1/3-4.

Forte piano. *SEE* Piano.

Foy, Martin. Dancing instructor and teacher of guitar, violin and the use of the small sword.
(18 Sep 79) 3/3; (25 Sep 79) 3/4; (2 Oct 79) 2/2; (6 Oct 79) 4/4.

Franceschini, Gaetano, fl.1774-1783.

_____. Concert to be performed June 9, 1783 "for the benefit of Signor Gaetano Franceschini. . . ."
(4 Jun 83) 3/2; (7 Jun 83) 2/4.
_____. Leader of band in theatre.
(21 Jun 83) 3/3; (2 Jul 83) 3/2; (5-9 Jul 83) 3/4; (12 Jul 83) 3/2;
(16 Jul 83) 3/1; (19-23 Jul 83) 3/2; (26 Jul 83) 2/4; (30 Jul 83)
3/2; (2 Aug 83) 2/3; (19 Jul 83) 3/3; (6 Aug 83) 3/2; (9 Aug 83)
2/2.
_____. Signior [sic] Franceschini to perform God save the king with variations in the theatre.
(9 Jul 83) 3/4.

Francis, Mr. Dancing in the theatre.
(6 May 73) 3/3; (29 Apr 73) 3/3; (13 May 73) 3/3; (3 Jun 73) 3/2; (10-17 Jun 73) 3/3; (1 Jul 73) 3/3; (8 Jul 73) 3/1.

The Free masons pocket book, being a curious collection of original masonic songs. . . . Published by Lewis and Horner. To be sold.
(15 May 82) 4/4; (25 May - 19 Jun 82) 4/4; (22 Jun - 31 Jul 82) 4/1.

The Free-mason's pocket book, being a curious collection of original masonic songs; to which is added a toast applicable to each song. ***This valuable book will not fail to be extremely acceptable to all lovers of the royal craft at the celebration of the festival of their renowned patron, St. John the Baptist, on Monday next the 24th. To be sold.
(22 Jun 82) 3/3.

Free mason's song. *SEE* "Come let us rejoice."

Free masons. *SEE ALSO* Church-music.

French country dances. *SEE* Dancing.

French horn. Instruments, to be sold.

_____. French horns, a pair of fine toned E horns.
(30 Sep 73) 3/4; (7 Oct 73) 4/3; (14 Oct 73) Supplement, 1/3.
_____. French horns, E, with crooks.
(14 Oct 73) 1/4; (11 Nov 73) Supplement, 1/1.
_____. "A pair of very fine toned concert French horns, with all the crooks complete, made by the celebrated Hoffmaster. The death of Hoffmaster six years ago, has made his horns invaluable. The lowest is twenty five pounds sterling. . . . "
(1 Aug 78) 1/4; (5 Aug 78) 4/4.
_____. French horns. "Wanted an excellent pair. The printer is ready to purchase them."
(7 Oct 78) 3/2.
_____. French horns (pairs, concert complete, concert).
(28 Oct 78) 2/3; (31 Oct 78) 4/1; (4 Nov 78) 1/4; (7 Nov 78) 4/3; (11 Nov 78) 1/4; (28 Aug 79) 2/2; (1 Sep 79) 2/4; (3 May 80) 3/3-4; (27 May 80) 3/3; (17 Jun 80) 4/2; (8 Jul 80) 3/4; (23 Dec 80) 3/4; (27 Dec 80 - 3 Jan 81) 4/3; (6 Jan 81) 2/2; (26 Sep 81) 4/1; (29 Sep 81) 4/2; (6-31 Oct 81) 4/2; (3-7 Nov 81) 4/4; (10-21 Nov 81) 4/2; (24 Nov 81) 4/4; (5 Dec 81 - 5 Jan 82) 4/4; (9 Jan 82) 3/3; (16 Jan 82) 1/2; (19 Jan 82) 4/4; (23 Jan - 23 Feb 82) 4/2; (23-27 Mar 82) 4/2; (13 Apr 82) 3/4; (24 Apr - 1 May 82) 1/3; (4-29 May 82) 1/1; (1 Jun 82) 1/3; (5 Jun 82) 1/2; (8 Jun 82) 1/1; (12-22 Jun 82) 4/1; (26 Jun - 13 Jul 82) 4/4; (17 Jul 82) 1/1; (20-31 Jul 82) 4/4; (3-17 Aug 82) 4/3; (21 Aug - 4 Sep 82) 4/1; (29 Dec 81 - 23 Feb 82) 1/1; (27 Feb 82) 4/3; (6-16 Mar 82) 1/2; (20 Mar 82) 4/2; (11 Sep 82) 3/4; (14-21 Sep 82) 1/2; (19 Oct 82) 2/4; (23 Oct 82) 1/1.

French horn. Accessories, to be sold.

_____. French horn crooks.
> (30 Sep 73) 3/4; (7 Oct 73) 4/3; (14 Oct 73) Supplement, 1/1; (14 Oct 73) 1/4; (11 Nov 73) Supplement, 1/1; (29 Sep 79) 2/3; (2 Oct 79) 3/4; (9 Oct 79) 3/4; (13 Oct 79) Supplement, 1/1; (3 Nov 79) Supplement, 2/1; (10-17 Nov 79) 4/4; (20-24 Nov 79) 1/4.

_____. French horn mouthpieces.
> (14 Oct 73) 1/4; (11 Nov 73) Supplement, 1/1; (29 Sep 79) 2/3; (2 Oct 79) 3/4; (9 Oct 79) 3/4; (13 Oct 79) Supplement, 1/1; (3 Nov 79) Supplement, 2/1; (10-17 Nov 79) 4/4; (20-24 Nov 79) 1/4.

_____. French horn shanks.
> (29 Sep 79) 2/3; (2 Oct 79) 3/4; (9 Oct 79) 3/4; (13 Oct 79) Supplement, 1/1; (3 Nov 79) Supplement, 2/1; (10-17 Nov 79) 4/4; (20-24 Nov 79) 1/4; (27 Oct 81) 3/4; (3-7 Nov 81) 4/4; (10-21 Nov 81) 4/2; (24 Nov 81) 4/4; (5 Dec 81 - 5 Jan 82) 4/4; (9 Jan 82) 3/3; (16 Jan 82) 1/2; (19 Jan 82) 4/4; (23 Jan - 23 Feb 82) 4/2; (23-27 Mar 82) 4/2; (13 Apr 82) 3/4; (24 Apr - 1 May 82) 1/3; (4-29 May 82) 1/1; (1 Jun 82) 1/3; (5 Jun 82) 1/2; (8 Jun 82) 1/1; (12-22 Jun 82) 4/1;, (26 Jun - 13 Jul 82) 4/4; (17 Jul 82) 1/1; (20-31 Jul 82) 4/4; (3-17 Aug 82) 4/3; (21 Aug - 4 Sep 82) 4/1.

French horn. Music, to be sold.

_____. French horn music.
> (28 Aug 79) 2/2; (1 Sep 79) 2/4.

French horn and clarinet music. *SEE* DRETZY; GALEOTTI, Salvatore *or* Stefano; GIORDANI, Tommaso.

French horn. Performers.

_____. French horn players wanted for band on board the *General Pattison*, private ship of war.
> (14 Apr 79) 2/4; (21 Apr 79) 4/3.

French horn. Performers. *SEE ALSO* Musicians. Wanted for a regiment.

French horn. Tutors or instructors, to be sold.

_____. French horn tutors or instructors.
> (14 Oct 73) 1/4; (11 Nov 73) Supplement, 1/1; (8 Sep 79) 2/4; (2 Oct 79) 2/3; (9 Oct 79) 3/4.

French horns (5). Surrendered by British at Yorktown.
> (26 Dec 81) 2/2.

French jigs. *SEE* Dancing.

"The Frenchmen came upon the coast." To the tune of Doodle-doo. Song lyric printed.
>(27 Nov 79) 3/3-4.

"From heav'n behold a charming ray." Song lyric printed.
>(3 Jun 82) 2/4.

"From Lewis, Monsieur Gerard came." Yankee Doodle's expedition to Rhode-Island. To the tune of Yankee Doodle. Song lyric printed.
>(3 Oct 78) 3/2.

GALEOTTI, Salvatore (fl.1760s) *or* Stefano (ca.1723-ca.1790). (GALLECTI; GLEOTTI)

_____. Six duets for two violins, to be sold.
>RISM G124: *Six sonatas for two violins, with a thorough bass for the organ or harpsichord. Five by Sigr. Salvatore Galleotti and one by Sigr. Christiano Giuseppi Lidardi.* London: Peter Welcker, 1762.
>RISM G132: *Six sonatas for two violins, with a thorough bass for the harpsichord . . . Opera IV.* London: Welcker, ca.1770.
>(22 Nov 77) 1/3-4

_____. Gleotti's fourteen new minuets for horns, violins and a bass, to be sold.
>RISM G136: *Twenty Italian minuets for two violins and a bass.* London: Henry Thorowgood.
>(20-23 Oct 79) 3/3; (3-10 Nov 79) 4/2; (17-20 Nov 79) 4/2; (24 Nov 79) 3/2; (27 Nov - 1 Dec 79) 4/2; (22 Dec 79 - 12 Jan 80) 4/3; (15 Jan 80) 2/4; (26 Jan 80) 3/3; (5 Feb 80) 3/4.

GALUPPI, Baldassare, 1706-1785.

_____. Overtures, to be sold.
>BUC II, p.751: *Six favourite overtures in six parts, for two violins, two French-horns, a tenor and bass. Composed by . . . Galuppi, St. Martini & Jomelli.* London: A. Hummel, ca.1770.
>RISM G307: *A favourite overture for the harpsichord.* London: C. and S. Thompson, 1770.
>(20-23 Oct 79) 3/3; (3-10 Nov 79) 4/2; (17-20 Nov 79) 4/2; (24 Nov 79) 3/2; (27 Nov - 1 Dec 79) 4/2; (22 Dec 79 - 12 Jan 80) 4/3; (15 Jan 80) 2/4; (26 Jan 80) 3/3; (5 Feb 80) 3/4.

Gardel of France. *SEE* Tetley, W. Birchall.

Garrick, David, 1717-1779. *SEE* SHIELD, William. Oxford Nancy bewitch'd, a ballad.

GARTH, John, ca.1722-ca.1810.

_____. Works by, to be sold.
>(28 Aug 79) 2/2; (1 Sep 79) 2/4;

_____. Sonatas for keyboard, to be sold.

RISM G434: *Six sonata's for the harpsichord, piano forte, and organ: with accompanyments for two violins, and a violoncello . . . Opera secunda.* London: R. Bremner . . . 1768.

(14 Oct 73) 1/4; (11 Nov 73) Supplement, 1/1.

_____. Sonatas for two German flutes or violins, to be sold.

RISM G434: See entry above.

RISM G440: *A second sett of six sonata's for the harpsichord, piano forte and organ; with accompanyments for two violins and a violoncello. Opera IV.* London: Welcker, 1772.

RISM G441: *A third sett of six sonatas for the harpsichord, piano forte, and organ, with accompanyments for two violins and a violoncello . . . Op. V.* London: Welcker.

RISM G442: *A fourth sett of six sonatas for the harpsichord, piano-forte and organ with accompaniements for two violins and a violoncello . . . Opera VI.* London: John Welcker, ca.1778.

RISM G443: *A fifth sett of six sonatas for the harpsichord, piano forte and organ with accompanyments for two violins and a violoncello . . . Op. VII.* London: Robson, for the author.

(20-23 Oct 79) 3/3; (3-10 Nov 79) 4/2; (17-20 Nov 79) 4/2; (24 Nov 79) 3/2; (27 Nov - 1 Dec 79) 4/2; (22 Dec 79 - 12 Jan 80) 4/3; (15 Jan 80) 2/4; (26 Jan 80) 3/3; (5 Feb 80) 3/4.

_____. Six voluntaries for keyboard, to be sold privately.

RISM G438: *Six voluntarys for the organ, piano forte or harpsichord . . . Opera terza.* London: Welcker, 1771.

(4 Oct 83) 2/2.

Gay, John, 1685-1732. *SEE* ARNE, Thomas Augustine. *The beggar's opera.*

GAZARDI.

_____. Works by, to be sold.

(28 Aug 79) 2/2; (1 Sep 79) 2/4.

GEMINIANI, Francesco, 1687-1762.

_____. Art of playing on the violin, to be sold.

RISM G1541: *The art of playing on the violin, containing all the rules necessary to attain a perfection on that instrument, with great variety of compositions . . . Opera IX.* London: R. Bremner, ca.1765.

(14 Oct 73) 1/4; (11 Nov 73) Supplement, 1/1.

_____. On good taste for violin, to be sold.

RISM G1538: *A treatise of good taste in the art of musick.* London, 1749.

(14 Oct 73) 1/4; (11 Nov 73) Supplement, 1/1.

_____. On true taste for violin, to be sold.

RISM G1537: *Rules for playing in a true taste on the violin, German flute, or violoncello and harpsicord, particularly the thorough bass. Exemplify'd in a variety of compositions on the subjects of English, Scotch and Irish tunes . . . Opera VIII.* London, ca.1739.

(14 Oct 73) 1/4; (11 Nov 73) Supplement, 1/1.

_____. A pocket book, for the violin, embellished with curious remarks, and excellent examples by the late celebrated Signior [sic] Geminiani, &c. To which are added a pleasing variety of songs, duets, and airs, judiciously collected from the most favourite operas, entertainments. To be published by Rivington.
    (11 Jul 78) 3/3; (25 Jul 78) 3/1; (20 Jan 81) 2/2; (31 Jan 81) 2/2; (11-14 Feb 81) 4/4; (24 Feb 81) 3/4.

General Pattison. Private ship of war. "Musical performers. Two French horns, two clarinets, two hautboys, one bassoon wanted to compleat the band on board. . . . Such as are deserving besides the opportunity of making their fortunes, will meet the best encouragement by applying to Charles Patton, Esq. on board the said vessel, or at the St. Andrew, on Cruger's wharf."
    (14 Apr 79) 2/4; (21 Apr 79) 4/3.

GERARD, James.

_____. Six sonatas for violin and German flute, to be sold.
    RISM G1614: *Six sonatas or duets for two German flutes or two violins.* London: J. Johnson, ca.1765.
    (22 Nov 77) 1/3-4; (20-23 Oct 79) 3/3; (3-10 Nov 79) 4/2; (17-20 Nov 79) 4/2; (24 Nov 79) 3/2; (27 Nov - 1 Dec 79) 4/2; (22 Dec 79 -12 Jan 80) 4/3; (15 Jan 80) 2/4; (26 Jan 80) 3/3; (5 Feb 80) 3/4.

Gerarde of London. *SEE* Tetley, W. Birchall.

GERLIN.

_____. Gerlin's tunes French songs and sonatas for guitar, to be sold.
    (20-23 Oct 79) 3/3; (3-10 Nov 79) 4/2; (17-20 Nov 79) 4/2; (24 Nov 79) 3/2; (27 Nov - 1 Dec 79) 4/2; (22 Dec 79 - 12 Jan 80) 4/3; (15 Jan 80) 2/4; (26 Jan 80) 3/3; (5 Feb 80) 3/4.

German dances. *SEE* Dancing.

German flute. Instruments, to be sold.

_____. Florio's German flutes, with all the keys.
    (3 May 80) 3/3-4; (27 May 80) 3/3; (17 Jun 80) 4/2; (8 Jul 80) 3/4.
_____. Florios German flutes, with six brass keys.
    (22 Nov 77) 1/3-4.
_____. Florios German flutes, with six silver keys.
    (22 Nov 77) 1/3-4.
_____. German flutes from 24s. to 94s. on the new and old construction.
    (30 Sep 73) 3/4; (7 Oct 73) 4/3; (14 Oct 73) Supplement, 1/3.
_____. German flutes of one, three and four keys, to be sold by Valentine Nutter.
    (31 Mar 79) 2/4; (7 Apr 79) 3/4; (23 Dec 80) 2/4; (30 Dec 80) 3/3.

_____. German flutes, Porter's and other English.
(3 May 80) 3/3-4; (27 May 80) 3/3, (17 Jun 80) 4/2; (8 Jul 80)
3/4.

_____. Potter's fine toned German flutes.
(22 Nov 77) 1/3-4.

_____. Potter's German flutes, new construction, two prices.
(22 Nov 77) 1/3-4.

_____. German flutes, to be sold by George Deblois, sen. & jun.
(18 Jul 78) 4/4; (22 Jul 78) 1/3.

_____. German flutes (with extra middle pieces; second, third and fourth; of
the most approved makers, workmanship, by the dozen or single
instruments; in mahogany cases with locks and keys).
(10 Jun 73) 3/2; (17 Jun 73) 4/2; (14 Oct 73) 1/4; (11 Nov 73)
Supplement, 1/1; (7 Apr 74) 3/1; (9 Feb 75) 2/4; (9 Mar 75) 3/4;
(16 Mar 75) 4/4; (21 Jul 75) 3/4; (22 Nov 77) 1/3-4; (28 Aug 79)
2/2; (1 Sep 79) 2/4; (29 Sep 79) 2/3; (2 Oct 79) 3/4; (9 Oct 79)
3/4; (13 Oct 79) Supplement, 1/1; (3 Nov 79) Supplement, 2/1;
(10-17 Nov 79) 4/4; (20-24 Nov 79) 1/4; (23 Dec 80) 3/4; (27 Dec
80 - 3 Jan 81) 4/3; (6 Jan 81) 2/2; (26 Sep 81) 4/1; (29 Sep 81)
4/2; (6-31 Oct 81) 4/2; (27 Oct 81) 3/4; (3-7 Nov 81) 4/4; (10-21
Nov 81) 4/2; (24 Nov 81) 4/4; (5 Dec 81 - 5 Jan 82) 4/4; (9 Jan
82) 3/3; (16 Jan 82) 1/2; (19 Jan 82) 4/4; (23 Jan - 23 Feb 82)
4/2; (23-27 Mar 82) 4/2; (13 Apr 82) 3/4; (24 Apr - 1 May 82)
1/3; (4-29 May 82) 1/1; (1 Jun 82) 1/3; (5 Jun 82) 1/2; (8 Jun 82)
1/1; 12-22 Jun 82) 4/1; (26 Jun - 13 Jul 82) 4/4; (17 Jul 82) 1/1;
(20-31 Jul 82) 4/1; (3-17 Aug 82) 4/3; (21 Aug - 4 Sep 82) 4/1;
(29 Dec 81 - 23 Feb 82) 1/1; (27 Feb 82) 4/3; (6-16 Mar 82) 1/2;
(20 Mar 82) 4/2; (11 Sep 82) 3/4; (14-21 Sep 82) 1/2; (19 Oct 82)
2/4; (23 Oct 82) 1/1; (7 Jun 83) 3/3; (11 Jun 83) 1/1; (14 Jun 83)
1/1.

German flute. Accessories, to be sold.

_____. German flute cases or covers.
(4 Oct 77) 4/2; (25 Oct 77) 4/4; (22 Nov 77) 1/3-4; (28 Aug 79)
2/2; (1 Sep 79) 2/4; (29 Sep 79) 2/3; (2 Oct 79) 3/4; (9 Oct 79)
3/4; (13 Oct 79) Supplement, 1/1; (3 Nov 79) Supplement, 2/1;
(10-17 Nov 79) 4/4; (20-24 Nov 79) 1/4.

_____. German flutes with extra middle pieces.
(22 Nov 77) 1/3-4.

_____. German flute mouthpieces.
(30 Sep 73) 3/4; (7 Oct 73) 4/3; (14 Oct 73) Supplement, 1/3; (14
Oct 73) 1/4; (11 Nov 73) Supplement, 1/1; (4 Oct 77) 4/2; (25 Oct
77) 4/4; (22 Nov 77) 1/3-4; (7 Jun 83) 3/3; (11-14 Jun 83) 1/1.

German flute. Music, to be sold.

_____. German flute, music for.
(30 Sep 73) 3/4; (7 Oct 73) 4/3; (14 Oct 73) Supplement, 1/3; (14
Oct 73) 1/4; (11 Nov 73) Supplement, 1/1; (28 Aug 79) 2/2;

(1 Sep 79) 2/4; (3 May 80) 3/3-4; (27 May 80) 3/3; (17 Jun 80) 4/2; (8 Jul 80) 3/4.

German flute and/or violin, music. *SEE ALSO* ALEXANDER, B.; BACH, Carl Philipp Emanuel; BACH, Johann Christian; BATES, William; BEM, Venceslav; BLANC; BLANCK, Nicholas; CAMPIONI, Carlo Antonio; CAPPELLETTI, Anthonio; CIRRI, Giovanni Battista; DAVIS, Thomas; FISCHER, Johann Christian; FISHER, Johann Abraham; FLORIO, Pietro Grassi; GALEOTTI, Salvatore *or* Stefano; GARTH, John; GERARD, James; GIARDINI, Felice; GIORDANI, Tommaso; *Golden pippen*; GRASSI, Florio; GRONEMAN, Johann Albert; GUERINI, Francesco; HASSE, Johann Adolph; HOLYOAK; HUMBLE, Maximilian; JUST, Johann August; KAMMEL, Anton; KERNTL, C.F.; KLÖFFLER, Johann Friedrich; LIDARTI, Christiano Giuseppe; MAGHERINI; MANCHINELLI, Domenico; MILLER, Edward; Minuets; MYSLIVEČEK, Josef; NARDINI, Pietro; NOFERI, Giovanni Battista; NUSSEN, Frederick; PATONI, Giovanni Battista; PESCH, Carl August; PLA, José; REID, John; REINARDS, William; RODIL, Antonio; SABBATINI, Luigi Antonio; SCHWINDL, Friedrich; STAMITZ, Karl Phillip *or* Johann Wenzel Anton; TACET, Joseph; TARTINI, Giuseppe; THUMOTH, Burk; VENTO, Mattia; WENDLING, Johann Baptist.

German flute. Performers.

_____. German flute played by escaped Negro slave, James Jackson.
    (12 Nov 83) 2/3.

German flute. Tutors or instructors, to be sold.

_____. German flute tutor. A new and excellent pocket book for the German flute and fiddle.
    (22 Nov 77) 1/3-4.
_____. German flute tutor. "A pocket book, for the German flute, containing necessary directions and remarks on that instrument, with an agreeable variety of celebrated airs, duets, and songs, collected from the favourite opera entertainments, &c composed by the most admired authors in two parts, each is sold separate." Published by Rivington.
    (11 Jul 78) 3/3; (25 Jul 78) 3/1; (20 Jan 81) 3/2; (31 Jan 81) 2/2; (10-17 Feb 81) 4/4; (24 Feb 81) 3/4.
_____. German flute tutor. "New instructions for the German flute, containing the easiest and most modern methods for learners to play; to which are added, a favourite collection of minuets, marches, songs, tunes, duets, &c. Also, the method of double-tonguing, and a complete scale and description of a new-invented German flute, with the additional keys, such as played on by two eminent masters, Florio and Tacet." Published by Rivington.
    (19 Aug 78) 2/3; (12 Sep 78) 1/1.

_____. German flutes with books of instruction, to be sold by Valentine Nutter.

  (31 Mar 79) 2/4; (7 Apr 79) 3/4; (23 Dec 80) 2/4; (30 Dec 80) 3/3.

_____. German flute tutors or instructors.

  (30 Sep 73) 3/4; (7 Oct 73) 4/3; (14 Oct 73) Supplement, 1/3; (14 Oct 73) 1/4; (11 Nov 73) Supplement, 1/1; (21 Jul 75) 3/4; (4 Oct 77) 4/2; (25 Oct 77) 4/4; (22 Nov 77) 1/3-4; (25 Jul 78) 3/1; (8 Sep 79) 2/4; (2 Oct 79) 2/3; (9 Oct 79) 3/4; (7 Jun 83) 3/3; (11 Jun 83) 1/1; (14 Jun 83) 1/1.

German flute. Teachers.

_____. German flute taught by William Charles Hulett.

  (12 Jan 75) 3/4; (19 Jan 75) 4/2.

Gherarde of London. *SEE* Tetley, W. Birchall.

GIARDINI, Felice, 1716-1796. (GIORDINI)

_____. Works by, to be sold.

  (28 Aug 79) 2/2; (1 Sep 79) 2/4.

_____. Concertos, Op. 4, to be sold.

  RISM G1941: *Trois concerts a violino principale, violino primo & secondo, alto & basse (deux cors de chasse ad libitum), Oeuvre quatrième.* Berlin: Johann Julius Hummel.

  (20-23 Oct 79) 3/3; (3-10 Nov 79) 4/2; (17-20 Nov 79) 4/2; (24 Nov 79) 3/2; (27 Nov - 1 Dec 79) 4/2; (22 Dec 79 - 12 Jan 80) 4/3; (15 Jan 80) 2/4; (26 Jan 80) 3/3; (5 Feb 80) 3/4.

_____. Concertos, Op. 15, to be sold.

  RISM G1939: *A concerto in 7 parts . . . Opera XV, No. 1(-6).* London: Welcker.

  (20-23 Oct 79) 3/3; (3-10 Nov 79) 4/2; (17-20 Nov 79) 4/2; (24 Nov 79) 3/2; (27 Nov - 1 Dec 79) 4/2; (22 Dec 79 - 12 Jan 80) 4/3; (15 Jan 80) 2/4; (26 Jan 80) 3/3; (5 Feb 80) 3/4.

_____. Duetts for violins and German flutes, Op. 13, to be sold.

  RISM G1929: *Sei duetti per due violini . . . Opera XIII.* London, 1767.

  (20-23 Oct 79) 3/3; (3-10 Nov 79) 4/2; (17-20 Nov 79) 4/2; (24 Nov 79) 3/2; (27 Nov - 1 Dec 79) 4/2; (22 Dec 79 - 12 Jan 80) 4/3; (15 Jan 80) 2/4; (26 Jan 80) 3/3; (5 Feb 80) 3/4.

_____. Quintettos, to be sold.

  RISM G1927: *Sei quintetti per cembalo, due violini, violoncello e basso . . . Opera XI.* London: Welcker.

  (20-23 Oct 79) 3/3; (3-10 Nov 79) 4/2; (17-20 Nov 79) 4/2; (24 Nov 79) 3/2; (27 Nov - 1 Dec 79) 4/2; (22 Dec 79 - 12 Jan 80) 4/3; (15 Jan 80) 2/4; (26 Jan 80) 3/3; (5 Feb 80) 3/4.

_____. Solos for violin, to be sold.

  RISM G1985: *Six favourite solos for the violin, with accompaniment for the harpsichord or violoncello, expressly composed for the use of gentlemen performers . . . book 2d.* London: Samuel, Anne & Peter Thompson.

RISM G1943: *Six solos for the violin and a bass . . . Opera 16.*
London: Robert Bremner.
RISM G1957: *Six solos for the violin and a bass . . . Opera XIX.*
London: John Welcker.
(14 Oct 73) 1/4; (11 Nov 73) Supplement, 1/1.

Giardini screw bows, to be sold.
(30 Sep 73) 3/4; (7 Oct 73) 4/3; (14 Oct 73) Supplement, 1/3; (14
Oct 73) 1/4; (11 Nov 73) Supplement, 1/1; (22 Nov 77) 1/3-4; (28
Aug 79) 2/2; (1 Sep 79) 2/4; (3 May 80) 3/3-4; (27 May 80) 3/3;
(17 Jun 80) 4/2; (8 Jul 80) 3/4.

GIORDANI, Tommaso, ca.1733-1806.

_____. Works by, to be sold.
(4 Oct 77) 4/2; (25 Oct 77) 4/4; (28 Aug 79) 2/2; (1 Sep 79) 2/4.
_____. Concerto for keyboard, Opera 14, to be sold.
RISM G2255: *Six concertos for the pianoforte or harpsichord . . .*
Op. XIV. London: Longman, Lukey & Broderip.
(22 Nov 77) 1/3-4.
_____. New concertos, Opera 19, to be sold.
RISM G2263: *Six concertos for a German-flute, two violins and bass*
. . . Op. XIX. London: Longman & Broderip.
(20-23 Oct 79) 3/3; (3-10 Nov 79) 4/2; (17-20 Nov 79) 4/2; (24
Nov 79) 3/2; (27 Nov - 1 Dec 79) 4/2; (22 Dec 79 - 12 Jan 80)
4/3; (15 Jan 80) 2/4; (26 Jan 80) 3/3; (5 Feb 80) 3/4.
_____. Concertos, Op. 23, to be sold.
RISM G2265: *A second sett of six concertos for the harpsichord or*
piano forte with accompaniments . . . Opera XXIII. London: Longman
& Broderip.
(20-23 Oct 79) 3/3; (3-10 Nov 79) 4/2; (17-20 Nov 79) 4/2; (24
Nov 79) 3/2; (27 Nov - 1 Dec 79) 4/2; (22 Dec 79 - 12 Jan 80)
4/3; (15 Jan 80) 2/4; (26 Jan 80) 3/3; (5 Feb 80) 3/4.
_____. 6 chamber concertos for German flute, to be sold.
RISM G2252: *Six chamber concerto's for the German flute accompa-*
nied by two violins & a bass with a figured bass for the harpsichord
. . . Opera III. London: John Johnston & Longman, Lukey & Co.
(14 Oct 73) 1/4; (11 Nov 73) Supplement, 1/1; (20-23 Oct 79) 3/3;
(3-10 Nov 79) 4/2; (17-20 Nov 79) 4/2; (24 Nov 79) 3/2; (27 Nov
- 1 Dec 79) 4/2; (22 Dec 79 - 12 Jan 80) 4/3; (15 Jan 80) 2/4; (26
Jan 80) 3/3; (5 Feb 80) 3/4.
_____. 6 duettos for the violoncello, to be sold.
RISM G2316: *Six duettos for two violoncellos . . . Op. XVIII.*
London: Longman & Broderip.
(20-23 Oct 79) 3/3; (3-10 Nov 79) 4/2; (17-20 Nov 79) 4/2; (24
Nov 79) 3/2; (27 Nov - 1 Dec 79) 4/2; (22 Dec 79 - 12 Jan 80)
4/3; (15 Jan 80) 2/4; (26 Jan 80) 3/3; (5 Feb 80) 3/4.
_____. Favourite overture for clarinets and oboes, to be sold.
RISM G2250: *A favourite overture in eight parts for clarinets or*
oboes obligato. London: Longman & Broderip.

(20-23 Oct 79) 3/3; (3-10 Nov 79) 4/2; (17-20 Nov 79) 4/2; (24 Nov 79) 3/2; (27 Nov - 1 Dec 79) 4/2; (22 Dec 79 - 12 Jan 80) 4/3; (15 Jan 80) 2/4; (26 Jan 80) 3/3; (5 Feb 80) 3/4.

_____. Favourite overture for French horn and clarinet, to be sold.
    (20-23 Oct 79) 3/3; (3-10 Nov 79) 4/2; (17-20 Nov 79) 4/2; (24 Nov 79) 3/2; (27 Nov - 1 Dec 79) 4/2; (22 Dec 79 - 12 Jan 80) 4/3; (15 Jan 80) 2/4; (26 Jan 80) 3/3; (5 Feb 80) 3/4.

_____. Quartettos for violin, to be sold.
    RISM G2274: *Six quartettos, four for two violins, a tenor and bass; and two for a German flute, violin, tenor & bass . . . Opera II.* London: John Johnston.
    RISM 2279: *Sei quartetti per due violini, viola e violoncello . . . Opera VIII.* London: Longman & Broderip.
    (14 Oct 73) 1/4; (11 Nov 73) Supplement, 1/1.

_____. Quintettos, to be sold.
    RISM G2271: *Sei quintetti per due violini, viola, violoncello, e cembalo obligato.* London: Welcker, 1771.
    (20-23 Oct 79) 3/3; (3-10 Nov 79) 4/2; (17-20 Nov 79) 4/2; (24 Nov 79) 3/2; (27 Nov - 1 Dec 79) 4/2; (22 Dec 79 - 12 Jan 80) 4/3; (15 Jan 80) 2/4; (26 Jan 80) 3/3; (5 Feb 80) 3/4.

_____. 6 sonatas for keyboard, to be sold.
    RISM 2292: *Six sonates for the harpsichord with an accompanyment for the violin . . . Opera V.* London: Welcker (Straight & Skillern.)
    RISM 2297: *Six sonatas for the harpsichord or piano forte, with an accompanyment for a violin or flute . . . Opera 24.* London: Longman & Broderip
    RISM 2302: *Six sonatas for the harpsichord or piano forte with an accompaniment for a violin . . . Opera XXVII.* London: John Preston.
    RISM G2308: *Six sonatas for the piano forte with an accompaniment for a violin . . . Op. XXXV.* London: Preston & Son.
    (14 Oct 73) 1/4; (11 Nov 73) Supplement, 1/1.

_____. Six sonatas for keyboard, Opera 10, to be sold.
    RISM 2294: *VI sonatas for the piano forte, harpsichord, or organ . . . Opera X.* London: Longman, Lukey & Broderip.
    (22 Nov 77) 1/3-4.

_____. Trios, Op. 12, to be sold.
    RISM G2282: *Six trios for a German flute, tenor & violoncello . . . Opera XII.* London: Longman, Lukey & Broderip.
    (20-23 Oct 79) 3/3; (3-10 Nov 79) 4/2; (17-20 Nov 79) 4/2; (24 Nov 79) 3/2; (27 Nov - 1 Dec 79) 4/2; (22 Dec 79 - 12 Jan 80) 4/3; (15 Jan 80) 2/4; (26 Jan 80) 3/3; (5 Feb 80) 3/4.

Giordini's violin bows. *SEE* Giardini screw bows.

GIRANDINI.

_____. Works by, to be sold.
    (28 Aug 79) 2/2; (1 Sep 79) 2/4.

The girdle. *SEE* ARNE, Thomas Augustine.

Glassado, to be sold.
>(29 Sep 79) 2/3; (2-9 Oct 79) 3/4; (13 Oct 79) Supplement, 1/1; (3 Nov 79) Supplement, 2/1; (10-17 Nov 79) 4/4; (20-24 Nov 79) 1/4.

Glees, new, to be sold.
>(28 Aug 79) 2/2; (1 Sep 79) 2/4.

Glees. *SEE ALSO* Catches.

GLEOTTI. *SEE* GALEOTTI, Salvatore *or* Stefano.

God save the king, to be played every hour during races on Asket Heath on November 13-16
>(11 Nov 80) 2/3.
>For fuller reference, *SEE* Sport.

God save the king with variations. *SEE* Franceschini, Gaetano.

Goelet, Peter, fl.1774-1783. *SEE* Violin. Accessories, to be sold.

Golden pippin, airs and songs in for German flute, to be sold.
>BUC I, p.388: *The golden pippin, an English burletta . . . adapted with the words for the German flute, violin or hoboy.* London: Longman, Lukey and Co. and J. Johnston, ca.1775.
>(14 Oct 73) 1/4, (11 Nov 73) Supplement, 1/1.

Golden pippin. English opera, keyboard/vocal edition, to be sold.
>BUC I, p.388: *The songs, duets, trio &c. in the Golden-pippin an English burletta . . . compiled from the works of the most celebrated master by the author of Midas.* London: Longman, Lukey, and Co. & J. Johnston, 1773.
>(14 Oct 73) 1/4; (11 Nov 73) Supplement, 1/1; (22 Nov 77) 1/3-4.

Golden pippin. SEE ALSO The new golden pippin.

"Good neighbors, if you'll give me leave." Song lyric printed.
>(22 Jan 80) 3/3-4.

GRAF, Christian Ernst, 1723-1804. (GRAAF; GRAFF; GRAFI)

_____. Music, to be sold.
>(4 Oct 77) 4/2; (25 Oct 77) 4/4.

_____. Simphonies for keyboard, to be sold.
>RISM G3320?: *Six simphonies à deux violons, taille, basse, deux flûtes et deux cors de chasse . . . Oeuvre XI.* London: Longman, Lukey & Co., 1771.
>RISM G3322?: *Six simphonies à diverses instruments . . . Oeuvre XVI.* Berlin: J.J. Hummel, ca.1775.
>(14 Oct 73) 1/4; (11 Nov 73) Supplement, 1/1.

GRAF, Friedrich Hartmann, 1727-1795. (GRAAF; GRAFF; GRAFI)

_____. Quartettos, to be sold.
> RISM 3361: *Six grand quartettos for two violins a tenor and violoncello obligato etc.* London: J. Betz, ca.1780.
>> (20-23 Oct 79) 3/3; (3-10 Nov 79) 4/2; (17-20 Nov 79) 4/2; (24 Nov 79) 3/2; (27 Nov - 1 Dec 79) 4/2; (22 Dec 79 - 12 Jan 80) 4/3; (15 Jan 80) 2/4; (26 Jan 80) 3/3; (5 Feb 80) 3/4.

_____. Six quartettos for a flute, violin, viola and violoncello, to be sold.
> RISM G3364: *Six favourite quartettos for a German flute, violin, viola and violoncello, etc.* London: Longman, Lukey and Broderip, ca. 1778.
>> (22 Nov 77) 1/3-4.

Gramachree Molly. *SEE* Scotch songs.

GRASSI, Florio.

_____. Sonatas for two German flutes or violins, Opera 2, to be sold.
> RISM G3545: *Six sonatas for two German flutes . . . Opera II.* London: The author.
>> (20-23 Oct 79) 3/3; (3-10 Nov 79) 4/2; (17-20 Nov 79) 4/2; (24 Nov 79) 3/2; (27 Nov - 1 Dec 79) 4/2; (22 Dec 79 - 12 Jan 80) 4/3; (15 Jan 80) 2/4; (26 Jan 80) 3/3; (5 Feb 80) 3/4.

GREENE, Maurice, 1696-1755. (GREEN)

_____. Ten voluntaries by Mr. Handell and Dr. Green for keyboard, to be sold privately.
> BUC II, p.1050: *A collection of voluntaries, for the organ or harpsicord. Composed by Dr. Greene, Mr. Travers & several other eminent masters. Book I . . . (Book II).* London: Longman Lukey & Co. (Longman and Broderip), ca.1775-1780.
>> (4 Oct 83) 2/2.

Green, Henry. *SEE* ARNE, Thomas Augustine. "When Britain on her sea-girt shore."

Griffiths, James. *SEE* Clarichord.

GRONEMAN, Johann Albert, ca.1710-1778.

_____. Sonatas for two German flutes or violins, 2d collection, to be sold.
> RISM G4661: *Six sonatas or duets for two German flutes or two violins . . . Opera 2d.* London: Thompson & Son.
>> (20-23 Oct 79) 3/3; (3-10 Nov 79) 4/2; (17-20 Nov 79) 4/2; (24 Nov 79) 3/2; (27 Nov - 1 Dec 79) 4/2; (22 Dec 79 - 12 Jan 80) 4/3; (15 Jan 80) 2/4; (26 Jan 80) 3/3; (5 Feb 80) 3/4.

GUERINI, Francesco, fl.1740–1770.

_____. Works by, to be sold.
(28 Aug 79) 2/2; (1 Sep 79) 2/4.
_____. Sonatas for two German flutes or violins, to be sold.
RISM G4858: *Six sonatas or duets for two violins, etc. Op. 5.*
London: A. Hummel, ca.1770.
RISM G4861: *Six sonatas for two violins with a thorough bass for the harpsichord . . . Opera VIII.* London: Welcker, ca.1770.
(20-23 Oct 79) 3/3; (3-10 Nov 79) 4/2; (17-20 Nov 79) 4/2; (24 Nov 79) 3/2; (27 Nov - 1 Dec 79) 4/2; (22 Dec 79 - 12 Jan 80) 4/3; (15 Jan 80) 2/4; (26 Jan 80) 3/3; (5 Feb 80) 3/4.

Guitar. Instruments, to be sold.

_____. Guitar, "of the finest tone, made by Preston, of his first quality, and highly ornamented as a present to a lady . . . price twelve guineas."
(24 May 80) 3/3.
_____. Guitar, to be sold by Benjamin Davies.
(2 Sep 74) 3/4.
_____. Guitars, three excellent, property of a gentleman going to Europe.
(11 Dec 82) 2/4.
_____. Guittars (elegant; of various sorts, and a large choice of them; of various qualities and prices; excellent tone, second hand).
(10 Jun 73) 3/2; (17 Jun 73) 4/2; (14 Oct 73) 1/4; (11 Nov 73) Supplement, 1/1; (7 Apr 74) 3/1; (21 Apr 74) 3/4; (5 May 74) 3/2; (2 Sep 74) 3/4; (21 Jul 75) 3/4; (4 Oct 77) 4/2; (25 Oct 77) 4/4; (22 Nov 77) 1/3-4; (25 Jul 78) 3/1; (21 Apr 79) 2/4; (24 Apr 79) 2/2; (28 Apr 79) 2/1; (5 Jul 79) 4/4; (8 May 79) 4/4; (7 Aug 79) Supplement, 1/1; (11 Aug 79) 4/3; (28 Aug 79) 2/2; (1 Sep 79) 2/4; (29 Sep 79) 2/3; (2-9 Oct 79) 3/4; (13 Oct 79) Supplement, 1/1; (3 Nov 79) Supplement, 2/1; (10-17 Nov 79) 4/4; (20-24 Nov 79) 1/4; (3 May 80) 3/3-4; (27 May 80) 3/3; (17 Jun 80) 4/2; (8 Jul 80) 3/4; (7 Oct 80) 2/4; (23 Dec 80) 3/4; (27-30 Dec 80) 4/3; (3 Jan 81) 4/3; (6 Jan 81) 2/2; (27 Oct 81) 3/4; (3-7 Nov 81) 4/4; (10-21 Nov 81) 4/2; (24 Nov 81) 4/4; (5 Dec 81 - 5 Jan 82) 4/4; (29 Dec 81 - 23 Feb 82) 1/1; (9 Jan 82) 3/3; (16 Jan 82) 1/2; (19 Jan 82) 4/4; (23 Jan - 23 Feb 82) 4/2; (27 Feb 82) 4/3; (6-16 Mar 82) 1/2; (20 Mar 82) 4/2; (23-27 Mar 82) 4/2; (13 Apr 82) 3/4; (24 Apr - 1 May 82) 1/3; (4-29 May 82) 1/1; (1 Jun 82) 1/3; (5 Jun 82) 1/2; (8 Jun 82) 1/1; (12-22 Jun 82) 4/1; (26 Jun - 13 Jul 82) 4/4; (17 Jul 82) 1/1; (20-31 Jul 82) 4/1; (3-17 Aug 82) 4/3; (21 Aug - 4 Sep 82) 4/1; (11 Sep 82) 3/4; (14-21 Sep 82) 1/2; (19 Oct 82) 2/4; (23 Oct 82) 1/1; (7 Jun 83) 3/3; (11 Jun 83) 1/1; (14 Jun 83) 1/1.

Guitar. Accessories, to be sold.

_____. Guitar cases.
(4 Oct 77) 4/2; (25 Oct 77) 4/4; (7 Oct 80) 2/4.
_____. Guitar strings in complete setts, to be sold by Valentine Nutter.
(23 Dec 80) 2/4; (30 Dec 80) 3/3.

_____. Guittars, German wire for.
    (14 Oct 73) 1/4; (11 Nov 73) Supplement, 1/1.
_____. Guittars, silk strings for.
    (14 Oct 73) 1/4; (11 Nov 73) Supplement, 1/1.
_____. Guittar strings, silver.
    (11 Nov 73) Supplement, 1/1.

_____. Guittar strings.
    (30 Sep 73) 3/4; (7 Oct 73) 4/3; (14 Oct 73) Supplement, 1/3; (21
    Apr 74) 3/4; (5 May 74) 3/2; (9 Feb 75) 2/4; (4 Oct 77) 4/2; (25
    Oct 77) 4/4; (22 Nov 77) 1/3-4; (28 Aug 79) 2/2; (1 Sep 79) 2/4;
    (29 Sep 79) 2/3; (2 Oct 79) 3/4; (9 Oct 79) 3/4; (13 Oct 79)
    Supplement, 1/1; (3 Nov 79) Supplement, 2/1; (10-17 Nov 79) 4/4;
    (20-24 Nov 79) 1/4; (3 May 80) 3/3-4; (27 May 80) 3/3; (17 Jun
    80) 4/2; (8 Jul 80) 3/4; (29 Dec 81 - 23 Feb 82) 1/1; (27 Feb 82)
    4/3; (6-16 Mar 82) 1/2; (20 Mar 82) 4/2.

Guitar.   Music, to be sold.

_____. Guittar music.
    (30 Sep 74) 3/4; (7 Oct 73) 4/3; (14 Oct 73) Supplement, 1/3; (14
    Oct 73) 1/4; (11 Nov 73) Supplement, 1/1; (22 Nov 77) 1/3-4; (28
    Aug 79) 2/2; (1 Sep 79) 2/4.

Guitar music. *SEE ALSO* ALCOCK, John, Doctor in music; ALCOCK, John,
the Younger; ARNE, Michael. *Cymon*; ARNE, Thomas Augustine. *The
ladies frolick* and *Love in a village*; ARNOLD, Samuel; BACH,
Johann Christian; BALENTINE; CARTER, Charles Thomas;
CITRACINI, Giovanni Battista; DIBDIN, Charles. *The padlock*;
FISCHER, Johann Christian; Ford, Miss; GERLIN; HAXBY, R.;
Hymns and songs sung at the Magdalen; A LADY; MENEZE;
MILGROVE; *The new golden pippin*; NOFERI, Giovanni Battista;
SCHUMANN, Friedrich Theodor; THACKRAY, Thomas.

Guitar.   Tutors or instructors, to be sold.

_____. A pocket book for the guitar.
    (7 Aug 79) Supplement, 1/2; (11 Aug 79) 4/3.
_____. A pocket book for the guitar. With directions, whereby every lady and
gentleman may become their own tuner. To which is added . . . an
entertaining collection of songs, duets, airs, minuets, marches. To be
published by Rivington.
    (11 Jul 78) 3/3; (25 Jul 78) 3/1; (20 Jan 81) 3/2; (31 Jan 81) 2/2;
    (17 Feb 81) 4/4; (24 Feb 81) 3/4.
_____. A pocket book with directions for teaching pupils the guittar, with
songs, duets, airs, marches.
    (22 Nov 77) 1/3-4.

_____. The pocket companion for the guittar.
  BUC II, p.800: *The pocket companion for the guittar. Containing a favourite collection of the best Italian, French and Scotch songs. Adapted for that instrument and the voice. Book II-VI.* London: J. Oswald, ca.1755.
  BUC II, p.800: *A Pocket companion for the guittar containing XL of the newest and most favourite minuets country-dances jiggs airs &c* . . . . London: T. Habgood, 1759.
  (19 Aug 78) 2/3; (12 Sep 78) 1/1.

_____. Guittar tutors.
  (30 Sep 73) 3/4; (7 Oct 73) 4/3; (14 Oct 73) Supplement, 1/3; (21 Apr 74) 3/4; (5 May 74) 3/2; (4 Oct 77) 4/2; (25 Oct 77) 4/4; (8 Sep 79) 2/4; (2 Oct 79) 2/3; (9 Oct 79) 3/4.

Guitar. Teachers.

_____. Guitar taught by William Charles Hulett.
  (12 Jan 75) 3/4; (19 Jan 75) 4/2.

_____. Guitar to be taught by Martin Foy.
  (18 Sep 79) 3/3; (25 Sep 79) 3/4; (2 Oct 79) 2/2; (6 Oct 79) 4/4.

HÄNDEL, Georg Friedrich, 1685-1759. (HANDEL; HANDELL)

_____. Music, to be sold.
  (4 Oct 77) 4/2; (25 Oct 77) 4/4.

_____. Voluntaries for the keyboard, to be sold.
  RISM H1454: *Six fugues or voluntarys for the organ or harpsicord . . . troisième ouvrage.* London: J. Walsh.
  RISM H1485: *Twelve voluntaries and fugues for the organ or harpsichord, with rules for tuning by the celebrated Mr. Handel, book IV.* London: Longman & Broderip.
  (14 Oct 73) 1/4; (11 Nov 73) Supplement, 1/1.

_____. Ten voluntaries by Mr. Händel and Dr. Green for keyboard, to be sold privately.
  BUC II, p.1050: *A collection of voluntaries, for the organ or harpsichord. Composed by Dr. Greene, Mr. Travers & several other eminent masters. Book I . . . (Book II).* London: Longman Lukey & Co. (Longman and Broderip), ca.1775-1780.
  (4 Oct 83) 2/2.

Händel, performance of the Hallelujah chorus from the *Messiah. SEE* Concerto spirituale.

Hallam, Miss, fl.1765-1773.

_____. Sings "The soldier tired."
  (6 May 73) 3/3.

_____. To sing "Vain is beauty's gawdy flowers" in Mr. Zedtwitz's concert.
  (6 May 73) 3/3.
  For fuller reference, *SEE* Concert (6 May 73).

Hallam, Miss. *SEE ALSO* ARNE, Thomas Augustine. *Comus* and *The way to keep him; The musical lady.*

Hallam, Mr. [Lewis Hallam, Jr.?, 1741-1808] *SEE* HOOK, James. *She stoops to conquer.*

HANDEL. *SEE* HÄNDEL, Georg Friedrich.

Hand organs. *SEE* Organ.

"Hark! hark! the bugle's lofty sound." To the tune of Hark! hark! the joy-inspiring horn. Song lyric printed.
    (23 Dec 78) 3/1-2.

Harlequin collector: or, the miller deceiv'd. Pantomime entertainment performed.
    (1 Jul 73) 3/3.

Harlequin's gambols. *SEE* FISHER, John Abraham. *The sylphs.*

Harmonic society.

_____. Members played instrumental parts in concert conducted by Zedtwitz.
    (6 May 73) 3/3.
    For fuller reference, *SEE* Concert (6 May 73).
_____. Involved in public concert to be held on April 28, 1774.
    (14 Apr 74) 3/3; (21 Apr 74) 3/2; (28 Apr 74) 2/2.
    For fuller reference, *SEE* Concert (14 Apr 74).

Harp. Instruments, to be sold.

_____. Harp, a very good, to be sold for four guineas.
    (8 Nov 83) 3/4.
_____. Harps.
    (26 Sep 81) 4/1; (29 Sep 81) 4/2; (6-31 Oct 81) 4/2; (29 Dec 81 - 23 Feb 82) 1/1; (27 Feb 82) 4/3; (6-16 Mar 82) 1/2; (20 Mar 82) 4/2.

Harp. *SEE ALSO* Welsh harp.

Harp. Accessories, to be sold.

_____. Harps strings.
    (3 May 80) 3/3-4; (27 May 80) 3/3; (17 Jun 80) 4/2; (8 Jul 80) 3/4; (23 Dec 80) 3/4; (27 Dec 80) 4/3; (30 Dec 80) 4/3; (3 Jan 81) 4/3; (6 Jan 81) 2/2.
_____. Harp wires.
    (29 Dec 81 - 23 Feb 82) 1/1; (27 Feb 82) 4/3; (6-16 Mar 82) 1/2; (20 Mar 82) 4/2.

Harp.   Music, to be sold.

_____.   Harp music.
     (14 Oct 73) 1/4; (11 Nov 73) Supplement, 1/1; (28 Aug 79) 2/2;
     1 Sep 79) 2/4.

Harp music.   *SEE ALSO* PARRY, John.

Harpsichord.   Instruments, to be sold.

_____.   Harpsichord, a fine ton'd double key'd.
     (12 Dec 78) 2/3.
_____.   Harpsichord, made by Harris, with two unison stops.
     (13-17 Apr 82) 3/4.
_____.   Harpsichord made by Kirkman, with three stops and a swell.
     (8 Dec 81) 3/4.
_____.   Harpsichord, the best instrument in America, old and ever highly
approved.   The lowest price is sixty guineas, a sum inferior to its
cost.
     (15 Sep 79) 2/4.
_____.   Harpsichord to be sold by Benjamin Davies.
     (2 Sep 74) 3/4.
_____.   Harpsichord.
     (7 Oct 78) 3/4; (23-26 Dec 78) 3/4; (30 Dec 78 - 9 Jan 79) 1/1;
     (29 Dec 79) 3/3; (1-8 Jan 80) 4/4; (12-15 Jan 80) 1/4; (3 May 80)
     3/3-4; (27 May 80) 3/3; (17 Jun 80) 4/2; (8 Jul 80) 3/4.
_____.   Harpsichords made, repaired and to be sold by Frederick Heyer.
     (11 Nov 73) 1/3.

Harpsichord.   Repaired and rented.

_____.   Harpsichord, spinett, or piano forte, wanted to hire.
     (9 Nov 82) 2/4.
_____.   Harpsichord, wanted to rent for the subscription concert season.
     (25 Jan 83) 3/3.
_____.   Harpsichords made, repaired and to be sold by Frederick Heyer.
     (11 Nov 73) 1/3.
_____.   Harpsichords, stringing, tuning, quilling by William Pearson, clock
and watch-maker.
     (14 Apr 74) 1/1; (21 Apr 74) 4/4.

Harpsichord.   Accessories, to be sold.

_____.   Harpsichord and spinnet tuning hammers.
     (14 Oct 73) 1/4; (11 Nov 73) Supplement, 1/1.
_____.   Harpsichord, crow quills.
     (4 Oct 77) 4/2; (25 Oct 77) 4/4.
_____.   Harpsichord desks.
     (14 Oct 73) 1/4; (11 Nov 73) Supplement, 1/1.
_____.   Harpsichord, steel tuning forks.
     (23 Dec 80) 3/4; (27 Dec 80 - 3 Jan 81) 4/3; (6 Jan 81) 2/2.

_____. Harpsichord string and wire.
(30 Sep 73) 3/4; (7 Oct 73) 4/3; (14 Oct 73) Supplement, 1/3; (14 Oct 73) 1/4; (11 Nov 73) Supplement, 1/1; (9 Feb 75) 2/4; (21 Jul 75) 3/4; (28 Aug 79) 2/2; (1 Sep 79) 2/4; (11 Sep 79) 2/3; (3 Nov 79) Supplement, 2/1; (29 Sep 79) 2/3; (2-9 Oct 79) 3/4; (13 Oct 79) Supplement, 1/1; (3 Nov 79) Supplement, 2/1; (10-17 Nov 79) 4/4; (20-24 Nov 79) 1/4; (23 Dec 80) 3/4; (27 Dec 80 - 3 Jan 81) 4/3; (6 Jan 81) 2/2; (29 Dec 81 - 23 Feb 82) 1/1; (27 Feb 82) 4/3; (6-16 Mar 82) 1/2; (20 Mar 82) 4/2.

Harpsichord. Music for, to be sold.

_____. Harpsichord music, to be sold by Valentine Nutter.
(23 Dec 80) 2/4; (30 Dec 80) 3/3.
_____. Harpsichord, music for.
(30 Sep 73) 3/4; (7 Oct 73) 4/3; (14 Oct 73) Supplement, 1/3; (14 Oct 73) 1/4; (11 Nov 73) Supplement, 1/1; (22 Nov 77) 1/3-4; (28 Aug 79) 2/2; (1 Sep 79) 2/4; (20-23 Oct 79) 3/3; (3-10 Nov 79) 4/2; (17-20 Nov 79) 4/2; (24 Nov 79) 3/2; (27 Nov - 1 Dec 79) 4/2; (22 Dec 79 -12 Jan 80) 4/3; (15 Jan 80) 2/4; (26 Jan 80) 3/3; (5 Feb 80) 3/4.

Harpsichord. Tutors or instructors, to be sold.

_____. Harpsichord tutors or instructors.
(30 Sep 73) 3/4; (7 Oct 73) 4/3; (14 Oct 73) Supplement, 1/3; (14 Oct 73) 1/4; (11 Nov 73) Supplement, 1/1; (21 Jul 75) 3/4; (25 Jul 78) 3/1; (8 Sep 79) 2/4; (2 Oct 79) 2/3; (9 Oct 79) 3/4.

Harpsichord. Teachers.

_____. Harpsichord lessons offerred by Mr. Biferi. "In a very short time, [he enables his pupils] to play . . . either pieces, sonatas, thorough bass, &c."
(1 Dec 74) 3/4; (8 Dec 74) 4/1.
For fuller reference, *SEE*, Biferi, Nicholas.
_____. Harpsichord to be taught by Mr. Biferi.
(30 Jun 74) 2/4; (7 Jul 74) 4/3.
For fuller reference, *SEE* Biferi, Nicholas.
_____. Harpsichord, used for teaching singing by Mr. Biferi.
(1 Dec 74) 3/4; (8 Dec 74) 4/1.
For fuller reference, *SEE* Biferi, Nicholas.

Harpsichord. Teachers. *SEE ALSO* Leadbetter, James.

Harris harpsichord to be sold, two unison stops.
(13-17 Apr 82) 3/4.

HASSE, Johann Adolph, 1699-1783.

_____.   Six sonatas for a German flute, violin and bass, to be sold.
RISM H2300: *Six sonatas for a German flute, violin, & base.*
Composed by Signor Hass [sic].   London: J. Tyther, 1745.
RISM H2301: *Six sonatas for a German flute, violin & bass . . . by*
Signor Hass [sic].   London: James Lewer, ca.1760.
(20-23 Oct 79) 3/3; (3-10 Nov 79) 4/2; (17-20 Nov 79) 4/2; (24
Nov 79) 3/2; (27 Nov - 1 Dec 79) 4/2; (22 Dec 79 - 12 Jan 80)
4/3; (15 Jan 80) 2/4; (26 Jan 80) 3/3; (5 Feb 80) 3/4.

Hautboy (Hautbois; Hoboy; Oboe).   Instruments, to be sold.

_____.   Hautboys.
(10 Jun 73) 3/2; (17 Jun 73) 4/2; (14 Oct 73) 1/4; (11 Nov 73)
Supplement, 1/1; (28 Aug 79) 2/2; (1 Sep 79) 2/4; (3 May 80)
3/3-4; (27 May 80) 3/3; (17 Jun 80) 4/2; (8 Jul 80) 3/4; (23 Dec
80) 3/4; (27 Dec 80) 4/3; (30 Dec 80) 4/3; (3 Jan 81) 4/3; (6 Jan
81) 2/2; (26 Sep 81) 4/1; (29 Sep 81) 4/2; (6-31 Oct 81) 4/2; (27
Oct 81) 3/4; (3-7 Nov 81) 4/4; (10-21 Nov 81) 4/2; (24 Nov 81)
4/4; (5 Dec 81 - 5 Jan 82) 4/4; (9 Jan 82) 3/3; (16 Jan 82) 1/2;
(19 Jan 82) 4/4; (23 Jan - 23 Feb 82) 4/2; (23-27 Mar 82) 4/2; (13
Apr 82) 3/4; (24 Apr - 1 May 82) 1/3; (4-29 May 82) 1/1; (1 Jun
82) 1/3; (5 Jun 82) 1/2; (8 Jun 82) 1/1; (12-22 Jun 82) 4/1; (26
Jun - 13 Jul 82) 4/4; (17 Jul 82) 1/1; (20-31 Jul 82) 4/1; (3-17
Aug 82) 4/3; (21 Aug - 4 Sep 82) 4/1; (29 Dec 81 - 23 Feb 82)
1/1; (27 Feb 82) 4/3; (6-16 Mar 82) 1/2; (20 Mar 82) 4/2.

Hautboy.   Accessories, to be sold.

_____.   Hautboy reed cases (with holes to deposit 6 of each of oboe reeds).
(14 Oct 73) 1/4; (11 Nov 73) Supplement, 1/1; (4 Oct 77) 4/2; (25
Oct 77) 4/4; (22 Nov 77) 1/3-4; (3 May 80) 3/3-4; (27 May 80)
3/3; (17 Jun 80) 4/2; (8 Jul 80) 3/4; (23 Dec 80) 3/4; (27 Dec 80)
4/3; (30 Dec 80) 4/3; (3 Jan 81) 4/3; (6 Jan 81) 2/2.
_____.   Hautboy reeds.
(30 Sep 73) 3/4; (7 Oct 73) 4/3; (14 Oct 73) Supplement, 1/3; (14
Oct 73) 1/4; (11 Nov 73) Supplement, 1/1; (21 Apr 74) 3/4; (5 May
74) 3/2; (4 Oct 77) 4/2; (25 Oct 77) 4/4; (22 Nov 77) 1/3-4; (25
Jul 78) 3/1; (3 May 80) 3/3-4; (27 May 80) 3/3; (17 Jun 80) 4/2;
(8 Jul 80) 3/4; (23 Dec 80) 2/4; (20 Dec 80) 3/3; (23 Dec 80) 3/4;
(27 Dec 80) 4/3; (30 Dec 80) 4/3; (3 Jan 81) 4/3; (6 Jan 81) 2/2.

Hautboy.   Music, to be sold.

_____.   Hautboy music.
(30 Sep 73) 3/4; (7 Oct 73) 4/3, (14 Oct 73) Supplement, 1/3; (28
Aug 79) 2/2; (1 Sep 79) 2/4.

Hautboy (Oboe) music.   *SEE ALSO* GIORDANI, Tommaso.

A hautboy concerto, to be performed between the play and farce in the theatre.
(19 Jul 80) 3/4.

Hautboy solo concerto. *SEE Love a-la-mode.*

Hautboy. Performers.

_____. Two hautboy players wanted for band on board the *General Pattison*, private ship of war.
(14 Apr 79) 2/4; (21 Apr 79) 4/3.

Hautboy. Tutors or instructors, to be sold.

_____. Hautboy tutors.
(30 Sep 73) 3/4; (7 Oct 73) 4/3; (14 Oct 73) Supplement, 1/3; (14 Oct 73) 1/4; (11 Nov 73) Supplement, 1/1; (8 Sep 79) 2/4; (2 Oct 79) 2/3; (9 Oct 79) 3/4.

HAWDON, Matthias, d.1787.

_____. Concerto for keyboard, to be sold.
RISM H2418: *Two concertos for the harpsicord, organ or piano forte, with accompaniments for two violins & a violoncello.* London: Longman, Lukey & Co.
RISM H2419: *Two concertos for the organ, or harpsichord, with instrumental parts.* London: Longman & Broderip.
(22 Nov 77) 1/3-4.

HAXBY, R.

_____. Haxby's easy airs for guitar, to be sold.
RISM H2438: *Twenty four easy airs for the guitar made on purpose for young beginners.* London: J. Longman & Co.
(14 Oct 73) 1/4; (11 Nov 73) Supplement, 1/1.

HAYDN, Franz Joseph, 1732-1809. (HAYDEN)

_____. Works by, to be sold.
(28 Aug 79) 2/2; (1 Sep 79) 2/4.
_____. Six quartettos for two violins, taille and bass, Opera 1, to be sold.
RISM H3437: *Six quatuor à deux violons, taille, et basse obligés . . . Opera I.* London: R. Bremner, 1772.
RISM H3439: *Six quartettos for two violins, tenor and violoncello obligato. Op. Ist.* London: Longman & Broderip, ca.1780.
(22 Nov 77) 1/3-4.
_____. Six quartettos for two violins, taille and bass, Opera 2, to be sold.
RISM H3442: *Six quatuor à deux violons, taille, et basse obligés . . . Opera II.* London: R. Bremner, 1772.
(22 Nov 77) 1/3-4.

_____. Six quartettos for a violin alto and bass Opera 5, to be sold.
   RISM H3340: *Six quatuor à flute violon alto, & basse . . . Opera quinta.*   London: R. Bremner, ca.1772.
   (22 Nov 77) 1/3-4.

_____. Quartettos, Op. 7, to be sold.
   RISM H3446: *VI Quatour* [sic] *. . . Opera VII.*   London: Longman, Lukey & Co.
   (20-23 Oct 79) 3/3; (3-10 Nov 79) 4/2; (17-20 Nov 79) 4/2; (24 Nov 79) 3/2; (27 Nov - 1 Dec 79) 4/2; (22 Dec 79 - 12 Jan 80) 4/3; (15 Jan 80) 2/4; (26 Jan 80) 3/3; (5 Feb 80) 3/4.

_____. Six quartettos for two violins, a tenor, and violoncello, Opera 10, to be sold.
   RISM H3604. *Six favorite quartettos for two violins, a tenor and violoncello . . . Op. X.*   London: R. Warnum, ca.1775.
   (22 Nov 77) 1/3-4.

_____. Sinfonie, to be performed.
   (27 Apr 82) 3/3.
   For fuller reference, *SEE* Concert (27 Apr 82).

_____. Trios, Op. 3, to be sold.
   RISM H3804: *Six trios for two violins & a bass . . . Opera 3.*   London: Longman, Lukey and Co., ca.1776.
   (20-23 Oct 79) 3/3; (3-10 Nov 79) 4/2; (17-20 Nov 79) 4/2; (24 Nov 79) 3/2; (27 Nov - 1 Dec 79) 4/2; (22 Dec 79 - 12 Jan 80) 4/3; (15 Jan 80) 2/4; (26 Jan 80) 3/3; (5 Feb 80) 3/4.

HAYES, Philip, 1708-1777 *or* 1738-1797.

_____. Concertos, to be sold.
   RISM H4884: *Six concertos, with accompaniments; for the organ, harpsichord or forte piano; to which is added a harpsicord sonata, etc.*   London: Printed for the author, 1769.
   (20-23 Oct 79) 3/3; (3-10 Nov 79) 4/2; (17-20 Nov 79) 4/2; (24 Nov 79) 3/2; (27 Nov - 1 Dec 79) 4/2; (22 Dec 79 - 12 Jan 80) 4/3; 15 Jan 80) 2/4; (26 Jan 80) 3/3; (5 Feb 80) 3/4.

HAYSARD.

_____. Works by, to be sold.
   (28 Aug 79) 2/2; (1 Sep 79) 2/4.

Hearts of oak.   *SEE* "Come cheer up, my lads";   "Here's a bumper brave boys."

Henry, Mr. [John Henry?, d.1795]   Singing as character Sir Callaghan O'Brallaghan in *Love a-la-mode.*
   (24 Jun 73) 3/4.

"Here's a bumper brave boys to the health of our king."   To the tune of Hearts of oak.   Song lyric printed.
   (17 May 79) 3/1.

Hey! my kitten, my kitten.   *SEE* "What did my phlogy, my phlogy."

HEYDEN.

____. Music, to be sold.
    (4 Oct 77) 4/2; (25 Oct 77) 4/4.

Heyer, Frederick. Maker of organs, harpsichords and spinets. In the Broad-Way, in the same house where Mr. George Cook, Sadler, lives, near St. Paul's Church.
    (11 Nov 73) 1/3.

HICKES, George. (HICKS)

____. Works by, to be sold.
    RISM H5236: *Six sonatas for the harpsichord or piano forte.*
London: Longman & Broderip for the author.
    (28 Aug 79) 2/2; (1 Sep 79) 2/4.

High life below stairs. SEE BATTISHILL, Jonathan.

Hob in the wall. English opera, harpsichord/vocal edition, to be sold.
    (22 Nov 77) 1/3-4.

Hob in the well. SEE BATES, William. *Flora, or Hob in the well.*

Hoboy. *SEE* Hautboy.

Hodge and Shober. *SEE* The American robin.

Hoffmaster, French horn maker. Died six years ago.
    (1 Aug 78) 1/4; (5 Aug 78) 4/4.

HOLYOAK.

____. Duettos for German flute, to be sold.
    (14 Oct 73) 1/4; (11 Nov 73) Supplement, 1/1.

HONAUR, Leontzi, ca.1735-?.

____. Works by, to be sold.
    (28 Aug 79) 2/2; (1 Sep 79) 2/4.

HOOK, James, 1747-1827.

____. Works, by to be sold.
    (28 Aug 79) 2/2; (1 Sep 79) 2/4.
____. How sweet the love that meets return. A favorite song. Sung by Mrs. Kennedy, at Vauxhall and set to music by Mr. Hook. The words by a lady. To be sold.

RISM H6885: *How sweet the love that meets return. A favorite song sung by Mrs. Kennedy at Vauxhall Gardens, etc.* London: J. Preston, ca.1783.

(22 Oct 83) 2/1.

_____. *The lady of the manor.* English opera, keyboard/vocal edition, to be sold.

RISM H6485: *The lady of the manor, a comic opera . . . for the voice, harpsichord or violin. The words written by Dr. Kenrick . . . Op. XX.* London: S.A. & P. Thompson, 1778.

(28 Aug 79) 2/2; (1 Sep 79) 2/4.

_____. *She stoops to conquer.* Mr. Hallam, singing as the character Tony Lumpkin in.

RISM H6509: *The wretch condemn'd. The favourite song sung by Mr. DuBellamy . . . in the comedy She stoops to conquer.* London: Welcker, etc., ca.1770.

(29 Jul 73) 3/4; (5 Aug 73) 3/2.

_____. *Too civil by half,* a farce, to be performed in the theatre.

RISM H6514: *The overture, songs and chorus, in the farce of Too civil by half . . . Opera XXV.* London: S.A. & P. Thompson, 1783.

(22 Oct 83) 3/2.

_____. *Trick upon trick, or, Harlequin skeleton,* a new pantomime entertainment, to be performed.

RISM H6517: *The songs and masque in the pantomime of Trick upon trick, as performed at Sadlers Wells.* London: C. & S. Thompson, 1772.

(24 Aug 83) 3/2; (30 Aug 83) 3/3.

HOOK, James. *SEE ALSO* Scotch songs. Down the burn Davy, love.

HOPKINSON, Francis, 1737-1791.

_____. "Arise! arise! your voices raise." *The temple of Minerva.* Oratorial entertainment, lyrics printed.*

(5 Jan 82) 2/1.

_____. "Sing to his shade a solemn strain." In memory of Mr. James Bremner. Song lyric printed.**

(28 Feb 81) 3/3.

_____. "Strain hard! Strain hard! Your voices raise." To the tune of Whiston and Ditton. *The temple of Cloacina.* Song lyric printed.*

(5 Jan 82) 2/2.

Horner (publisher). *SEE* The Free masons pocket book.

---

*For modern edition, *SEE: America Independent, or, The temple of Minerva,* edited by Gillian Anderson (Washington, DC: C.T. Wagner Music Publishers,1978).

**There is a photocopy of a manuscript in the Library of Congress (M1621.H, copy 2, case) called *In memory of James Bremner.* A note has been added which says "copyright Paul G. and Henry C. Woehlcke, 1931."

Hornpipe, to be performed in the theatre.
(9 June 81) 2/2.

Hornpipe, to be performed in the theatre between play and farce.
(2 Jun 81) 2/4.

Hornpipes, single, double and treble. To be taught by W. Birchall Tetley.
(3 Nov 74) 3/4; (10 Nov 74) 4/4.
For fuller reference, *SEE* Tetley, W. Birchall.

Hornpipes. *SEE ALSO* Dancing.

Hosanna to the Son of David. *SEE* Church-music.

Hosier's ghost. *SEE* A medley for the light infantry.

Hot stuff. *SEE* "Come, each death-doing dog who dare venture his neck."

"How merrily we live that shepherds be." *SEE* SHIELD, William. *The flitch of bacon.*

How much superior beauty awes. *SEE* "As tyrant power and slavish fear."

"How oft we've seen in every form." Song lyric printed.
(8 Jan 80) 2/2.

"How sweet the love that meets return." *SEE* HOOK, James.

HUCHALL.

_____. Works by, to be sold.
(28 Aug 79) 2/2; (1 Sep 79) 2/4.

Hulett, William Charles, d.1785.

_____. Selling tickets for concert and ball, 4 January 1774.
(23 Dec 73) 3/4; (30 Dec 73) 4/1.
_____. Involved in public concert to be held on 28 April 1774.
(14 Apr 74) 3/3; (21 Apr 74) 3/2; (25 Apr 74) 2/2.
For fuller reference, *SEE* Concert (14 Apr 74).
_____. Teacher of violin, guittar, German flute and dancing. 20 year resident of N.Y.C. Announces reopening of school in Broad St.
(12 Jan 75) 3/4; (19 Jan 75) 4/2.
_____. To perform in concert, 4 April 1775.
(30 Mar 75) 2/3.
_____. Son, 10 years old, singing a duet in concert.
(6 May 73) 3/3.
For fuller reference, *SEE* Concert (6 May 73).

Hulett, William Charles. *SEE ALSO* Dancing.

Hulett, Young Mr. To dance a rigadoon with Miss Sodi.
> (19 May 74) 3/3; (26 May 74) 2/4.
> For fuller reference, *SEE* Concert (19 May 74).

Hull's Assembly Room. Concerts, rehearsals, and balls.
> (6 May 73) 3/3; (2 Dec 73) 3/4; (9 Dec 73) 3/4; (16 Dec 73) 4/3;
> (23 Dec 73) 3/4; (30 Dec 73) 4/1; (19 May 74) 3/3; (26 May 74)
> 2/4; (23 Feb 75) 3/2; (2 Mar 75) 2/3; (9 Mar 75) 2/4; (16 Mar 75)
> 1/2; (23 Mar 75) 3/3; (30 Mar 75) 2/3; (20 Apr 75) 3/3.

Hull's Long Room. *SEE* ARNE, Michael. *Cymon*; DIBDIN, Charles. *The
padlock.*

HUMBLE, Maximilian.

_____. Works by, to be sold.
> (28 Aug 79) 2/2; (1 Sep 79) 2/4.

_____. Six duets for two violins, to be sold.
> RISM H7883: *Six duets for two violins . . . (Op. VI).* London:
> Longman, Lukey and Co. . . . and John Johnston, ca.1775.
> (22 Nov 77) 1/3-4.

_____. Sonatas for two German flutes or violins, 2d sett, to be sold.
> RISM H7875: *A second sett of six sonatas for two violins with a
> thorough bass for the harpsichord.* London: Welcker.
> (20-23 Oct 79) 3/3; (3-10 Nov 79) 4/2; (17-20 Nov 79) 4/2; (24
> Nov 79) 3/2; (27 Nov - 1 Dec 79) 4/2; (22 Dec 79 - 12 Jan 80)
> 4/3; (15 Jan 80) 2/4; (26 Jan 80) 3/3; (5 Feb 80) 3/4.

_____. Sonatas for two German flutes or violins, 4th sett, to be sold.
> RISM H7878: *A fourth sett of six sonatas for two violins and a
> thorough bass.* London: Welcker.
> (20-23 Oct 79) 3/3; (3-10 Nov 79) 4/2; (17-20 Nov 79) 4/2; (24
> Nov 79) 3/2; (27 Nov - 1 Dec 79) 4/2; (22 Dec 79 - 12 Jan 80)
> 4/3; (15 Jan 80) 2/4; (26 Jan 80) 3/3; (5 Feb 80) 3/4.

_____. Six sonatas for violin and German flute, Opera 7, to be sold.
> RISM H7881: *A favorite set of sonatas for two violins, violoncello
> or a thorough bass for the harpsichord . . . Op. VII.* London: Longman,
> Lukey & Co.
> (22 Nov 77) 1/3-4.

_____. Sonatas for two German flutes or violins, Op. 7, to be sold.
> RISM H7881: See entry above.
> (20-23 Oct 79) 3/3; (3-10 Nov 79) 4/2; (17-20 Nov 79) 4/2; (24
> Nov 79) 3/2; (27 Nov - 1 Dec 79) 4/2; (22 Dec 79 - 12 Jan 80)
> 4/3; (15 Jan 80) 2/4; (26 Jan 80) 3/3; (5 Feb 80) 3/4.

_____. Trios, 5th set, to be sold.
> RISM H7880: *A fifth sett of trios for two violins and a violoncello.*
> London: Welcker.
> (20-23 Oct 79) 3/3; (3-10 Nov 79) 4/2; (17-20 Nov 79) 4/2; (24
> Nov 79) 3/2; (27 Nov - 1 Dec 79) 4/2; (22 Dec 79 - 12 Jan 80)
> 4/3; (15 Jan 80) 2/4; (26 Jan 80) 3/3; (5 Feb 80) 3/4.

Humphreys, James, jun. (publisher). *SEE* LINLEY, Thomas, the Elder. *The duenna.*

Hunting horns, to be sold.
>(3 May 80) 3/3-4; (27 May 80) 3/3; (17 Jun 80) 4/2; (8 Jul 80) 3/4.

Hunting horns. *SEE ALSO* English hunting horns.

Hunting song, new, to be performed in theatre after the third act of a comedy.
>(2 Jun 81) 2/4.

"Huzza! Huzza then cry'd a skinner." Song lyric printed.
>(3 Feb 74) 1/2.

Hyde, Mrs.

_____. Singing a song in the theatre.
>(5 May 82) 3/3; (8 May 82) 3/2.

_____. Singing "Bright author" in theatre.
>(27 Sep 83) 3/4.

_____. Sings "If 'tis joy to wound a lover"; "The lark's shrill notes"; and "Soldier tir'd of wars alarms."
>(27 Apr 82) 3/3.
>For fuller reference, *SEE* Concert (27 Apr 82).

Hymns and songs sung at the Magdalen for the guitar, to be sold.
>BUC I, p.522: *The hymns anthems and tunes with the ode used at the Magdalen Chapel. Set for the organ harpsichord, voice German-flute or guitar. Bk. 1.* London: Henry Thorowgood, ca.1765.
>BUC I, p.523: *A companion to the Magdalen-Chapel, containing the hymns, psalms, ode and anthems, used there, set for the harpsichord, voice, German-flute or guitar. The music composed by the most eminent masters.* London: Henry Thorowgood, ca.1770.
>(14 Oct 73) 1/4; (11 Nov 73) Supplement, 1/1.

"If fortune would smile, and I cannot complain." *SEE* ARNE, Thomas Augustine.

"If 'tis joy to wound a lover."

_____. Song in the theatre, performed between the play and the farce.
>BUC I, p.539: *If 'tis joy to wound a lover. Sung by Mrs. Pinto.* London: R. Falkener, ca.1770.
>(2 Mar 82) 2/3.

_____. To be sung by Mrs. Hyde.
>BUC I, p.539: See entry above.
>(27 Apr 82) 3/3.
>For fuller reference, *SEE* Concert (27 Apr 82).

If you can caper as well as you modulate. *SEE* "Thus, having buried the daemon of enmity."

"In Esop's days, when all things spoke." Song lyric printed.
(19 Sep 78) 2/1.

In memory of Mr. James Bremner. *SEE* HOPKINSON, Francis. "Sing to his shade a solemn strain."

"An independent and a page." Song lyric printed.
(3 Feb 74) 1/2.

Institution of the garter. SEE DIBDIN, Charles.

Instrumental music, taught and composed. *SEE* Biferi, Nicholas.

The Irish widow. SEE VERNON, Joseph.

"It was on Mr. Peroy's land." To the tune of Yankee doodle. Song lyric printed.
(11 Nov 78) 3/1-2.

Jackson, James. Escaped Negro slave, plays on the German flute and fife.
(12 Nov 83) 2/3.

JACKSON, William, 1730-1803.

_____. Eight sonatas for keyboard, Opera 10, to be sold.
BUC I, p.551: *Eight sonatas for the harpsichord accompanied with two violins, a tenor and bass . . . Opera X.* London: Longman and Broderip, 1773.
(22 Nov 77) 1/3-4.
_____. Six sonatas for keyboard, to be sold.
BUC I, p.551: *Six sonatas for the harpsichord accompanied with a violin.* London: Printed for John Johnson, 1760.
(22 Nov 77) 1/3-4.

Jamaica Accession Ball. *SEE* Ball.

Jane Shore, play in the theatre after which was sung "Bucks have at ye all".
(19 Jul 80) 3/4.

Jigs. *SEE* Dancing.

Jingle, Bob. [Pseudonym for Francis Hopkinson?] *SEE* The Association. . . .

Jockey to the fair. *SEE* Scotch songs.

JOMMELLI, Niccolò, 1714-1774.

_____. Works by, to be sold.
    (28 Aug 79) 2/2; (1 Sep 79) 2/4.
_____. Overtures, to be sold.
    RISM J595: *The periodical overture in 5 parts . . . number XIV.*
London: Robert Bremner.
    RISM J597: *The periodical overture in 8 parts . . . number XIX.*
London: Robert Bremner.
    RISM J601: *The favorite periodical overture and chaconne . . .
adapted for the harpsichord or piano forte by W. Smethergall.* London:
Longman & Broderip, for the editor.
    (20-23 Oct 79) 3/3; (3-10 Nov 79) 4/2; (17-20 Nov 79) 4/2; (24
Nov 79) 3/2; (27 Nov - 1 Dec 79) 4/2; (22 Dec 79 - 12 Jan 80)
4/3; (15 Jan 80) 2/4; (26 Jan 80) 3/3; (5 Feb 80) 3/4.

"Joy to great Congress, joy an hundred fold." Song lyric printed.
    (6 Nov 79) 2/2-3.

Jubilate Deo. *SEE* Church-music.

The jubilee. SEE DIBDIN, Charles.

JUST, Johann August, ca.1750-1791.

_____. Works by, to be sold.
    (28 Aug 79) 2/2; (1 Sep 79) 2/4.
_____. Concertos, to be sold.
    RISM J758: *Six concerts pour les amateurs de musique sur le
clavecin avec l'accompagnement de deux violons, taille, basse, et deux
cors de chasse ad libitum . . . Oeuvre IV.* London: Longman, Lukey &
Co.
    RISM J773: *Concerto for the harpsichord with accompanyments for
two violins, a basse, two oboes or flutes and two horns ad libitum.*
London: J. Bland.
    RISM J786: *A concerto for all performers & admirers of the violin,
in seven parts (viz) violin principal, violin primo, violin secondo, two
horns, tenor and bass.* London: Longman, Lukey & Co.
    (20-23 Oct 79) 3/3; (3-10 Nov 79) 4/2; (17-20 Nov 79) 4/2; (24
Nov 79) 3/2; (27 Nov - 1 Dec 79) 4/2; (22 Dec 79 - 12 Jan 80)
4/3; (15 Jan 80) 2/4; (26 Jan 80) 3/3; (5 Feb 80) 3/4.
_____. Divertiments for the violin, to be sold.
    RISM J743: *Six divertissemens pour le clavecin, avec
l'accompagnement d'un violon . . . Oeuvre I.* London: A. Hummel,
Longman, Lukey & Co.
    RISM J761: *Six divertissemens pour le clavecin ou le piano forte,
avec l'accompagnement d'un violon obligé . . . Oeuvre sixième.* Den
Haag: Burchard Hummel & Sohn.
    (14 Oct 73) 1/4; (11 Nov 73) Supplement, 1/1.

_____. Six divertimentos for keyboard, to be sold.

    RISM J744: *Six divertimentos pour le clavecin, avec l'accompagnement d'un violon . . . Oeuvre I.* London: Longman, Lukey & Co.

    RISM J750: *Six divertimentos, pour le clavecin, avec l'accompagnement d'un violon . . . Oeuvre (II).* London: Longman, Lukey & Co.

    (22 Nov 77) 1/3-4.

_____. Duettinos for two German flutes or violins, to be sold.

    RISM J788: *Six duettino's* [sic] *for the German flutes or violins.* London: Longman, Lukey & Co.

    (20-23 Oct 79) 3/3; (3-10 Nov 79) 4/2; (17-20 Nov 79) 4/2; (24 Nov 79) 3/2; (27 Nov - 1 Dec 79) 4/2; (22 Dec 79 - 12 Jan 80) 4/3; (15 Jan 80) 2/4; (26 Jan 80) 3/3; (5 Feb 80) 3/4.

_____. Overtures, to be sold.

    RISM J771: *Six overtures for 2 violins, 2 oboes or flutes, 2 horns, viola and figured bass for the harpsichord . . . Opera 8.* London.: Longman & Broderip.

    (20-23 Oct 79) 3/3; (3-10 Nov 79) 4/2; (17-20 Nov 79) 4/2; (24 Nov 79) 3/2; (27 Nov - 1 Dec 79) 4/2; (22 Dec 79 - 12 Jan 80) 4/3; (15 Jan 80) 2/4; (26 Jan 80) 3/3; (5 Feb 80) 3/4.

_____. Six sonatas for keyboard, Opera 2, to be sold.

    RISM J749: *Six sonatas pour le clavecin avec l'accompagnement d'un violon . . . Op. 2d.* London: Longman, Lukey & Co.

    (22 Nov 77) 1/3-4.

_____. Six sonatinas for keyboard, Opera 5, to be sold.

    RISM J759: *Six sonatinas for the harpsichord, with an accompaniement for a violin . . . Opera V.* London: Longman, Lukey & Co.

    (22 Nov 77) 1/3-4.

_____. Sonatinos [sic] for the violin, to be sold.

    RISM J759: See entry above.

    (14 Oct 73) 1/4; (11 Nov 73) Supplement, 1/1.

KAMMEL, Anton, 1730-1787. (KAMMELL; Antonio; Antonin)

_____. Works by, to be sold.

    (4 Oct 77) 4/2; (25 Oct 77) 4/4; (28 Aug 79) 2/2; (1 Sep 79) 2/4.

_____. Six duets for two violins, to be sold.

    RISM K83: *Six duets for two violins . . . Opera II.* London: Welcker.

    RISM K104: *Six duetts for two violins . . . Opera 5th.* London: Welcker.

    RISM K138: *Six duettos for two violins . . . Opera XI.* London: John Welcker.

    (22 Nov 77) 1/3-4.

_____. Nottornos, Opera 6, to be sold.

    RISM K110: *Six notturnos for two violins and a bass . . . Opera VI.* London: Longman & Broderip.

    (20-23 Oct 79) 3/3; (3-10 Nov 79) 4/2; (17-20 Nov 79) 4/2; (24 Nov 79) 3/2; (27 Nov - 1 Dec 79) 4/2; (22 Dec 79 - 12 Jan 80) 4/3; (15 Jan 80) 2/4; (26 Jan 80) 3/3; (5 Feb 80) 3/4.

_____. Quartetto for violino, to be performed.
RISM K98: *Six quartettos for two violins, a tenor and violoncello obligato . . . Opera IV.* London: Longman & Broderip.
(27 Apr 82) 3/3.
For fuller reference, *SEE* Concert (27 Apr 82).

_____. Six quartettos for two violins and violoncello obligato, Opera 4, to be sold.
RISM K98: See entry above.
(22 Nov 77) 1/3-4.

_____. Second set of quartettos, Opera 7, to be sold.
RISM K117: *A second sett of six quartettos for two violins, a tenor and violoncello obligato . . . Opera VII.* London: John Welcker.
(22 Nov 77) 1/3-4.

_____. Sonatas for two German flutes or violins, Op. 7, to be sold.
RISM K117: See entry above.
RISM K121: *Trois quatuors à flûte, violon, taille & violoncelle . . . Oeuv: XIV.* Berlin: Johann Julius Hummel, No. 497.

KELLY, Lord, 1732-1781. [Thomas Alexander Erskine, Sixth Earl of Kelly]

_____. Overtures for keyboard, to be sold.
BUC I, p.319: *The overture . . . adapted for the harpsichord or piano forte by Sigr. Corri & Sutherland.* Edinburgh, ca.1785. Op. 1, No. 1-3.
(14 Oct 73) 1/4; (11 Nov 73) Supplement, 1/1.

KELWAY, Joseph, ca.1702-1782.

_____. Works by, to be sold.
(28 Aug 79) 2/2; (1 Sep 79) 2/4.

Kennedy, Mrs. *SEE* HOOK, James. How sweet the love that meets return.

KERNTL, C. F.

_____. Duetts for German flute, to be sold.
RISM K464: *Six duets for two German flutes.* London: Longman, Lukey & Co.
(14 Oct 73) 1/4; (11 Nov 73) Supplement, 1/1.

_____. Duetts for German flute, to be sold.
RISM K464: *Six duets for two German flutes.* London: Longman, Lukey & Co.
(20-23 Oct 79) 3/3; (3-10 Nov 79) 4/2; (17-20 Nov 79) 4/2; (24 Nov 79) 3/2; (27 Nov - 1 Dec 79) 4/2; (22 Dec 79 - 12 Jan 80) 4/3; (15 Jan 80) 2/4; (26 Jan 80) 3/3; (5 Feb 80) 3/4.

_____. Six sonatas for violin and German flute, to be sold.
RISM K461: *Six sonatas for two German flutes, or two violins and a bass.* London: Longman & Broderip.
(22 Nov 77) 1/3-4.

_____. Six sonatas for two German flutes or violins, to be sold.
RISM K461: See entry above.
(20-23 Oct 79) 3/3; (3-10 Nov 79) 4/2; (17-20 Nov 79) 4/2; (24 Nov 79) 3/2; (27 Nov - 1 Dec 79) 4/2; (22 Dec 79 - 12 Jan 80) 4/3; (15 Jan 80) 2/4; (26 Jan 80) 3/3; (5 Feb 80) 3/4.

Keyboard. *SEE* Harpsichord; Organ; Piano; Spinnet.

Keyboard Music. *SEE* ALCOCK, John, Doctor in Music; BACH, Carl Philipp Emanuel; BACH, Johann Christian; BOCCHERINI, Luigi; BORGHESE, Antonio D.R.; EICHNER, Ernst; ESHER; FISHER, Johann Abraham; FOOTE; GARTH, John; GIORDANI, Tommaso; GRAF, Christian Ernst; HÄNDEL, Georg Friedrich; HAWDON, Matthias; JACKSON; JUST, Johann August; KELLY, Lord; PARRY, John; PASQUALI, Nicolò; Periodical overtures; SCHUMANN, Friedrich Theodor; SCHWINDL, Friedrich; TAYLOR, Raynor.

The king and the miller of Mansfield. *SEE* ARNE, Thomas Augustine.

King Arthur. *SEE* ARNE, Thomas Augustine.

"King Hancock sat in regal state." To the tune of The watry god. Song lyric printed.
(1 Aug 81) 2/1.

Kirkman harpsichord, with three stops and a swell, to be sold.
(8 Dec 81) 3/4.

Kitty fell. *SEE* "Some muse assist me to relate."

KLÖFFLER, Johann Friedrich, 1725-1790. (KLOFFLER)

_____. Concertos, to be sold.
RISM K929: *A concerto for the harpsichord or piano forte with accompaniments for two violins, two horns, two German flutes or oboes, a tenor & violoncello.* London: William Napier.
(20-23 Oct 79) 3/3; (3-10 Nov 79) 4/2; (17-20 Nov 79) 4/2; (24 Nov 79) 3/2; (27 Nov - 1 Dec 79) 4/2; (22 Dec 79 - 12 Jan 80) 4/3; (15 Jan 80) 2/4; (26 Jan 80) 3/3; (5 Feb 80) 3/4.

_____. Duetts for two German flutes, to be sold.
RISM K934: *Six duets for two German flutes.* London: Longman, Lukey & Co.
(20-23 Oct 79) 3/3; (3-10 Nov 79) 4/2; (17-20 Nov 79) 4/2; (24 Nov 79) 3/2; (27 Nov - 1 Dec 79) 4/2; (22 Dec 79 - 12 Jan 80) 4/3; (15 Jan 80) 2/4; (26 Jan 80) 3/3; (5 Feb 80) 3/4.

KREUSSER, Georg Anton, 1746-1810.

_____. Concertos, to be sold.
(20-23 Oct 79) 3/3; (3-10 Nov 79) 4/2; (17-20 Nov 79) 4/2; (24 Nov 79) 3/2; (27 Nov - 1 Dec 79) 4/2; (22 Dec 79 - 12 Jan 80) 4/3; (15 Jan 80) 2/4; (26 Jan 80) 3/3; (5 Feb 80) 3/4.

The ladies' frolick. SEE ARNE, Thomas Augustine. *The lady's* [sic] *frolick.*

The ladle. English opera, harpsichord/vocal edition, to be sold.
(22 Nov 77) 1/3-4.

Lads and lasses. SEE BATES, William. *Flora, or, Hob in the well.*

A LADY.

_____. Twelve lessons for the guitar, to be sold.
(14 Oct 73) 1/4; (11 Nov 73) Supplement, 1/1.

The lady of the manor. SEE HOOK, James.

The lady's frolick. SEE ARNE, Thomas Augustine.

The lark's shrill notes.

_____. To be performed.
BUC II, p.595: *The lark's shrill notes. Sung by Mrs. Vincent, etc.* London: ca.1770.
(27 Apr 82) 3/3.
For fuller reference, *SEE* Concert (27 Apr 82).
_____. To be sung in the theatre.
BUC II, p.595: See entry above.
(24 Aug 83) 3/2.

Leadbetter, James. Teacher of the organ, harpsichord, and spinnet.
(6 May 73) 2/2; (13 May 73) 4/1; (20 May 73) Supplement, 2.

"Let songs of triumph every voice employ." Song lyric printed.
(24 Nov 79) 2/2-3.

Lethe, or Aesop in the shades, a farce. Mercury, (with songs) played by Miss Wall, to be performed in the theatre.
BUC II p.615: *The card invites. Sung by Mrs. Clive in Lethe.* London: ca.1760.
Ye mortals whom fancies and troubles perplex. A song in Lethe. Sung by Mr. Beard in the character of Mercury. London: 1749. IN: *Gentleman's magazine*, Vol. XIX, p.232.
(6 Aug 83) 3/1.

LEVERIDGE, Richard, ca.1670-1758.

_____. *The recruiting officer.* "In the third act, and in the character of Serjeant Kite, will be introduced the favourite songs of O what a charming thing's a battle. To which will be added *Love a-la-mode*."
(6 May 80) 2/4.

_____. *The recruiting officer.* "The fife and drum, a favourite song to be sung during the epilogue."
(6 Mar 82) 3/3; (9 Mar 82) 3/3.

Lewis and Horner (publishers). *SEE* The Free masons pocket book.

LIDARTI, Christiano Giuseppe, 1730-1793.

_____. Six sonatas for violin and German flute, to be sold.
RISM L2358: *Six sonatas for two German flutes or violins with a thorough bass for the harpsichord.* London: Welcker, ca.1770.
(22 Nov 77) 1/3-4.

_____. Sonatas for two German flutes or violins, to be sold.
RISM L2358: See entry above.
(20-23 Oct 79) 3/3; (3-10 Nov 79) 4/2; (17-20 Nov 79) 4/2; (24 Nov 79) 3/2; (27 Nov - 1 Dec 79) 4/2; (22 Dec 79 - 12 Jan 80) 4/3; (15 Jan 80) 2/4; (26 Jan 80) 3/3; (5 Feb 80) 3/4.

LIDEL, Andreas, d.before 1789. (LIDL; LINDEL)

_____. Trios, Op. 1, to be sold.
RISM L2367: *Six trios for a violin or flauto, violin secondo, and violoncello obligato . . . Opera Imo.* London: Longman, Lukey & Broderip.
(20-23 Oct 79) 3/3; (3-10 Nov 79) 4/2; (17-20 Nov 79) 4/2; (24 Nov 79) 3/2; (27 Nov - 1 Dec 79) 4/2; (22 Dec 79 - 12 Jan 80) 4/3; (15 Jan 80) 2/4; (26 Jan 80) 3/3; (5 Feb 80) 3/4.

"Life of the hero, as well as of the sage." "Ame du héros et du sâge." Song lyric printed.
(24 Dec 83) 2/4, 3/1-2.

Lilies of France. *SEE* "Come, each death-doing dog who dare venture his neck."

LINDEL. *SEE* LIDEL, Andreas.

LINLEY, Thomas, the Elder, 1733-1795.

_____. *The camp.* English opera, keyboard/vocal edition, to be sold.
RISM L2447: *The camp, an entertainment . . . N.B.: The favorite song in The school for scandals is printed at the end of his book by permission of the author.* London: S. & A. Thompson, 1778.
(28 Aug 79) 2/2; (1 Sep 79) 2/4.

_____. Nancy of the dale, a song performed in the theatre between the second and third acts.
    RISM L2449: *(The camp.) Nancy of the dale. Sung by Mr. Web-ster, etc.* London: S. A. & P. Thompson, ca.1780.
    (26 Jan 82) 3/3.

_____. *The duenna.* English opera, to be sold.
    RISM L2460: *The duenna or double elopement, a comic-opera . . . for the voice, harpsichord, or violin.* London: C. and S. Thompson, 1775.
    (4 Oct 77) 4/2; (25 Oct 77) 4/4.

_____. *The duenna.* English opera, keyboard/vocal edition, to be sold.
    RISM L2460: See entry above.
    (22 Nov 77) 1/3-4; (28 Aug 79) 2/2; (1 Sep 79) 2/4.

_____. *The duenna,* a new comic opera, just published by James Humphreys, jun. and Valentine Nutter, to be sold.
    RISM L2460: See entry above.
    (13 Feb 79) 3/4; (10 Mar 79) 3/3; (24 Mar 79) 3/3; (31 Mar 79) 4/3; (21 Apr 79) 3/2.

Lionel and Clarissa. SEE DIBDIN, Charles.

"Listen to that swelling noise!" *SEE* A medley for the light infantry.

LOMBARDINI. *SEE* SIRMEN, Maddalena Laura.

The London songster, a songbook, to be sold.
    (7 Jun 83) 3/3; (11 Jun 83) 1/1; (14 Jun 83) 1/1.

Loosley, Brooklyn Hall. Declares financial failure.
    (9 Apr 83) 3/3.

Loosley's Tavern.

_____. Band of martial music to attend celebration of Prince of Wales's birthday.
    (9 Aug 80) 3/3; (12 Aug 80) 2/2.

_____. Site of subscription assembly.
    (1 Feb 83) 3/4; (19 Feb 83) 3/3; (26 Feb 83) 3/4; (12 Mar 83) 3/3.

"Loud howls the storm! the vex'd Atlantic roars!" Song lyric printed.
    (11 Jul 81) 2/1-4.

Louvre [i.e. Loure]. *SEE* Dancing. Taught by William Charles Hulett *and by* W. Birchall Tetley.

Love a-la-mode.

_____. Betweeen the play and the farce will be performed a solo concerto on the hautbois.
    (29 May 80) 3/3; (1 Apr 80) 3/3.

_____. To be performed.
>(6 May 80) 2/4; (20 Feb 82) 2/4; (23 Feb 82) 3/3.

Love in a village. *SEE* ARNE, Thomas Augustine.

Lovely nymph with variations. *SEE* Scotch songs.

Lumps of pudding. *SEE* A medley for the light infantry.

The lying valet. Singing by Miss Wall.
>(21 Jun 83) 3/3.

LYON, James, 1735-1794.

_____. Urania, a new edition of. "The best collection of psalm tunes, hymns, and anthems extant, on thick paper, is just published. Price 12s." To be sold by Noel and Hazard.
>DLC, M2116.L99: *Urania, or a choice collection of psalm-tunes, anthems, and hymns, from the most approved authors, with some entirely new: in two, three and four parts, the whole peculiarly adapted to the use of churches, and private families: to which are prefix'd the plainest, & most necessary rules of psalmody.* Philadelphia, 1761.
>(16 Dec 73) 3/4.

MacGIBBON, William, ca.1690-1756.

_____. Music by, to be sold.
>(4 Oct 77) 4/2; (25 Oct 77) 4/4.
_____. Scots tunes, to be sold.
>RISM M27: *A collection of Scots tunes for the violin or German-flute and a bass for the violoncello or harpsichord . . . With some additions by R. Bremner. Book I (-IV).* London: R. Bremner, 1762.
>(21 Apr 74) 3/4; (5 May 74) 3/2.
_____. Scots tunes for voice, to be sold.
>RISM M27: See entry above.
>(22 Nov 77) 1/3-4.

Mackenzie, John. (M'Kenzie) *SEE* Concert (9 Sep 80); White Conduit House.

MAGHERINI.

_____. Trios for German flute, to be sold.
>RISM M129: *Six trios for violins or German flutes and a bass, composed in a familiar stile.* London: Longman, Lukey & Co.
>(14 Oct 73) 1/4; (11 Nov 73) Supplement, 1/1.

MAHON, John, ca.1749-1834. (MAHAN; MAHOY)

_____. Works by, to be sold.
>(28 Aug 79) 2/2; (1 Sep 79) 2/4

_____. Clarenetto solo concerto, to be performed.
>   RISM M166: *Mahon's 2nd concerto for the clarinett, hoboy, German flute or violin: in all its parts.* London: J. Bland, ca.1795.
>   (27 Apr 82) 3/3.
>   For fuller reference, *SEE* Concert (27 Apr 82).

_____. Concertos, to be sold.
>   (20-23 Oct 79) 3/3; (3-10 Nov 79) 4/2; (17-20 Nov 79) 4/2; (24 Nov 79) 3/2; (27 Nov - 1 Dec 79) 4/2; (22 Dec 79 - 12 Jan 80) 4/3; (15 Jan 80) 2/4; (26 Jan 80) 3/3; (5 Feb 80) 3/4.

Maid of the mill. SEE ARNOLD, Samuel.

Maid of the oaks. SEE BARTHÉLÉMON, François Hippolyte.

MALDERE, Pierre van, 1729-1768.

_____. Concertos, Op. 4th, to be sold.
>   RISM M215: *Six favourite overtures in 8 parts for 2 violins, 2 oboes, 2 horns, viola, and a figured bass for the harpsichord . . . Opera 4th.* London: I. Iohnston, ca.1770.
>   (20-23 Oct 79) 3/3; (3-10 Nov 79) 4/2; (17-20 Nov 79) 4/2; (24 Nov 79) 3/2; (27 Nov - 1 Dec 79) 4/2; (22 Dec 79 - 12 Jan 80) 4/3; (15 Jan 80) 2/4; (26 Jan 80) 3/3; (5 Feb 80) 3/4.

_____. Overture for violin, to be sold.
>   RISM M215: See entry above.
>   (14 Oct 73) 1/4; (11 Nov 73) Supplement, 1/1.

MANCINELLI, Domenico, d.1802. (MANCHINELLI)

_____. Works by, to be sold.
>   (28 Aug 79) 2/2; (1 Sep 79) 2/4.

_____. Eight duets for two violins and German flutes, Opera 2, to be sold.
>   RISM M277?: *Eight duets for two German flutes, or violins, or a German flute & violin . . . Opera lst.* London: Longman, Lukey & Co.
>   RISM M278: *Dodici duetti per due flauti o fagotti . . . Opera IIa.* Paris: Mme. Berault.
>   (22 Nov 77) 1/3-4.

_____. Duetts for violins and German flutes, Opera 2d and 3d, to be sold.
>   RISM M277?: See entry above.
>   RISM M280?: *Six sonatas for two German flutes, or violins . . . Opera III.* London: Longman, Lukey & Broderip.
>   (20-23 Oct 79) 3/3; (3-10 Nov 79) 4/2; (17-20 Nov 79) 4/2; (24 Nov 79) 3/2; (27 Nov - 1 Dec 79) 4/2; (22 Dec 79 - 12 Jan 80) 4/3; (15 Jan 80) 2/4; (26 Jan 80) 3/3; (5 Feb 80) 3/4.

_____. Six sonatas for violin and German flute, Opera 3, to be sold.
>   RISM M280: See entry above.
>   (22 Nov 77) 1/3-4.

_____. Sonatas for two German flutes or violins Op. 3, to be sold.
>   RISM M280: See entry above.

(20-23 Oct 79) 3/3; (3-10 Nov 79) 4/2; (17-20 Nov 79) 4/2; (24 Nov 79) 3/2; (27 Nov - 1 Dec 79) 4/2; (22 Dec 79 - 12 Jan 80) 4/3; (15 Jan 80) 2/4; (26 Jan 80) 3/3; (5 Feb 80) 3/4.

Marches, new to be sold.
(28 Aug 79) 2/2; (1 Sep 79) 2/4.

Marches, for young adepts on the German flute, fiddle, guittar, hautboy, etc., to be sold.
(20-23 Oct 79) 3/3; (3-10 Nov 79) 4/2; (17-20 Nov 79) 4/2; (24 Nov 79) 3/2; (27 Nov - 1 Dec 79) 4/2; (22 Dec 79 - 12 Jan 80) 4/3; (15 Jan 80) 2/4; (26 Jan 80) 3/3; (5 Feb 80) 3/4.

MARDINO. *SEE* NARDINO.

"Mark yon wretch submissive bending." *SEE* A medley for the light infantry.

MARTINI. *SEE* SAMMARTINI, Giovanni Battista *and* Giuseppe.

A Mason's anthem. *SEE* Wools, Mr.

The mayor of Garrat. SEE Country dance. Conclusion to. . . .

Mazzanti, Signiora [sic]. Notice of public performance to be held, first April 24, then April 28, 1774. Signiora Mazzanti to sing Italian and English songs.
(14 Apr 74) 3/3; (21 Apr 74) 3/2; (25 Apr 74) 2/2.
For fuller reference, *SEE* Concert (14 Apr 74).

A medley for the light infantry. Song lyric printed. "Behold with what ardor to action they press" To the tune of Away to the copse. "Listen to that swelling noise!" To the tune of By the gayly circling glass. "Mark yon wretch submissive bending" To the tune of Hosier's ghost. "Soldier whilst the flowing bowl" To the tune of Over the hills and far away. "We've shewn them full oft' of what stuff we are made" To the tune of Lumps of pudding.
LBM, G311.(152): *A favourite medley for the light infantry. By a soldier, written at New-York.* London: W. Napier, ca.1780.
(23 Jan 79) 3/3.
SEE ALSO "For battle prepar'd in their country's just cause."
MENEZE.

_____. Collection of Italian, French and English songs and duetts, for guitar, to be sold.
(20-23 Oct 79) 3/3; (3-10 Nov 79) 4/2; (17-20 Nov 79) 4/2; (24 Nov 79) 3/2; (27 Nov - 1 Dec 79) 4/2; (22 Dec 79 - 12 Jan 80) 4/3; (15 Jan 80) 2/4; (26 Jan 80) 3/3; (5 Feb 80) 3/4.
_____. Divertiments, for guitar, Op. 1, to be sold.
(20-23 Oct 79) 3/3; (3-10 Nov 79) 4/2; (17-20 Nov 79) 4/2; (24 Nov 79) 3/2; (27 Nov - 1 Dec 79) 4/2; (22 Dec 79 - 12 Jan 80) 4/3; (15 Jan 80) 2/4; (26 Jan 80) 3/3; (5 Feb 80) 3/4.

Messiah, grand chorus. *SEE* Concerto spirituale.

Midas. English opera, keyboard/vocal edition, to be sold.
>BUC II, p.674: *A comic opera . . . For the harpsichord, voice, German flute, violin, or guitar.* London: I. Walsh, 1764.
>(14 Oct 73) 1/4; (11 Nov 73) Supplement, 1/1.

MILGROVE. (MILLGROVE)

_____. 40 lessons, for one or two guittars, to be sold.
>(14 Oct 73) 1/4; (11 Nov 73) Supplement, 1/1.

MILLER, Edward, 1735-1807.

_____. Six solos for violin and German flute, to be sold.
>RISM M2786: *Six solos for a German flute, with a thorough bass for the harpsichord or violoncello.* London: J. Johnson, 1763.
>(22 Nov 77) 1/3-4.

_____. Solos for German flute, to be sold.
>RISM M2786: See entry above.
>(14 Oct 73) 1/4; (11 Nov 73) Supplement, 1/1.

MILLGROVE. *SEE* MILGROVE.

The minstell. *SEE* The minstrell.

[The minstrell]. An entire new song book, called The minstell [sic]. Being a new and valuable collection of the most admired English songs, duets, and cantatas, with the most favourite Scots songs, to be sold.
>BUC I, p.494: *The minstrell. A collection of songs selected from the reliques of ancient poetry . . . Book I. Op. XXXI.* London: J. Preston, 1784
>(12 Oct 82) 1/3; (16-19 Oct 82) 1/2; (23 Oct 82) 1/1; (16-23 Nov 82) 4/3; (7 Jun 83) 3/3; (11-14 Jun 83) 1/1.

Minuet, to be taught by W. Birchall Tetley.
>(3 Nov 74) 3/4; (10 Nov 74) 4/4.
>For fuller reference, *SEE* Tetley, W. Birchall.

Minuets and country dances, at birthday ball in London, described.
>(2 Sep 83) 2/1-2.

Minuets.

_____. Dutch, for German flute, to be sold.
>(14 Oct 73) 1/4; (11 Nov 73) Supplement, 1/1.

_____. For young adepts on the German flute, fiddle, guitar, hautboy, &c, to be sold.
>(20-23 Oct 79) 3/3; (3-10 Nov 79) 4/2; (17-20 Nov 79) 4/2; (24 Nov 79) 3/2; (27 Nov - 1 Dec 79) 4/2; (22 Dec 79 - 12 Jan 80) 4/3; (15 Jan 80) 2/4; (26 Jan 80) 3/3; (5 Feb 80) 3/4.

_____. New, to be sold.
    (21 Apr 74) 3/4; (5 May 74) 3/2; (28 Aug 79) 2/2; (1 Sep 79) 2/4.
_____. 24, Italian and Spanish for violin, to be sold.
    (14 Oct 73) 1/4; (11 Nov 73) Supplement, 1/1.

Minuets. *SEE ALSO* Dance books; Dancing. Taught by William Charles Hulett *and by* William Birchall Tetley; Dancing School.

Minuette Dauphine. *SEE* Dancing. Taught by William Charles Hulett.

MISLIWECKEK. *SEE* MYSLIVEČEK, Josef.

Miss in her teens. SEE ARNE, Thomas Augustine.

The mock doctor.

_____. *The mock doctor*, to be performed. In the character of Leander will be introduced two songs.
    BUC II, p.681: *The mock doctor: or the dumb lady cur'd. A comedy. Done from Molière . . . with the musick prefix'd to each song. A new edition with additional songs.* London: A. Millar, 1761.
    (5 Feb 81) 2/4.
_____. *The mock doctor*, a farce, with the character of Dorcas, with the songs in character, by a young lady.
    BUC II, p.681: See entry above.
    (23 Jan 82) 2/2; (30 Jan 82) 3/1; (2 Feb 82) 2/4; (20 Mar 82) 3/4;
    (23 Mar 82) 3/3.

A moral song. *SEE* ARNE, Thomas Augustine. "If fortune would smile."

Murphy, Mr. *SEE The citizen.*

The muses mirror, two volumes, to be sold.
    (28 Aug 79) 2/2; (1 Sep 79) 2/4.

Music, taught in J. and M. Tanner's boarding school for young ladies.
    (24 Feb 74) 3/3; (3 Mar 74) 4/2; (21 Mar 74) 3/3; (14 Apr 74) 4/4.

Music, taught by William Charles Hulett.
    (12 Jan 75) 3/4; (19 Jan 75) 4/2.

Music, to be sold.

_____. Music, a variety, both printed and in manuscript, to be sold by Benjamin Davies.
    (2 Sep 74) 3/4.
_____. Music, most kinds.
    (10 Jun 73) 3/2; (17 Jun 73) 4/2; (30 Sep 73) 3/4; (7 Oct 73) 4/3;
    (14 Oct 73) Supplement, 1/4; (14 Oct 73) 1/4; (11 Nov 73) Supplement, 1/1; (4 Oct 77) 4/2; (25 Oct 77) 4/4; (22 Nov 77) 1/3-4; (28 Aug 79) 2/2; (1 Sep 79) 2/4; (11 Sep 79) 2/3; (3 Nov 79)

Supplement, 2/1; (20-23 Oct 79) 3/3; (3-10 Nov 79) 4/2; (17-20 Nov 79) 4/2; (24 Nov 79) 3/2; (27 Nóv - 1 Dec 79) 4/2; (22 Dec 79 - 12 Jan 80) 4/3; (15 Jan 80) 2/4; (26 Jan 80) 3/3; (5 Feb 80) 3/4; (29 Apr 80) 3/4; (3 May 80) 3/3-4; (27 May 80) 3/3; (17 Jun 80) 4/2; (8 Jul 80) 3/4; (27 Oct 81) 3/4; (3-7 Nov 81) 4/4; (10-21 Nov 81) 4/2; (24 Nov 81) 4/4; (5 Dec 81 - 5 Jan 82) 4/4; (9 Jan 82) 3/3; (16 Jan 82) 1/2; (19 Jan 82) 4/4; (23 Jan - 23 Feb 82) 4/2; (23-27 Mar 82) 4/2; (13 Apr 82) 3/4; (24 Apr - 1 May 82) 1/3; (4-29 May 82) 1/1; (1 Jun 82) 1/3; (5 Jun 82) 1/2; (8 Jun 82) 1/1; (12-22 Jun 82) 4/1; (26 Jun - 13 Jul 82) 4/4; (17 Jul 82) 1/1; (20-31 Jul 82) 4/1; (3-17 Aug 82) 4/3; (21 Aug - 4 Sep 82) 4/1; (11 Sep 82) 3/4; (14-21 Sep 82) 1/2; (19 Oct 82) 2/4; (23 Oct 82) 1/1.

Music books, to be sold.

_____. Music books, to be sold by George Deblois, sen. & jun.
(18 Jul 78) 4/4; (22 Jul 78) 1/3.
_____. Music books, blank, ruled for all sorts of instruments of all sizes.
(30 Sep 73) 3/4; (7 Oct 73) 4/3; (14 Oct 73) Supplement, 1/3; (14 Oct 73) 1/4; (11 Nov 73) Supplement, 1/1; (21 Jul 75) 3/4; (28 Aug 79) 2/2; (1 Sep 79) 2/4; (23 Dec 80) 3/4; (27 Dec 80 - 3 Jan 81) 4/3; (6 Jan 81) 2/2; (8 Jan 83) 3/2.
_____. Music books, ruled, bound, of various sizes for different instruments.
(29 Sep 79) 2/3; (2-9 Oct 79) 3/4; (13 Oct 79) Supplement, 1/1; (3 Nov 79) Supplement, 2/1; (10-17 Nov 79) 4/4; (20-24 Nov 79) 1/4.
_____. Musick books, &c. "A printed catalogue of articles in the above, and other branches sold by James Rivington, may be had by applying at his house."
(4 Oct 80) 3/4; (7 Oct 80) 1/4; (11-18 Oct 80) 4/2; (1-8 Nov 80) 2/4; (18-25 Nov 80) 4/4; (16 Dec 80) 2/3.
_____. Two music books covered with brown leather, lost . . . two dollars reward offered.
(15 Jun 82) 2/4; (19 Jun 82) 3/3.

Music desks, to be sold.

_____. Music desks, to be sold by Benjamin Davies.
(2 Sep 74) 3/4.

Music paper, to be sold.

_____. Musick paper of all sorts ruled.
(4 Oct 77) 4/2; (25 Oct 77) 4/4.
_____. Music paper of various kinds.
(22 Nov 77) 1/3-4.
_____. Musick paper, ruled, bound in small or large volumes.
(11 Sep 79) 2/3; (3 Nov 79) Supplement, 2/1.
_____. Music paper, ruled.
(3 May 80) 3/3-4; (27 May 80) 3/3; (17 Jun 80) 4/2; (8 Jul 80) 3/4; (23 Dec 80) 3/4; (27 Dec 80 - 3 Jan 81) 4/3; (6 Jan 81) 2/2;

(27 Oct 81) 3/4; (3-7 Nov 81) 4/4; (10-21 Nov 81) 4/2; (24 Nov 81) 4/4; (5 Dec 81 - 5 Jan 82) 4/4; (9 Jan 82) 3/3; (16 Jan 82) 1/2; (19 Jan 82) 4/4; (23 Jan - 27 Mar 82) 4/2; (13 Apr 82) 3/4; (24 Apr - 1 May 82) 1/3; (4-29 May 82) 1/1; (1 Jun 82) 1/3; (12-22 Jun 82) 4/1; (26 Jun -13 Jul 82) 4/4; (17 Jul 82) 1/1; (20-31 Jul 82) 4/1; (3-17 Aug 82) 4/3; (21 Aug - 4 Sep 82) 4/1; (29 Dec 81 - 23 Feb 82) 1/1; (27 Feb 82) 4/3; (6-16 Mar 82) 1/2; (20 Mar 82) 4/2.

Music pens, to be sold.
(23 Dec 80) 3/4; (27 Dec 80 - 3 Jan 81) 4/3; (6 Jan 81) 2/2.

Music pens. *SEE ALSO* Pens.

Music performed for 4th of July celebration in Philadelphia.
(12 Jul 83) 3/1.

Music teachers. *SEE* Biferi, Nicholas; Bull, Amos; Cozani, Mrs.; Foy, Martin; Hulett, William Charles; Leadbetter, James; Pearson, William; Tanner, J. and M.; Thompson, Robert; Zedtwitz, Harman.

Musical clock with mahogany case, to be sold by Frederick Roberts.
(2 Sep 83) 3/2; (10 Sep 83) 4/1.

Musical clock, to be sold by Michael Roberts.
(18 Oct 83) 3/2; (22 Oct 83) 3/3; (25 Oct 83) 2/4; (29 Oct 83) 2/4.

Musical instruments, to be sold.
(14 Oct 73) 1/4; (11 Nov 73) Supplement, 1/1; (22 Nov 77) 1/3-4; (20-23 Oct 79) 3/3; (11 Sep 79) 2/3; (29 Sep 79) 2/3; (2-9 Oct 79) 3/4; (13 Oct 79) Supplement, 1/1; (3 Nov 79) 4/2; (3 Nov 79) Supplement, 2/1; (10 Nov 79) 4/2; (10-17 Nov 79) 4/4; (17-29 Nov 79) 4/2; (20-24 Nov 79) 1/4; (24 Nov 79) 3/2; (27 Nov - 1 Dec 79) 4/2;, (22 Dec 79 - 12 Jan 80) 4/3; (15 Jan 80) 2/4; (26 Jan 80) 3/3; (5 Feb 80) 3/4; (29 Apr 80) 3/4; (7 Oct 80) 2/4; (26 Sep 81) 4/1; (29 Sep 81) 4/2; (6-31 Oct 81) 4/2; (29 Dec 81) 1/1; (7 Jun 83) 3/3; (11-14 Jun 83) 1/1.

Musical instruments. *SEE ALSO* Bagpipe; Barrel organ; Bassoon; Bugle horn; Clarichord; Clarinet; Classado; Common flute; Cornet; Drum; English flute; Fiddle; Fiddle, tenor; Fife; Flute; French horn; German flute;, Glassado; Guitar; Harp; Harpsichord; Hautboy; Hunting horn; Organ; Pastorale; Piano; Pitch pipes; Spinnet; Sticcado; Sticcado pastorale; Tabor and pipes; Tenor fiddle; Trumpet; Viola; Violin; Violoncello; Voice flutes; Welsh harp.

The musical lady. Miss Hallam singing a song as the character Sephy.
BMC II, p.178: *Love's a sweet and soft musician. A favourite song sung by Miss Pope, in The musical lady.* London: 1773. IN: *London magazine,* Nov. 1773.
(29 Jul 73) 3/4.

Musicians wanted.

_____. Wanted to compleat the band on board the *General Pattison*, private ship of war. Two French horns, two clarinets, two hautboys, one bassoon.
>(14 Apr 79) 2/4; (21 Apr 79) 4/3.
>For fuller reference, *SEE General Pattison*.

_____. Wanted for a regiment. "Two good horns, a clarinet, a bassoon, and a person capable of directing a band, to all of whom good encouragement will be given."
>(18 Jul 78) 3/1; (22 Jul 78) 4/3; (25 Jul 78) 1/2; (29 Jul 78) 4/2; (1 Aug 78) 1/1; (5 Aug 78) 4/1; (8 Aug 78) 1/2; (12 Aug 78) 4/4; (15 Aug 78) 1/2; (19 Aug 78) 4/3; (22 Aug 78) 1/2; (26 Aug 78) 4/2; (29 Aug 78) 1/4; (2 Sep 78) 4/4; (5 Sep 78) 1/4; (9 Sep 78) 4/3; (12 Sep 78) 1/3.

Mutes, to be sold.
>(28 Aug 79) 2/2; (1 Sep 79) 2/4.

"My dear brother Ned, we are knock'd o' the head." Song lyric printed.
>(28 Dec 82) 2/3.

"My soldiers all." Song lyric printed.
>(23 Mar 82) 3/1-2.

MYSLIVEČEK, Josef, 1737-1781. (MISLIWECKEK)

_____. Trios for the German flute, to be sold.
>BUC II, p.722: *Six trios, three for a German flute, bassoon or violoncello and three for two German flutes or violins bassoons or violoncello by Mislewecek, Venturini and Leo.* London: J. Bland, ca.1795.
>(14 Oct 73) 1/4; (11 Nov 73) Supplement, 1/1.

NAIR. [James Nares?, 1715-1783]

_____. Works by, to be sold.
>(28 Aug 79) 2/2; (1 Sep 79) 2/4.

Nancy of the dale. *SEE* LINLEY, Thomas, the Elder.

NARDINI, Pietro, 1722-1793. (NARDENI)

_____. Duetts for violins and German flutes, to be sold.
>BUC II, p.724: *6 sonatas or duets for two violins . . . by Sig. Nardini and Ferar. Opera secunda.* London: I. Walsh, ca.1765.
>RISM N42: *Six sonatas for two German flutes or two violins and bass.* London: R. Bremner.
>(20-23 Oct 79) 3/3; (3-10 Nov 79) 4/2; (17-20 Nov 79) 4/2; (24 Nov 79) 3/2; (27 Nov - 1 Dec 79) 4/2; (22 Dec 79 - 12 Jan 80) 4/3; (15 Jan 80) 2/4; (26 Jan 80) 3/3; (5 Feb 80) 3/4.

NARDINO. (MARDINO)

_____. Sinfonie, to be performed.
(28 Apr 82) 3/3.
For fuller reference, *SEE* Concert (27 Apr 82).

NARES, James. *SEE* NAIR.

"Near his meridian pomp the sun." Song lyric printed.
(30 Aug 80) 3/1-2.

A new and excellent pocket book for the German flute and fiddle, to be sold.
(22 Nov 77) 1/3-4.

A new collection of songs, with the music and tune printed to each book, to
be sold.
(25 Sep 79) 3/3; (29 Sep 79) 2/4; (2 Oct 79) 2/4.

A new collection of songs, with the music and tune printed to each, to be sold
with other books of amusement.
(24 Nov 79) 3/4.

The new golden pippin. Airs in, for guitar, to be sold.
(14 Oct 73) 1/4; (11 Nov 73) Supplement, 1/1.

The new golden pippin. SEE ALSO The golden pippin.

New instructions for the German flute. *SEE* German flute. Tutors.

New instructions for the violin. *SEE* Violin. Tutors.

The new merry companion, a much esteemed song book, to be sold.
BUC II, p.729: *The new merry companion or complete modern
songster: being a select collection of . . . songs, lately sung at the
theatres . . . also a collection of the most esteem'd catches and glees.
Set to musick.* London: John Wheble, ca.1775.
BUC II, p.729: *The new merry companion: . . . the second edition
with considerable additions.* London: Wallis and Stonehouse, ca.1778.
(2 Jul 83) 4/1; (5 Jul 83) 4/1.

A new song on Doctor Lucas. *SEE* "What did my phlogy, my phlogy."

Noel and Hazard. *SEE* LYON, James.

NOFERI, Giovanni Battista, fl.1750-1781. (NOSERI)

_____. Works by, to be sold.
(28 Aug 79) 2/2; (1 Sep 79) 2/4.

_____. Six duetts for guitar, to be sold.
  (20-23 Oct 79) 3/3; (3-10 Nov 79) 4/2; (17-20 Nov 79) 4/2; (24 Nov 79) 3/2; (27 Nov - 1 Dec 79) 4/2; (22 Dec 79 - 12 Jan 80) 4/3; (15 Jan 80) 2/4; (26 Jan 80) 3/3; (5 Feb 80) 3/4.

_____. Six duets for violins, to be sold.
  RISM N741: *Six sonatas or duets for two violins . . . Opera IV.* London: Welcker.
  (22 Nov 77) 1/3-4.

_____. Six lessons for guitar, to be sold.
  RISM N757: *Six sonatas or lessons for the guitar . . . Opera 12.* London: Longman, Lukey & Co.
  (14 Oct 73) 1/4; (11 Nov 73) Supplement, 1/1.

_____. Six sonatas or lesson for guittar, to be sold.
  RISM N757: See entry above.
  (22 Nov 77) 1/3-4.

_____. Six lessons for guitar, Op. 12, to be sold.
  RISM N757: See entry above.
  (20-23 Oct 79) 3/3; (3-10 Nov 79) 4/2; (17-20 Nov 79) 4/2; (24 Nov 79) 3/2; (27 Nov - 1 Dec 79) 4/2; (22 Dec 79 - 12 Jan 80) 4/3; (15 Jan 80) 2/4; (26 Jan 80) 3/3; (5 Feb 80) 3/4.

_____. Sonatas for two German flutes or violins, Opera 10, to be sold.
  RISM N754: *Six sonatas for two violins with a thorough bass for the harpsichord . . . Opera 10th.* London: Welcker.
  (20-23 Oct 79) 3/3; (3-10 Nov 79) 4/2; (17-20 Nov 79) 4/2; (24 Nov 79) 3/2; (27 Nov - 1 Dec 79) 4/2; (22 Dec 79 - 12 Jan 80) 4/3; (15 Jan 80) 2/4; (26 Jan 80) 3/3; (5 Feb 80) 3/4.

NOSERI. *SEE* NOFERI, Giovanni Battista.

"Not all delights the bloody spear." Song lyric printed.
  (23 Sep 80) 2/1-2.

Nottingham ale. *SEE* "When faction, in league with the treacherous Gaul."

NOTTORNE.

_____. Sonatas for two violins and a bass, to be sold.
  (20-23 Oct 79) 3/3; (3-10 Nov 79) 4/2; (17-20 Nov 79) 4/2; (24 Nov 79) 3/2; (27 Nov - 1 Dec 79) 4/2; (22 Dec 79 - 12 Jan 80) 4/3; (15 Jan 80) 2/4; (26 Jan 80) 3/3; (5 Feb 80) 3/4.

Nottornos. *SEE* AGUS, Giuseppe; KAMMEL, Anton.

"Now Titan rais'd his flaming head." Song lyric printed.
  (26 Jun 79) 1/2-4.

NUSSEN, Frederick.

_____. Works by, to be sold.
  (28 Aug 79) 2/2, (1 Sep 79) 2/4.

_____. Sonatas for two German flutes or violins, to be sold.
RISM N815: *Six sonatas for two violins, violoncello or harpsicord
. . . Opera 2da.* London: John Walsh.
(20-23 Oct 79) 3/3; (3-10 Nov 79) 4/2; (17-20 Nov 79) 4/2; (24
Nov 79) 3/2; (27 Nov - 1 Dec 79) 4/2; (22 Dec 79 - 12 Jan 80)
4/3; (15 Jan 80) 2/4; (26 Jan 80) 3/3; (5 Feb 80) 3/4.

Nutter, Valentine. *SEE* Bassoon. Accessories; Drum heads; Fiddle. Accessories.
Strings; Flute. Music; German flute. Instruments; German flute.
Tutors; Guitar. Accessories. Strings; Harpsichord. Music; LINLEY,
Thomas, the Elder. *The duenna*; St. Cecilia's songs; Songbooks;
Violin. Accessories; Violin. Music; Watts's hymns.

"O mother dear Jerusalem." *SEE* "Come let us run at once they cry."

"O what a charming thing's a battle." *SEE* LEVERIDGE, Richard. *The
recruiting officer.*

"O wherefore, brother Jonathan." Set to music by Signora Carolina. Song lyric
printed.
(27 Sep 80) 3/1.

Oboe. *SEE* Hautboy.

Ode for the new-year, 1780. *SEE* "Old time flew panting by, in full career";
"When rival nations first descried."

O'Hara, K. (compiler). *SEE The golden pippin.*

"The old English cause knocks at every man's door." To the tune of The
cut-purse. Song lyric printed.
(29 Jan 80) 3/4.

"Old time flew panting by, in full career." Song lyric printed.
(1 Jan 80) 3/3.

"Old time flew panting by, in full career." Ode for the new year, 1780. Song
lyric printed.
(11 Mar 80) 3/2-3.

Old women ground young, a pantomimical interlude with dancing, to be performed in theatre.
(20 Sep 83) 2/4.

"On Calvert's plains new faction reigns." To the tune of The Abbot of
Canterbury, or Wilkes's wriggle. Song lyric printed.
(5 Jan 75) 2/2.

"On this day our countrymen, ages before ye." To the tune of the Roast beef
of old England. Song lyric printed.
(2 May 81) 2/3-4.

Opera airs. *SEE* A pocket book for the violin; A pocket book for the German flute.

Opera glasses, for sale.
> (25 Dec 79 - 15 Jan 80) 1/1; (29 Jan 80) 4/1.

Operas, English. Keyboard/vocal editions, to be sold.
> (14 Oct 73) 1/4; (11 Nov 73) Supplement, 1/1; (22 Nov 77) 1/3-4.

Operas, pantomimes & plays with incidental music. *SEE:*

> *The apprentice.*
> ARNE, Michael. *Cymon; The fathers or goodnatured man; Maid of the mill.*
> ARNE, Thomas Augustine. *Artaxerxes; The beggars's opera; Comus; Elfrida; The king and the miller of Mansfield; King Arthur; The ladies' frolick; Love in a village; Miss in her teens; Thomas and Sally; The way to keep him.*
> ARNOLD, Samuel. *The portrait.*
> BARTHÉLÉMON, François Hippolyte. *Maid of the oaks.*
> BATES, William. *Flora, or Hob in the well.*
> BATTISHILL, Jonathan. *High life below stairs.*
> *The buck, or the Englishman in Paris.*
> *The butterfly.*
> *The captive.*
> *The citizen.*
> *The devil to pay.*
> DIBDIN, Charles. *Damon and Phillida; The deserter; The institution of the garter; The jubilee; Lionel and Clarissa; The padlock; Pigmy revels; Poor Vulcan; The Quaker; The recruiting serjeant; The touchstone; The wedding ring.*
> *Edgar and Emmeline.*
> FISHER, John Abraham. *The sylphs, or Harlequin's gambols.*
> *The golden pippin.*
> *Harlequin collector, or, the miller deceiv'd.*
> *Hob in the wall.*
> HOOK, James. *The lady of the manor; She stoops to conquer; Too civil by half; Trick upon trick.*
> *The ladle.*
> *Lethe, or Aesop in the shades.*
> LEVERIDGE, Richard. *The recruiting officer.*
> LINLEY, Thomas, the Elder. *The camp; The duenna.*
> *Love a-la-mode.*
> *The lying valet.*
> *Midas.*
> *The mock doctor.*
> *Musical lady.*
> *New golden pippin.*
> OSWALD, James. *The reprisals, or the tars of old England.*
> PICCINNI, Niccolò. *La buona figliuola.*
> PURCELL, Daniel. *Beaux stratagem.*

Shakespeare's ode.
SHIELD, William. *The flitch of bacon.*
VERNON, Joseph. *The Irish widow; The witches.*

Orchestra. *SEE* Concerto spirituale.

Organ. Instruments, to be sold.

_____. Organ, chamber. Made and to be sold by Frederick Heyer. ". . .
may, in a short time, be compleatly finished and enlarged . . . so as to
suit a place of . . . worship."
(11 Nov 73) 1/3.
_____. Organ, chamber.
(12 Dec 78) 2/3; (23-26 Dec 78) 3/4; (30 Dec 78 - 9 Jan 79) 1/1;
(7 Dec 82) 3/1; (11 Dec 82) 3/3.
_____. Organ, a hand . . . with two barrels, playing sixteen tunes.
(9 Jun 79) 2/4; (12-19 Jun 79) 4/4; (23 Jun 79) 3/4; (10 Jul 79)
3/1.
_____. Organ, a hand.
(29 Sep 79) 4/1.
_____. Organ elegant well-toned for private sale by Loosley, Brooklyn-Hall.
(9 Apr 83) 3/3.

Organ. Instruments wanted.

_____. Organ, for a country church.
(1 Jul 73) 3/4; (8 Jul 73) 4/3.
_____. Organ, a good hand.
(1 May 79) 2/4.

Organ. Music, to be sold.

_____. Organ music.
(14 Oct 73) 1/4; (11 Nov 73) Supplement, 1/1; (22 Nov 77) 1/3-4.

Organ teachers. *SEE* Leadbetter, James.

Organs, hand or barrel, tuned and repaired. *SEE* Pearson, William.

OSWALD, James, 1711-1769.

_____. *The reprisals, or the tars of old England* with the songs in character,
to be performed.
BUC II, p.748: *From the man whom I love. A favourite song in
The reprisal. Sung by Miss Macklin, etc.* London, ca.1757.
BUC II, p.886: *Let ye nymphs still avoid. Sung by Miss Macklin in
Ye reprisal.* London, ca.1757.
BUC II, p.886: *The tars of old England. Sung by Mr. Beard, in
The reprisal, etc.* London, 1757.
(22 Nov 80) 2/3; (25 Nov 80) 3/4 (performance postponed); (29 Nov
80) 2/3.

"Our farce is now finish'd, your sport's at an end." To the tune of Derry
    down. Song lyric printed.
        (24 Oct 78) 3/1.

Over the hills and far away. *SEE* A medley for the light infantry.

Overture. *SEE* Concerto spirituale.

Overtures. *SEE* ABEL, Carl Friedrich; DEZÈDE, Nicolas Alexandre;
    GALEOTTI, Salvatore *or* Stefano ; GALUPPI, Baldassare;
    GIORDANI, Tommaso; JOMMELLI, Niccolò; JUST, Johann August;
    KELLY, Lord; MALDERE, Pierre van; PHILIDOR, François André
    Danican; SAMMARTINI, Giuseppe.

Oxfordshire Nancy bewitch'd. A ballad. *SEE* SHIELD, William.

The padlock. SEE DIBDIN, Charles.

Pantomime dance, called, *The Wapping landlady; or, Jack in distress*, to be
    performed in the theatre.
        (6 Aug 83) 3/1.

Pantomime entertainment. *SEE Harlequin collector*; HOOK, James. *Trick upon
    trick*; VERNON, Joseph. *The witches or, the birth, vagaries and death
    of Harlequin.*

Pantomimes. *SEE* Operas, pantomimes, etc.

Pantomimical interlude. *SEE Old women ground young.*

Paper ruled for musick. *SEE* Music paper.

PARRY, John, ca.1710-1782.

_____. Airs for harp, to be sold.
    RISM P946: *A collection of Welsh, English & Scotch airs with new
    variations, also four new lessons for the harp or harpsichord. . . . To
    which are added twelve airs for the guittar. . . .* London: Welcker, ca.
    1776.
        (14 Oct 73) 1/4; (11 Nov 73) Supplement, 1/1.
_____. Airs for keyboard, to be sold.
    RISM P946: See entry above.
    (14 Oct 73) 1/4; (11 Nov 73) Supplement, 1/1.

PASQUALI, Nicolò, ca.1718-1757.

_____. Art of fingering for keyboard, to be sold.
    RISM P993: *The art of fingering the harpsichord, illustrated with
    examples in notes. To which is added, an approved method of tuning
    that instrument.* Edinburgh: Robert Bremner.
        (14 Oct 73) 1/4; (11 Nov 73) Supplement, 1/1.

_____. Thorough bass for keyboard, to be sold.
  RISM P994: *Thorough-bass made easy; or, practical rules for finding
  & applying its various chords with little trouble; together with variety
  of examples in notes, shewing the manner of accompanying concertos,
  solos, songs, and recitatives.* London: Robert Bremner.
  (14 Oct 73) 1/4; (11 Nov 73) Supplement, 1/1.

Pastorales, to be sold.
  (23 Dec 80) 3/4; (27 Dec 80 - 3 Jan 81) 4/3; (6 Jan 81) 2/2.

PATONI, Giovanni Battista.

_____. Sonatas for German flute, to be sold.
  (14 Oct 73) 1/4; (11 Nov 73) Supplement, 1/1.

Pearson, William. Clock and watch maker.

_____. "Teaches vocal and instrumental music; strings, quills, and tunes
  harpsichords, spinnets, claricords and hand or barrel-organs. At the
  dial in Hanover-Square."
  (14 Apr 74) 1/1; (21 Apr 74) 4/4.
_____. "Clock and watch-maker from London; at the Dial in Hanover-Square,
  New-York, next door to Mr. Gerardus Beekman. He likewise teaches
  vocal and instrumental music."
  (29 Sep 74) 4/3; (15 Dec 74) 4/4.

PECK, James, fl.18th-early 19th centuries.

_____. Works by, to be sold.
  (28 Aug 79) 2/2; (1 Sep 79) 2/4.

Pens.

_____. Brass pens to rule musick staves, to be sold.
  (29 Sep 79) 2/3; (2-9 Oct 79) 3/4; (13 Oct 79) Supplement, 1/1; (3
  Nov 79) Supplement, 2/1; (10-17 Nov 79) 4/4; (20-24 Nov 79) 1/4.
_____. Five line pens, to be sold by Benjamin Davies.
  (2 Sep 74) 3/4
_____. Pens for ruling music, to be sold.
  (14 Oct 73) 1/4; (11 Nov 73) Supplement, 1/1; (4 Oct 77) 4/2; (25
  Oct 77) 4/4; (25 Aug 79) 2/2; (1 Sep 79) 2/4.

Pens. *SEE ALSO* Music pens.

PEPUSCH, John Christopher, 1667-1752. *SEE* ARNE, Thomas Augustine. *The
  beggar's opera.*

PERGOLESI, Giovanni Battista, 1710-1736.

_____. Works by, to be sold.
  (28 Aug 79) 2/2; (1 Sep 79) 2/4.

Periodical overtures for keyboard, to be sold.
>   (22 Nov 77) 1/3-4.

PESCH, Carl August.

_____.   Sonatas for two German flutes or violins, Opera 2d, to be sold.
>   RISM P1523: *Six sonatas à deux violons & basse . . . Oeuvre second.*
>   London: Welcker.
>   (20-23 Oct 79) 3/3; (3-10 Nov 79) 4/2; (17-20 Nov 79) 4/2; (24
>   Nov 79) 3/2; (27 Nov - 1 Dec 79) 4/2; (22 Dec 79 - 12 Jan 80) 4/3;
>   (15 Jan 80) 2/4; (26 Jan 80) 3/3; (5 Feb 80) 3/4.

PHILIDOR, François André Danican, 1726-1795.   (PHILIDER)

_____.   Overtures, to be sold.
>   (20-23 Oct 79) 3/3; (3-10 Nov 79) 4/2; (17-20 Nov 79) 4/2; (24
>   Nov 79) 3/2; (27 Nov - 1 Dec 79) 4/2; (22 Dec 79 - 12 Jan 80)
>   4/3; (15 Jan 80) 2/4; (26 Jan 80) 3/3; (5 Feb 80) 3/4.

Phillips, David.   *SEE* Clarichord.

Piano.   Instruments, to be sold.

_____.   Forte piano, price £32, and another, price £27.
>   (30 Sep 73) 3/4; (7 Oct 73) 4/3; (14 Oct 73) Supplement, 1/3.
_____.   Piano forte, of good tone, with a set of fresh strings.
>   (9 Dec 78) 2/4, (12 Dec 78) 4/1.
_____.   Forte piano, to be sold with other furniture at the home of William
Wade in the town of Jamaica, opposite Betts's Tavern.
>   (21 Aug 82) 3/2; (24-28 Aug 82) 4/1; (31 Aug 82) 1/1.
_____.   Forte pianos, of excellent tones, from £27 to £32.
>   (14 Oct 73) 1/4; (11 Nov 73) Supplement, 1/1.
_____.   Forte pianos.
>   (7 Apr 74) 3/1; (23-26 Dec 78) 3/4; (30 Dec 78 - 9 Jan 79) 1/1; (3
>   May 80) 3/3-4; (27 May 80) 3/3; (17 Jun 80) 4/2; (8 Jul 80) 3-4.

Piano.   Instruments wanted.

_____.   Piano forte, spinett, or harpsichord, wanted for hire.
>   (9 Nov 82) 2/4.

Piano.   Accessories, to be sold.

_____.   Strings.
>   (30 Sep 73) 3/4; (7 Oct 73) 4/3; (14 Oct 73) Supplement, 1/3; (29
>   Sep 79) 2/3; (2-9 Oct 79) 3/4; (13 Oct 79) Supplement, 1/1; (3 Nov
>   79) Supplement 2/1; (10-17 Nov 79) 4/4; (20-24 Nov 79) 1/4.
_____.   Sets of strings.
>   (28 Aug 79) 2/2; (1 Sep 79) 2/4.

_____. Wire.
>(14 Oct 73) 1/4; (11 Nov 73) Supplement, 1/1; (11 Sep 79) 2/3; (3 Nov 79) Supplement, 2/1; (23 Dec 80) 3/4; (27 Dec 80 - 3 Jan 81) 4/3; (6 Jan 81) 2/2.

_____. German wire.
>(14 Oct 73) 1/4; (11 Nov 73) Supplement, 1/1.

Piano. Music, to be sold.

_____. Piano forte music.
>(30 Sep 73) 3/4; (7 Oct 73) 4/3; (14 Oct 73) Supplement, 1/3; (14 Oct 73) 1/4; (11 Nov 73) Supplement, 1/1; (22 Nov 77) 1/3-4.

Piano Music. *SEE ALSO* ALCOCK, John, Doctor in Music; BACH, Carl Philipp Emanuel; BACH, Johann Christian; BOCCHERINI, Luigi; BORGHESE, Antonio; EICHNER, Ernst; FISCHER, Johann Christian; FOOTE; GARTH, John; GIORDANI, Tommaso; HAWDON, Matthias; HAYES, Philip; JOMMELLI, Niccolò; KELLY, Lord; KLÖFFLER, Johann Friedrich; SCHWINDL, Friedrich; SMETHERGELL, William; TAYLOR, Raynor.

Piano. Tutors, to be sold.

_____. Piano forte tutors.
>(30 Sep 73) 3/4; (7 Oct 73) 4/3; (14 Oct 73) Supplement, 1/3; (14 Oct 73) 1/4; (11 Nov 73) Supplement, 1/1; (8 Sep 79) 2/4; (2 Oct 79) 2/3; (9 Oct 79) 3/4.

PICCINNI, Niccolò, 1728-1800. (PICCINI)

_____. *La buona figliuola.* Opera, keyboard/vocal edition, to be sold.
>BUC II, p.782: *La buona figliuola. Opera comica, etc.* London: R. Bremner, 1767.
>(14 Oct 73) 1/4; (11 Nov 73) Supplement, 1/1.

"A pigeon who'd think it, alas! a fine trinket." Song lyric printed.
>(17 Feb 74) 2/3.

The pigmy revels. *SEE* DIBDIN, Charles.

Pipes and tabors. *SEE* Tabor and pipes.

Pitch-pipes, to be sold.
>(14 Oct 73) 1/4; (11 Nov 73) Supplement, 1/1.

PLA, José.

_____. Works by, to be sold.
>(28 Aug 79) 2/2; (1 Sep 79) 2/4.

_____. Concertos for two German flutes or hautboys, to be sold.
  RISM P2493: *A favourite concerto for two German flutes, or hautboys*. London: Longman & Broderip.
  (22 Nov 77) 1/3-4.

_____. 6 sonatas for violin and German flute, book 1, to be sold.
  RISM P2497: *Six sonatas for two German flutes or violins, composed in a pleasing agreeable style*. *Book I*. London: Richard Bride.
  (22 Nov 77) 1/3-4.

_____. Sonatas for two German flutes or violins, Op. 1, to be sold.
  RISM P2497: See entry above.
  (20-23 Oct 79) 3/3; (3-10 Nov 79) 4/2; (17-20 Nov 79) 4/2; (24 Nov 79) 3/2; (27 Nov - 1 Dec 79) 4/2; (22 Dec 79 - 12 Jan 80) 4/3; (15 Jan 80) 2/4; (26 Jan 80) 3/3; (5 Feb 80) 3/4.

_____. Six sonatas for violin and German flute, to be sold.
  RISM P2496: *Six sonatas for two German flutes or two violins and a bass*. London: Welcker.
  (22 Nov 77) 1/3-4.

_____. 6 sonatas for two German flutes or violins, to be sold.
  RISM P2496: See entry above.
  (20-23 Oct 79) 3/3; (3-10 Nov 79) 4/2; (17-20 Nov 79) 4/2; (24 Nov 79) 3/2; (27 Nov - 1 Dec 79) 4/2; (22 Dec 79 - 12 Jan 80) 4/3; (15 Jan 80) 2/4; (26 Jan 80) 3/3; (5 Feb 80) 3/4.

A pocket book for the German flute. *SEE* German flute. Tutors, to be sold.

A pocket book for the guitar. *SEE* Guitar. Tutors, to be sold.

A pocket book for the violin. *SEE* GEMINIANI, Francesco; Violin. Tutors, to be sold.

A pocket book with directions for teaching pupils the guitar. *SEE* Guitar. Tutors, to be sold.

The pocket companion for the guittar. *SEE* Guitar. Tutors, to be sold.

The pocket companion for the violin. *SEE* Violin. Tutors, to be sold.

Poor Vulcan. *SEE* DIBDIN, Charles.

Porter's . . . English and German flutes. *SEE* English, or common, flute. Instruments, to be sold; German flute. Instruments, to be sold.

The portrait. *SEE* ARNOLD, Samuel.

Potter's German flutes. *SEE* German flute. Instruments, to be sold.

Preston, maker of guitar. *SEE* Guitar. Instruments, to be sold.

"The prophet, as became a reverend seer." The sacrifice. Song lyric printed.
  (2 Jan 79) 3/2.

Psalm 133 anthem. *SEE* Church-music.

Psalmody, to be taught. *SEE* Bull, Amos;   Thompson, Robert.

Psalmody, taught to the children in the charity school.
    (25 Oct 83) 3/1.

PUGNANI, Giulio Gaetano Gerolamo, 1731-1798.   (PUGGANI)

____.   Works by, to be sold.
    (28 Aug 79) 2/2; (1 Sep 79) 2/4.
____.   Trios, Op. 8 [*i.e.* Op. 9], to be sold.
    RISM P5600: *Six trios for two violins and a violoncello . . . Opera
IX*. London: Welcker.
    (20-23 Oct 79) 3/3; (3-10 Nov 79) 4/2; (17-20 Nov 79) 4/2; (24
Nov 79) 3/2; (27 Nov - 1 Dec 79) 4/2; (22 Dec 79 - 12 Jan 80)
4/3; (15 Jan 80) 2/4; (26 Jan 80) 3/3; (5 Feb 80) 3/4.

PURCELL, Daniel, ca.1663-1717.

____.   *Beaux stratagem*, between the fourth and fifth act, will be a song.
    BUC II, p.855: *The trifle: a new song, etc. (Words from G.
Farquahr's "Beaux strategem")*. London, ca.1707.
    (26 Feb 80) 3/4.
____.   *Beaux strategem*, comedy, to be performed in the theatre.
    BUC II, p.855: See entry above.
    (6 Aug 83) 3/2.

The Quaker. *SEE* DIBDIN, Charles.

QUANTZ, Johann Joachim, 1697-1773.

____.   Works by, to be sold.
    (28 Aug 79) 2/2; (1 Sep 79) 2/4.

Quartets, to be sold.
    (29 Dec 81 - 23 Feb 82) 1/1; (27 Feb 82) 4/3; (6-16 Mar 82) 1/2;
(20 Mar 82) 4/2.

Quartets. *SEE ALSO* ABEL, Carl Friedrich;   BACH, Johann Christian;   BEM,
    Venceslav;   CIRRI, Giovanni Battista;   DAVAUX, Jean Baptiste;
    GIORDANI, Tommaso;   GRAF, Friedrich Hartmann;   HAYDN, Franz
    Joseph;   KAMMEL, Anton;   RICCI, Francesco Pasquale;   RICHTER,
    Franz Xaver;   TOESCHI, Carlo Giuseppi;   WANHALL, Jan Baptiste.

Quartettos, string, to be sold.
    (22 Nov 77) 1/3-4.

Quills.

_____. Crow, to be sold.
>   (30 Sep 73) 3/4; (7 Oct 73) 4/3; (14 Oct 73) Supplement, 1/3; (14 Oct 73) 1/4; (11 Nov 73) Supplement, 1/1; (22 Nov 77) 1/3-4.

_____. Crow, for harpsichords, to be sold.
>   (4 Oct 77) 4/2; (25 Oct 77) 4/4.

_____. Crow and raven, to be sold.
>   (28 Aug 79) 2/2; (1 Sep 79) 2/4; (29 Sep 79) 2/3; (2-9 Oct 79) 3/4; (13 Oct 79) Supplement, 1/1; (3 Nov 79) Supplement, 2/1; (10-17 Nov 79) 4/4; (20-24 Nov 79) 1/4; (23 Dec 80) 3/4; (27 Dec 80 - 3 Jan 81) 4/3; (6 Jan 81) 2/2.

Quintets, to be sold.
>   (29 Dec 81 - 23 Feb 82) 1/1; (27 Feb 82) 4/3; (6-16 Mar 82) 1/2; (20 Mar 82) 4/2.

Quintets. *SEE ALSO* BACH, Johann Christian;   COCCHI, Gioacchino;   GIARDINI, Felice;   GIORDANI, Tommaso.

RAMBACH, F. Xaver Max.

_____. Works by, to be sold.
>   (28 Aug 79) 2/2; (1 Sep 79) 2/4.

_____. Duetts for violins, Op. 6, to be sold.
>   RISM R118: *Six duets for two violins . . . Opera VI.*   London: Welcker, ca.1775.
>   (20-23 Oct 79) 3/3; (3-10 Nov 79) 4/2; (17-20 Nov 79) 4/2; (24 Nov 79) 3/2; (27 Nov - 1 Dec 79) 4/2; (22 Dec 79 - 12 Jan 80) 4/3; (15 Jan 80) 2/4; (26 Jan 80) 3/3; (5 Feb 80) 3/4.

Ramsay, Allan. *SEE* STUART, A.

Ranelagh Gardens. *SEE* White Conduit house.

The recruiting officer. *SEE* LEVERIDGE, Richard.

The recruiting serjeant. *SEE* DIBDIN, Charles.

REID, John, 1721-1807.

_____. Music by, to be sold.
>   (4 Oct 77) 4/2; (25 Oct 77) 4/4.

_____. Solos for German flute, to be sold.
>   RISM R997: *Six solos for a German flute, hautboy or violon, with a thorough bass for the harpsichord.*   London: J. Oswald, ca.1770.
>   (14 Oct 73) 1/4; (11 Nov 73) Supplement, 1/1.

REINARDS, William.

_____. 2 pocket duets for violins and German flutes, to be sold.
RISM R1069: *Six duets for two German flutes or violins.*
London: Welcker, 1768.
(20-23 Oct 79) 3/3; (3-10 Nov 79) 4/2; (17-20 Nov 79) 4/2; (24
Nov 79) 3/2; (27 Nov - 1 Dec 79) 4/2; (22 Dec 79 - 12 Jan 80)
4/3; (15 Jan 80) 2/4; (26 Jan 80) 3/3; (5 Feb 80) 3/4.

"Rejoice, Americans, rejoice!" Song lyric printed.
(5 Dec 78) 3/2.

The reprisals. SEE OSWALD, James.

Resin boxes, to be sold.
(30 Sep 73) 3/4; (7 Oct 73) 4/3; (14 Oct 73) Supplement, 1/3.

Resin boxes. *SEE ALSO* Rosin boxes.

RETZEL, August Johann.

_____. Works by, to be sold.
(28 Aug 79) 2/2; (1 Sep 79) 2/4.
_____. Concertos, to be sold.
(20-23 Oct 79) 3/3; (3-10 Nov 79) 4/2; (17-20 Nov 79) 4/2; (24
Nov 79) 3/2; (27 Nov - 1 Dec 79) 4/2; (22 Dec 79 - 12 Jan 80)
4/3; (15 Jan 80) 2/4; (26 Jan 80) 3/3; (5 Feb 80) 3/4.

RHODIT.

_____. Works by, to be sold.
(28 Aug 79) 2/2; (1 Sep 79) 2/4.

RICCI, Francesco Pasquale, 1732-1817.

_____. Concertos, to be sold.
(20-23 Oct 79) 3/3; (3-10 Nov 79) 4/2; (17-20 Nov 79) 4/2; (24
Nov 79) 3/2; (27 Nov - 1 Dec 79) 4/2; (22 Dec 79 - 12 Jan 80)
4/3; (15 Jan 80) 2/4; (26 Jan 80) 3/3; (5 Feb 80) 3/4.
_____. Quartettos, Op. 8, to be sold.
RISM R1266: *Sei quartetti à due violini, viola, & basso . . . Opera
VIII.* London: Welcker, ca.1770.
(20-23 Oct 79) 3/3; (3-10 Nov 79) 4/2; (17-20 Nov 79) 4/2; (24
Nov 79) 3/2; (27 Nov - 1 Dec 79) 4/2; (22 Dec 79 - 12 Jan 80)
4/3; (15 Jan 80) 2/4; (26 Jan 80) 3/3; (5 Feb 80) 3/4.
_____. Trios, Op. 16, to be sold.
(20-23 Oct 79) 3/3; (3-10 Nov 79) 4/2; (17-20 Nov 79) 4/2; (24
Nov 79) 3/2; (27 Nov - 1 Dec 79) 4/2; (22 Dec 79 - 12 Jan 80)
4/3; (15 Jan 80) 2/4; (26 Jan 80) 3/3; (5 Feb 80) 3/4.

RICHTER, Franz Xaver, 1709-1789. (RITCHER)

_____. Works by, to be sold.
    (28 Aug 79) 2/2; (1 Sep 79) 2/4.
_____. Concertos, Op. 3, to be sold.
    RISM R1344?: *Six concertos for the harpsichord, in five parts viz. violino primo, violino secondo, viola and violoncello obligato.* London: F. Pasquali, ca.1765.
    RISM R1345: *Six concerto's* [sic] *for the harpsichord with accompaniments, etc.* London: J. Longman and Co., ca.1770.
    (20-23 Oct 79) 3/3; (3-10 Nov 79) 4/2; (17-20 Nov 79) 4/2; (24 Nov 79) 3/2; (27 Nov - 1 Dec 79) 4/2; (22 Dec 79 - 12 Jan 80) 4/3; (15 Jan 80) 2/4; (26 Jan 80) 3/3; (5 Feb 80) 3/4.
_____. Quartettos, to be sold.
    RISM R1347: *Six quartetto's for two violins, tenor and violoncello.* London: J. Longman & Co., 1768.
    (20-23 Oct 79) 3/3; (3-10 Nov 79) 4/2; (17-20 Nov 79) 4/2; (24 Nov 79) 3/2; (27 Nov - 1 Dec 79) 4/2; (22 Dec 79 - 12 Jan 80) 4/3; (15 Jan 80) 2/4; (26 Jan 80) 3/3; (5 Feb 80) 3/4.

Rigadoon. *SEE* Concert. To be performed May 26, 1774; Dancing. Taught by William Charles Hulett.

RITCHER. *SEE* RICHTER, Franz Xaver.

Rivington, James, 1724-1802. *SEE* Concert (25 Nov 78); GEMINIANI, Francesco. A pocket book; German flute. Tutors; Guitar. Tutors, to be sold. A pocket book for the guitar; Music books, to be sold. Musick books, &c.; Songs naval and military; WILLIAMS, Aaron. Williams and Tansurs psalmody.

The roast beef of old England. *SEE* "On this day our countrymen, ages before ye."

Roberts, Frederick. *SEE* Musical clock.

Roberts, Michael. *SEE* Musical clock.

RODIL, Antonio.

_____. Sonatas for two German flutes or violins, to be sold.
    RISM R1819: *Sei duetti per due flauti traversi.* Paris: Bignon.
    (20-23 Oct 79) 3/3; (3-10 Nov 79) 4/2; (17-20 Nov 79) 4/2; (24 Nov 79) 3/2; (27 Nov - 1 Dec 79) 4/2; (22 Dec 79 - 12 Jan 80) 4/3; (15 Jan 80) 2/4; (26 Jan 80) 3/3; (5 Feb 80) 3/4.

Rosin boxes, to be sold.
    (14 Oct 73) 1/4; (11 Nov 73) Supplement, 1/1; (4 Oct 77) 4/2; (25 Oct 77) 4/4; (22 Nov 77) 1/3-4; (29 Sep 79) 2/3; (2-9 Oct 79) 3/4; (13 Oct 79) Supplement, 1/1; (3 Nov 79) Supplement, 2/1; (10-17 Nov 79) 4/4; (20-24 Nov 79) 1/4.

Rosin boxes. *SEE ALSO* Resin boxes.

Roubalet's tavern.

_____. Site of subscription concert series.
(16 Jan 82) 3/4; (19 Jan 82) 2/4; (23 Jan 82) 2/1; (11 May 82) 3/3.
_____. Site of subscription assembly.
(8 Jan 83) 3/2; (11 Jan 83) 3/1; (22 Jan 83) 3/3; (25 Jan 83) 3/4.
_____. Site of concert.
(30 Nov 82) 3/4; (25 Jan 83) 3/3; (29 Jan 83) 3/4; (1 Feb 83) 3/4.
_____. Site of two proposed concerts by Mr. Brown.
(2 Aug 83) 2/3; (13 Aug 83) 3/3.
For fuller reference, *SEE* Concert (2 Aug 83).

The roundelay, a songbook to be sold.
(7 Jun 83) 3/3; (11-14 Jun 83) 1/1.

"Rouse, Britons! at length." To the tune of Derry down. Song lyric printed.
(27 Nov 79) 2/2.

Roussell, Mr. Dancing in the theatre.
(16 Aug 83) 2/2.

Rule Britannia. *SEE* "As bending o'er the azure tide"; "When Britain, by
divine command"; "When rival nations first decried."

RUSH, George, fl.1760-1780.

_____. Works by, to be sold.
(28 Aug 79) 2/2; (1 Sep 79) 2/4.

SABBATINI, Luigi Antonio, 1732-1809.

_____. 2 pocket duets for violins and German flutes, to be sold.
(20-23 Oct 79) 3/3; (3-10 Nov 79) 4/2; (17-20 Nov 79) 4/2; (24
Nov 79) 3/2; (27 Nov - 1 Dec 79) 4/2; (22 Dec 79 - 12 Jan 80)
4/3; (15 Jan 80) 2/4; (26 Jan 80) 3/3; (5 Feb 80) 3/4.

The sacrifice. *SEE* "The prophet, as became a reverend seer"; "As tyrant
power and slavish fear"; "Thus, having buried the daemon of enmity."

St. Cecilia's songs, to be sold by Valentine Nutter.
(22 Mar 80) 3/4.

St. John the Baptist. *SEE* The Free-mason's pocket book.

SAMMARTINI, Giovanni Battista, 1700/01-1775. (SAN MARTINI; MARTINI)

_____. Sonatas for violin, to be sold.

RISM S685: *Sei sonate di cembalo e violino . . . dedicate a Sua Excellenza La Signora Marchesana di Rockingamme.* London, 1766. (14 Oct 73) 1/4; (11 Nov 73) Supplement, 1/1.

SAMMARTINI, Giuseppe, 1693-1751. (SAN MARTINI; MARTINI)

_____. Overtures, to be sold.
RISM S703: *Eight overtures (Op.7) in eight parts for violins, hoboys, French horns, &c. with a thorough bass for the harpsicord or violoncello. . . .* London: I. Walsh [1752].
RISM S711: *Eight overtures and six grand concertos in seven parts for four violins, a tenor, violoncello and a thorough bass for the harpsichord, etc. Opera decima.* London: John Johnson [1756].
(20-23 Oct 79) 3/3; (3-10 Nov 79) 4/2; (17-20 Nov 79) 4/2; (24 Nov 79) 3/2; (27 Nov - 1 Dec 79) 4/2; (22 Dec 79 - 12 Jan 80) 4/3; (15 Jan 80) 2/4; (26 Jan 80) 3/3; (5 Feb 80) 3/4.

SAN MARTINI. *SEE* SAMMARTINI, Giovanni Battista *and* Giuseppe.

Saw you my father, saw you my mother. *SEE* Scotch songs.

"Says Satan to Jemmy, I hold you a bet." Song lyric printed.
(2 Mar 82) 3/1.

Scammadine. *SEE* Bassoon. Instruments, to be sold.

School for teaching music, dancing. *SEE* Biferi, Nicholas.

School for teaching psalmody and every other part of vocal church music. *SEE* Thompson, Robert.

SCHUMANN, Friedrich Theodor, fl.1760-1780. (SCHUMAN)

_____. English, French and Italian songs for guitar, to be sold.
RISM S2428: *A second set of English, French and Italian songs adapted for the guitar, etc.* London: R. Bremner, ca.1770
(20-23 Oct 79) 3/3; (3-10 Nov 79) 4/2; (17-20 Nov 79) 4/2; (24 Nov 79) 3/2; (27 Nov - 1 Dec 79) 4/2; (22 Dec 79 - 12 Jan 80) 4/3; (15 Jan 80) 2/4; (26 Jan 80) 3/3; (5 Feb 80) 3/4.
_____. Three sonatas for keyboard, Opera 3, to be sold.
RISM S2407: *Three sonatas for the harpsichord with accompanyments for a violin or German flute, etc. Opera III.* London: Printed for the author, 1770.
(22 Nov 77) 1/3-4.
_____. 38 lessons, with six French and Italian songs for guitar, to be sold.
RISM S205: *Thirty eight lessons, with an addition of six French & Italian songs for the guittar . . . Opera Ist.* London: Michal Rauche & Co., 1763.
(20-23 Oct 79) 3/3; (3-10 Nov 79) 4/2; (17-20 Nov 79) 4/2; (24 Nov 79) 3/2; (27 Nov - 1 Dec 79) 4/2; (22 Dec 79 - 12 Jan 80) 4/3; (15 Jan 80) 2/4; (26 Jan 80) 3/3; (5 Feb 80) 3/4.

SCHWINDL, Friedrich, 1737-1786. (SWINDL)

_____. Works by, to be sold.
  (28 Aug 79) 2/2; (1 Sep 79) 2/4.
_____. Choice airs for violin, to be sold.
  RISM S2602: *Airs choises des opéras français*. . . . Den Haag:
Burchard Hummel.
  (14 Oct 73) 1/4; (11 Nov 73) Supplement, 1/1.
_____. Concertos Opera 1 and 9, to be sold.
  RISM S2548: *Six simphonies in eight parts. Opera prima*. London:
Longman, Lukey & Co., ca.1775.
  RISM S2552: *Trois simphonies . . . Op. 9*. Den Hague: Burchard
Hummel, ca.1775.
  (20-23 Oct 79) 3/3; (3-10 Nov 79) 4/2; (17-20 Nov 79) 4/2; (24
  Nov 79) 3/2; (27 Nov - 1 Dec 79) 4/2; (22 Dec 79 - 12 Jan 80)
  4/3; (15 Jan 80) 2/4; (26 Jan 80) 3/3; (5 Feb 80) 3/4.
_____. Six duets for violin and violoncello, to be sold.
  RISM S2596: *Sei duetti per violino e violoncello . . . Opera VI*.
London: Longman, Lukey et Co., ca.1775.
  (22 Nov 77) 1/3-4.
_____. Four sonatas for keyboard, to be sold.
  RISM S2579: *Four sonatas for the harpsichord or piano forte with
an accompanyment for a violin and violoncello, Opera VIII*. London:.
Longman, Lukey & Co., ca.1776.
  (22 Nov 77) 1/3-4.
_____. Six sonatas for violin and German flute, Opera 5, to be sold.
  RISM S2575: *Six sonatas for two violins and bass . . . Opa. 5th*.
London: J. Longman & Co., 1769.
  (22 Nov 77) 1/3-4.

Scotch songs.

_____. A collection of ancient and modern Scotch songs, book, to be sold.
  (25 Sep 79) 3/3; (29 Sep 79) 2/4; (2 Oct 79) 2/4.
_____. A collection of ancient and modern Scotch songs, to be sold.
  (24 Nov 79) 3/4.

Scots songs.

_____. A collection of Scots songs in two volumes, to be sold.
  BUC II, p.937: *A collection of Scots songs. Adapted for a voice &
harpsichord*. Edinburgh: Neil Stewart, 1782.
  BUC II, p.937: *Thirty Scots songs, adapted for a voice and
harpsichord. The words by Allen Ramsay. Book Ist. (Book 2d)*.
Edinburgh: N. Stewart, ca.1780.
  (11 Aug 79) 2/2; (21 Aug 79) 3/4; (25 Aug 79) 2/2.
_____. Down the burn Davy, love; Saw you my father, saw you my mother;
  Thro' the wood laddie; Lovely nymph with variations; The banks of the
  dee; There's nae luck about the house; Jockey to the fair; Gramachree
  Molly; with many others set for the violin, German flute and guitar, to
  be sold.

BMC I, p.726: *The banks of the Dee. A favorite song. (Words by J. Tait, to a tune called Langolee.)* London, ca.1780.

BMC II, p.677: *Down the burn Davy, love. A favorite Scotch song. (words by. R. Crawford, music by J. Hook) sung at Vauxhall.* London, ca.1770.

BMC I, p.84: *Gramachree Molly. A favourite Irish air.* London, 1774. IN: *The London magazine,* Sept. 1774.

BUC II, p.674: *Lovely nymph. A favourite song, as sung by Mr. Du Bellamy . . . in the character of Apollo in Midas at the Theatre-Royal, Covent Garden.* London: R. Falkener, 1772.

BUC II, p.923: *Saw you my father. A favorite Scotch song.* London: R. Falkner, ca.1772.

BUC I, p.29: *There's nae luck about the house. A favorite Scotch song.* London: R. B[remner], ca.1770.

BUC I, p.58: *Through the wood laddie. As early I walk'd on the first day of May.* London, ca.1760.

BUC II, p.738: *Thro' the wood laddie. Oh Sandy why leaves thou thy Nelly. [Song, words by A. Ramsey, music by M. Arne]* Sung by Miss Wright at Vauxhall. London, ca.1765.

(19 Feb 80) 1/4.

Scots songs. *SEE ALSO* The minstrell; Song book; STUART, A.

Scots tunes. *SEE* MacGIBBON, William.

"See France and Spain to battle dare." Song lyric printed.
(5 Jan 80) 2/3.

"See yon black cloud that big with tempest lows." Song lyric printed.
(22 May 82) 2/4.

The seige of Savannah. *SEE* "Come let us rejoice."

Shakespeare's ode. English opera, harpsichord/vocal edition, to be sold.
(22 Nov 77) 1/3-4.

SHARP, Francis.

_____. Works by, to be sold.
(28 Aug 79) 2/2; (1 Sep 79) 2/4.

She stoops to conquer. SEE HOOK, James.

SHIELD, William, 1748-1829.

_____. *The flitch of bacon.* English opera. Keyboard/vocal edition, to be sold.
RISM S2980: *The flitch of bacon. A comic opera . . . part . . . composed and part compiled by W. Shield, etc.* London: William Napier, 1778.
(28 Aug 79) 2/2; (1 Sep 79) 2/4.

_____. *The flitch of bacon*, the favourite song in, adapted for the guitar and voice, and for one, two or three German flutes, to be sold.

　BUC I, p.340: *How merrily we live. The favorite glee in The flitch of bacon . . . adapted for a guitar and voice and for one two or three Gn. flutes.* London: Longman and Broderip, ca.1780.

　(19 Feb 80) 1/4.

_____. Oxfordshire Nancy bewitch'd. A ballad. By the late Mr. Garrick. "Tho' I'm slim, and am young, and was lively and fair." Song lyrics printed.

　RISM S3285: *A collection of songs, sung at Vauxhall by Mrs. Weichsell, to which is added . . . Oxfordshire Nancy, written by the late David Garrick.* London: W. Napier, ca.1780.

　(5 Jan 80) 2/3.

"Sing to his shade a solemn strain." *SEE* Hopkinson, Francis.

Singing. Tutors or instructors for, to be sold.

　(14 Oct 73) 1/4; (11 Nov 73) Supplement, 1/1; (8 Sep 79) 2/4; (2 Oct 79) 2/3; (9 Oct 79) 3/4.

Singing after the Italian way. *SEE* Biferi, Nicholas.

SIRMEN, Maddalena Laura, 1735-1785. (LOMBARDINI; SYRMEN)

_____. Sonatas for 2 violins, to be sold.

　RISM S3547: *Six sonates à deux violons . . . Oeuvre quatriem [!].* Den Haag: Burchard Hummel.

　(20-23 Oct 79) 3/3; (3-10 Nov 79) 4/2; (17-20 Nov 79) 4/2; (24 Nov 79) 3/2; (27 Nov - 1 Dec 79) 4/2; (22 Dec 79 - 12 Jan 80) 4/3; (15 Jan 80) 2/4; (26 Jan 80) 3/3; (5 Feb 80) 3/4.

Skellorn, Richard. Brass founder, bell maker. Beaver-Street, near the King's Statue.

　(11 May 75) 2/4; (18 May 75) 4/1; (1 Jun 75) 4/3; (22 Jun 75) 4/4.

SMETHERGELL, William, fl.18th century. (SMITHERGILL)

_____. Works by, to be sold.

　(28 Aug 79) 2/2; (1 Sep 79) 2/4.

_____. Concertos, to be sold.

　RISM S3629: *Six concertos for the harpsichord or piano forte, with accompaniments for two violins & a violoncello.* London: Printed for the author, ca.1775.

　(20-23 Oct 79) 3/3; (3-10 Nov 79) 4/2; (17-20 Nov 79) 4/2; (24 Nov 79) 3/2; (27 Nov - 1 Dec 79) 4/2; (22 Dec 79 - 12 Jan 80) 4/3; (15 Jan 80) 2/4; (26 Jan 80) 3/3; (5 Feb 80) 3/4.

Smile Britannia. *SEE* All hail! Britannia hail!

SMITH.

_____. Works by, to be sold.
    (28 Aug 79) 2/2; (1 Sep 79) 2/4.

Smith, Albert. Instrument maker. "Has removed from Nassau-Street, No. 20, to Gold-Street, No. 45, where he carries on turning and musical instrument making; umbrello making; covering and repairing as usual . . . ."
    (14 May 83) 2/1.

SMITHERGILL. *SEE* SMETHERGELL, William.

SODERINI. (SODORINI)

_____. Works by, to be sold.
    (28 Aug 79) 2/2; (1 Sep 79) 2/4.
_____. Trios, to be sold.
    (20-23 Oct 79) 3/3; (3-10 Nov 79) 4/2; (17-20 Nov 79) 4/2; (24 Nov 79) 3/2; (27 Nov - 1 Dec 79) 4/2; (22 Dec 79 - 12 Jan 80) 4/3; (15 Jan 80) 2/4; (26 Jan 80) 3/3; (5 Feb 80) 3/4.

Sodi, Miss. To dance with Mr. Sodi and the young Mr. Hulett.
    (19 May 74) 3/3; (26 May 74) 2/4.
    For fuller reference, *SEE* Concert (19 May 74).

Sodi, Pietro.

_____. Dancing-master, "lately arrived from London . . . will teach the minuet, the louvre [i.e. loure], the Dauphin minuet, the German dance, called L'allemande, the cotillon of his composition, and other figured dances, in a short time: he has been dancing-master in all the courts in Europe, and last at London."
    (5 May 74) 3/2.
_____. To perform after a concert May 26, 1774. Concert for his benefit.
    (19 May 74) 3/3; (26 May 74) 2/4.
    For fuller referemce, *SEE* Concert (19 May 74).

SODORINI. *SEE* SODERINI.

The soldier tir'd of wars alarms. *SEE* ARNE, Thomas Augustine. *Artaxerxes*; Concert "of vocal and instrumental music . . ."; Hallam, Miss; Hyde, Mrs.

"Soldier whilst the flowing bowl." *SEE* A medley for the light infantry.

Solos, to be sold.
    (29 Dec 81 - 23 Feb 82) 1/1; (27 Feb 82) 4/3; (6-16 Mar 82) 1/2; (20 Mar 82) 4/2.

"Some muse assist me to relate," To the tune of Blubber Hall, alias Kitty fell.
  Song lyric printed.
     (21 Jul 74) 1/4.

Sonatas. *SEE* AGAZZI, Gaetano; ALEXANDER, B.; BACH, Carl Philipp
     Emanuel; BACH, Johann Christian; BISCHOFF, I.C.; BOCCHERINI,
     Luigi; BORGHESE, Antonio; CAMPIONI, Carlo Antonio;
     CAPPELLETTI, Anthonio; CIRRI, Giovanni Battista; DREZTY;
     EICHNER, Ernst; GARTH, John; GERARD, James; GERLIN;
     GIORDANI, Tommaso; GRASSI, Florio; GRONEMAN, Johann Albert;
     GUERINI, Francesco; HASSE, Johann Adolph; HUMBLE, Maximilian;
     JUST, Johann August; KAMMEL, Anton; KERNTL, C.F.; LIDARTI,
     Christiano Giuseppe; MANCINELLI, Domenico; NOFERI, Giovanni;
     NOTTORNE; NUSSEN, Frederick; PESCH, Carl August; PLA, José;
     RODIL, Antonio; SAMMARTINI, Giovanni Battista; SCHUMANN,
     Friedrich Theodor; SCHWINDL, Friedrich; SIRMEN, Maddalena
     Laura; STAMITZ, Karl Phillip *or* Johann Wenzel Anton; VENTO,
     Mattia; WENDLING, Johann Baptist.

A song book, "This day is published, a new and select collection of the best
     English, Scots, and Irish songs, catches, duets, and cantatas . . . 354
     songs bound in red, only one dollar." To be sold.
     (7 Jun 80) 2/4; (10 Jun 80) 2/4; (24 Jun 80) 4/4.

Song, by a young lady, to be performed in the theatre.
     (5 Jan 82) 3/3; (9-12 Jan 82) 3/2; (16 Jan 82) 3/4; (19-23 Jan 82)
     2/2.

Song lyrics printed in the newspaper. *SEE:*

     "All hail! Britannia hail."
     "And so, you've been courting the muses, my boy."
     "Arise! arise! your voices raise."
     "As bending o'er the azure tide."
     "As for his religion he could mix."
     "As his worm eaten volumes old time tumbled o'er."
     "As Spain's proud monarch sat in state."
     "As tyrant power and slavish fear."
     "Behold this badge the female test."
     "Behold with what ardor to action they press."
     "The cloud is burst, behold a clearer sky!"
     "Come cheer up, my lads, let us haste to the main."
     "Come, each death-doing dog who dare venture his neck."
     "Come let us rejoice."
     "Come let us run at once they cry."
     "Come, my boys, in jovial strain."
     "Could I the abundance of my sorrow show."
     "For battle prepar'd in their country's just cause."
     "The Frenchmen came upon the coast."
     "From heav'n behold a charming ray."
     "From Lewis, Monsieur Gerard came."

"Good neighbors, if you'll give me leave."
"Hark! Hark! the bugle's lofty sound."
"Here's a bumper brave boys to the health of our king."
"How oft we've seen in every form."
"Huzza! Huzza then cry'd a skinner."
"If fortune would smile, and I cannot complain."
"In Esop's days, when all things spoke."
"An independent and a page."
"It was on Mr. Peroy's land."
"Joy to great Congress, joy an hundred fold."
"King Hancock sat in regal state."
"Let songs of triumph every voice employ."
"Life of the hero, as well as of the sage."
"Listen to that swelling noise."
"Loud howls the storm! the vex'd Atlantic roars!"
"Mark yon wretch submissive bending."
"My dear brother Ned, we are knock'd o' the head."
"My soldiers all."
"Near his meridian pomp the sun."
"Not all delights the bloody spear."
"Now Titan rais'd his flaming head."
"O wherefore, brother Jonathan."
"The old English cause knocks at every man's door."
"Old time flew panting by, in full career."
"On Calvert's plains new faction reigns."
"On this day our countrymen, ages before ye."
"Our farce is now finish'd, your sport's at an end."
"A pigeon who'd think it, alas! a fine trinket."
"The prophet, as became a reverend seer."
"Rejoice, Americans, rejoice.!"
"Rouse, Britons! at length."
"Says Satan to Jemmy, I hold you a bet."
"See France and Spain to battle dare."
"See yon black cloud that big with tempest lows."
"Sing to his shade a solemn strain."
"Soldier whilst the flowing bowl."
"Some muse assist me to relate."
"Strain hard! strain hard! your voices raise."
"Sure never, my Lord, was a time more distressing."
"There's gin and there's bran-dy, and heigh doodle-dandy."
"There's Pop-li-cola, that lags of a tory."
"They tremble at an equal press."
"The third day of June in the year sixty-seven."
"Tho' the fate of battle on to-morrow wait."
"Thus, having buried the daemon of enmity."
"To drive the kine one summer's morn."
"The trembling muse her grateful lays."
"Troddle, troddle, 'tis got in my noodle."
"'Twas on the twenty fourth of May."
"Upon my word it's very hard."
"We've shewn them full oft' of what stuff we are made."

"What a hubbub is here, my dear father, of late."
"What did my phlogy, my phlogy."
"What though last year be past and gone."
"When ancient Rome, the empress of the world."
"When at first this land I prest."
"When Britain, by divine command."
"When Britain on her sea-girt shore."
"When faction, in league with the treacherous Gaul."
"When Hawke, the British Neptune reign'd."
"When rival nations first descried."
"When royal George rul'd o'er this land."
"Which of my sons, proclaim'd war's god."
"Whilst all with duteous zeal contend."
"Who dares--tho' ev'n of patriot name."
"With flames they threaten to destroy."
"The world can bear witness, that nothing cou'd ruffle."
"Would you know what a whig is, and always was."
"Ye Devonshire lads, and ye lasses."
"Your boy, my good master, is happy to find."

Songbooks, a few newest . . . of different sorts, to be sold by Valentine
     Nutter.
         (31 Mar 79) 2/4; (7 Apr 79) 3/4.

Songbooks, to be sold. *SEE ALSO* The American robin; A bullfinch; The
     convivial songster; The London songster; The minstrell; A new
     collection of songs; The new merry companion; The roundelay; Scotch
     songs; Song book; Songs naval and military; The songster's
     companion; STUART, A.; The syren; Vocal music.

Songs. To be sold.

_____. Great number of single songs adapted to the various humours and
     affections of the mind, to be sold.
         (4 Oct 77) 4/2; (25 Oct 77) 4/4.
_____. New, to be sold.
         (21 Apr 74) 3/4; (5 May 74) 3/2; (28 Aug 79) 2/2; (1 Sep 79) 2/4.
_____. Set to music, a vast variety of modern. . . . To be sold.
         (22 Nov 77) 1/3-4.

Songs "for the navy and army and for St. George's day, the anniversary of
     which is to be celebrated on Friday next. . . . In this collection are to
     be found the most celebrated and animating songs in our language
     . . . ." To be sold.
         (21 Apr 79) 3/4.

Songs "for the navy and army." *SEE ALSO* Songs naval and military.

Songs, to be performed in the theatre. *SEE* Hallam, Miss; Hyde, Mrs.;
     Storer, Miss; Wall, Miss; Wools, Mr.

Songs, to be performed or to be sold:

The banks of the Dee. *SEE* Scotch songs.
Bright author of my present flame. *SEE* Travers, John.
Bucks have at ye all. *SEE Jane Shore*, play in the theatre.
Catches. *SEE Tamerlane.*
Down the burn Davy, love. *SEE* Scotch songs.
Ellen a roon. *SEE* Ailen a roon.
English. *SEE* Mazzanti, Signoria; *The minstrell*; Song book.
The entered apprentices song. *SEE* The entered apprentices song.
The fife and drum. *SEE* LEVERIDGE, Richard. *The recruiting officer*.
God save the king. *SEE* Sport.
Gramachree Molly. *SEE* Scotch songs.
How merrily we live that shepherds be. *SEE* SHIELD, William. *The flitch of bacon.*
How sweet the love that meets return. *SEE* HOOK, James.
If 'tis joy to wound a lover. *SEE* If 'tis joy to wound a lover.
Irish. *SEE* Song book.
Italian. *SEE* Mazzanti, Signoria [sic].
Jockey to the fair. *SEE* Scotch songs.
Lads and lasses. *SEE* BATES, William. *Flora, or Hob in the well.*
The lark's shrill notes. *SEE* The lark's shrill notes.
Lovely nymph with variations. *SEE* Scotch songs.
A mason's anthem. *SEE* Wools, Mr.
Nancy of the dale. *SEE* LINLEY, Thomas, the Elder.
O what a charming thing's a battle. *SEE* LEVERIDGE, Richard. *The recruiting officer.*
Oxfordshire Nancy bewitch'd. *SEE* SHIELD, William.
Saw you my father, saw you my mother. *SEE* Scotch songs.
Scots. *SEE* The minstrell; Scotch songs; Song book.
The soldier tired of war's alarms. *SEE* ARNE, Thomas Augustine. *Artaxerxes*; Hallam, Miss.
Sweet echo. *SEE* Arne, Thomas Augustine. *Comus.*
Tally ho. *SEE* Carter, Charles Thomas.
Theatrical. *SEE The apprentice*; ARNE, Thomas Augustine. *The king and the miller of Mansfield* and *Miss in her teens; Chronontonthologos; The citizen; The devil to pay; Edgar and Emmeline;* PURCELL, Daniel. *Beuax strategem;* VERNON, Joseph. *The Irish widow; Zara.*
There's nae luck about the house. *SEE* Scotch songs.
Thro' the wood laddie. *SEE* Scotch songs.
To thee, O gentle sleep. *SEE Tamerlane.*
Vain is beauty's gawdy flowers. *SEE* Hallam, Miss.

Songs naval and military. Printed by James Rivington. To be sold.
  LOW, p.12-13: *Songs naval and military.* New York: James Rivington, 1779.
    (6 Mar 79) 3/4; (10 Mar 79) 4/1; (24 Mar - 7 Apr 79) 4/1; (10-14 Apr 79) 1/4.

Songs naval and military. *SEE ALSO* Songs "for the navy and army."

Songs. *SEE ALSO* Concerto spirituale; GEMINIANI, Francesco. A pocket
    book for the violin; Scots songs; Vocal music.

The songster's companion, a new collection of chançons, to be sold with other
    literary amusements.
        (13 Nov 79) 3/4; (17 Nov 79) Supplement, 1/2; (27 Nov 79)
        Supplement, 1/3; (1 Dec 79) Supplement, 1/3; (22 Dec 79) 3/3; (29
        Dec 79) 2/3, (5-12 Jan 80) 2/4.

Spinnet (Spinet). Instruments, to be sold.

_____. Spinets. Made and repaired by Frederick Heyer.
        (11 Nov 73) 1/3.
_____. Spinnet. To be sold by Benjamin Davies.
        (2 Sep 74) 3/4.
_____. Spinnet. To be sold by Mr. Biferi.
        (1 Dec 74) 3/4; (8 Dec 74) 4/1.
        For fuller reference, *SEE* Biferi, Nicholas.
_____. Spinnet, a good . . . . Between Beekman and Buling slips,
    Water-Street.
        (19 Apr 83) 2/2.
_____. Spinnet.
        (2 Jul 83) 3/4.
_____. Spinnet. To be sold at private sale.
        (16 Aug 83) 3/4.
_____. Spinnet. "In the best order, fit for a capital performer. It is in full
    compass five octaves from double G. to G. in Alt." To be sold
    privately.
        (4 Oct 83) 2/2.

Spinnet. Instruments wanted.

_____. Spinett, harpsichord or piano forte, wanted for hire.
        (9 Nov 82) 2/4.

Spinnet. Music, to be sold.

_____. Music.
        (14 Oct 73) 1/4; (11 Nov 73) Supplement, 1/1.

Spinnet. Accessories, to be sold.

_____. German wire.
        (14 Oct 73) 1/4; (11 Nov 73) Supplement, 1/1.
_____. Harpsichord and spinnet tuning hammers.
        (14 Oct 73) 1/4; (11 Nov 73) Supplement, 1/1.

Spinnet. Repair.

_____. Stringing, quilling and tuning by William Pearson, clock and watch-maker.
     (14 Apr 74) 1/1; (21 Apr 74) 4/4.

Spinnet teachers. *SEE* Leadbetter, James.

Sport, three days. "On Monday the 13th of November, will be run for on Asket Heath. . . . Purse of sixty pounds. . . . N.B. A band of musick will attend, and God save the king will be played every hour during the races."
     (11 Nov 80) 2/3.

STAMITZ, Karl Philipp? (1745-1801) *or* Johann Wenzel Anton? (1717-1757).

_____. Concertos for violin, to be sold.
     RISM S4558: *Deux concerto à violon principal, premier et second dessus, alto et basse, hautbois ou flûtes et deux cors ad libitum . . . Oeuvre XII.* Paris: Bailleux.
     RISM S4611: *Concerto de violon à plusieurs instruments . . . Oeuvre (9).* Paris: De La Chevardière, ca.1765.
     RISM S4612: *Concerto de violon à plusieurs instruments . . . Oeuvre (10e).* Paris: De La Chevardière.
     (14 Oct 73) 1/4; (11 Nov 73) Supplement, 1/1.
_____. Concertos, to be sold.
     RISM S4611: See entry above.
     RISM S4612: See entry above.
     RISM S4614: *A favorite concerto for the German flute with instrumental parts. . . .* London: Welcker, ca.1770.
     RISM S4606: *Six concertos for the harpsicord, organ, or piano-forte, with instrumental parts.* London: Longman, Lukey & Co., ca.1775.
     (20-23 Oct 79) 3/3; (3-10 Nov 79) 4/2; (17-20 Nov 79) 4/2; (24 Nov 79) 3/2; (27 Nov - 1 Dec 79) 4/2; (22 Dec 79 - 12 Jan 80) 4/3; (15 Jan 80) 2/4; (26 Jan 80) 3/3; (5 Feb 80) 3/4.
_____. Duetts for German flutes, to be sold.
     RISM S4540: *Six duetts for two German flutes . . . Op. 27.* London: John Preston.
     RISM S4623: *Six duetts for two German flutes.* London: Longman, Lukey & Co.
     (14 Oct 73) 1/4; (11 Nov 73) Supplement, 1/1; (20-23 Oct 79) 3/3; (3-10 Nov 79) 4/2; (17-20 Nov 79) 4/2; (24 Nov 79) 3/2; (27 Nov - 1 Dec 79) 4/2; (22 Dec 79 - 12 Jan 80) 4/3; (15 Jan 80) 2/4; (26 Jan 80) 3/3; (5 Feb 80) 3/4.
_____. Sinfonie, to be performed.
     RISM S4407: *Six sinfonies à grand orchestre, deux violons, alto et basso, deux hautbois et deux cors de chasse ad libitum . . . Oeuvre XIII.* London: Printed for Mr. Charles Stamitz at Mrs. Dall's, 1781.

RISM S4591: *VI sinfonies or overtures in eight parts for violins, French horns, &c., with a bass for the harpsicord or violoncello.* London: I. Walsh, etc., ca.1765.

> (27 Apr 82) 3/3.
> For fuller reference, *SEE* Concert (27 Apr 82).

_____. Sonatas for two German flutes or violins, to be sold.

> RISM S4619: *Six sonatas en trios pour un flûte, un violon et basse . . . Oeuvre posthume . . . l'on peut jouer les trois dernières sonates à deux violons ou deux flûtes et basse.* Paris: Taillart l'aîné (gravé par Mme. Oger.)
> (20-23 Oct 79) 3/3; (3-10 Nov 79) 4/2; (17-20 Nov 79) 4/2; (24 Nov 79) 3/2; (27 Nov - 1 Dec 79) 4/2; (22 Dec 79 - 12 Jan 80) 4/3; (15 Jan 80) 2/4; (26 Jan 80) 3/3; (5 Feb 80) 3/4.

Sticcado, to be sold.

> (28 Aug 79) 2/2; (1 Sep 79) 2/4; (29 Sep 79) 2/3; (2-9 Oct 79) 3/4; (13 Oct 79) Supplement, 1/1; (3 Nov 79) Supplement, 2/1; (10-17 Nov 79) 4/4; (20-24 Nov 79) 1/4; (23 Dec 80) 3/4; (27 Dec 80 - 3 Jan 81) 4/3; (6 Jan 81) 2/2.

Sticcado pastorale. "New instruction for playing on," to be sold.

> (8 Sep 79) 2/4; (2 Oct 79) 2/3; (9 Oct 79) 3/4.

Storer, Miss.

_____. Singing a song as the character Lucinda in *The buck, or the Englishman in Paris.*

> (29 Apr 73) 3/3.

_____. Singing a song in a concert.

> (6 May 73) 3/3.
> For fuller reference, *SEE* Concert (6 May 73).

Storer, Miss. *SEE ALSO* Ailen a roon.

"Strain hard! Strain hard! Your voices raise." *SEE* HOPKINSON, Francis.

Strings, instrumental, to be sold.

> (7 Apr 74) 3/1; (22 Nov 77) 1/3-4; (11 Sep 79) 2/3; (3 Nov 79) Supplement, 2/1; (20-23 Oct 79) 3/3; (3 Nov 79) 4/2; (3 Nov 79) Supplement, 2/1; (10 Nov 79) 4/2; (17-20 Nov 79) 4/2; (24 Nov 79) 3/2; (27 Nov - 1 Dec 79) 4/2; (22 Dec 79 - 12 Jan 80) 4/3; (15 Jan 80) 2/4; (26 Jan 80) 3/3; (5 Feb 80) 3/4.

Strings of all sorts, to be sold.

> (11 Sep 82) 3/4; (14-21 Sep 82) 1/2; (19 Oct 82) 2/4; (23 Oct 82) 1/1.

STUART, A.

_____. Allan Ramsay's collection of Scots songs, to be sold.
  BUC II, p.987: *Musick for Allan Ramsay's collection of Scots songs. Set by A. Stuart & engraved by R. Cooper.* Edinburgh: Allan Ramsay, 1724.
  (11 Aug 79) 2/2; (21 Aug 79) 2/4; (25 Aug 79) 2/2.
_____. Ramsay's Scots songs, A songbook, to be sold.
  BUC II, p.937: *Thirty Scots songs, adapted for a voice, and harpsichord. The words by Allen Ramsay. Book 1st. [Thirty Scots songs . . . Book 2d.] 2 bk.* Edinburgh: N. Stewart, ca.1780.
  (7 Jun 83) 3/3; (11 Jun 83) 1/1; (14 Jun 83) 1/1.

Subscription assemblies. *SEE* Assembly. Subscription assembly.

Subscription concerts. *SEE* Concert. Subscription concert.

"Sure never, my lord, was a time more distressing." Song lyric printed.
  (8 Jan 80) 2/2.

Sweet echo. *SEE* ARNE, Thomas Augustine. *Comus.*

SWINDL. *SEE* SCHWINDL, Friedrich.

The sylphs. SEE FISHER, Johann Abraham.

Symphonies. *SEE* BACH, Johann Christian; FISHER, Johann Abraham; GRAF, Christian Ernst; HAYDN, Franz Joseph; NARDINO; STAMITZ, Karl Philipp *or* Johann Wenzel Anton; TOESCHI, Carlo Giuseppi.

Symphony. *SEE* Concerto spirituale.

The syren. *SEE* ARNE, Thomas Augustine.

SYRMEN. *SEE* SIRMEN, Maddalena Laura.

Tabor (tabour) and pipes. To be sold.

_____. Tabor and pipes for country dances.
  (22 Nov 77) 1/3-4.
_____. Tabors (tabours) and pipes.
  (10 Jun 73) 3/2; (17 Jun 73) 4/2; (14 Oct 73) 1/4; (11 Nov 73) Supplement, 1/1; (21 Jul 75) 3/4; (22 Nov 77) 1/3-4; (3 May 80) 3/3-4; (27 May 80) 3/3; (17 Jun 80) 4/2; (8 Jul 80) 3/4; (23 Dec 80) 3/4; (27 Dec 80 - 3 Jan 81) 4/3; (6 Jan 81) 2/2.

TACET, Joseph.

_____. Music by, to be sold.
  (4 Oct 77) 4/2; (25 Oct 77) 4/4.

_____. Divertiments, to be sold.
     RISM T5: *Six divertimentis . . . for the German flute . . . with a thorough bass for the harpsichord . . . Opera 4ta.* London: Printed for the author, 1769.
     (21 Apr 74) 3/4; (5 May 74) 3/2.

_____. Duets & preludes for German flute, to be sold.
     RISM T6: *Six duette for two German flutes or violins. . . .* London: Welcker, ca.1770.
     RISM T10: *Thirty six preludes in different keys for the German flute, hoboy or violin, with minuets, variations, &c.* London: Longman, Lukey & Co., 1771.
     (14 Oct 73) 1/4; (11 Nov 73) Supplement, 1/1.

_____. 39 [sic] preludes for German flute, violin, or hautboy, to be sold.
     RISM T10: See entry above.
     (22 Nov 77) 1/3-4.

Tally ho. *SEE* CARTER, Charles Thomas.

Tamerlane, to be performed. "In act the fourth will be introduced the favourite song of 'To thee, o gentle sleep.' Between the play and entertainment, will be sung some favourite catches."
     BUC II, p.994: *To thee oh! gentle sleep. Sung by Mr. Lowe in Tamerlane.* London, ca.1750.
     (19 Feb 80) 3/3; (23 Feb 80) 2/3.

Tanner, J. and M. Advertise their boarding school for young ladies which instructs them in music, dancing and every other polite accomplishment.
     (24 Feb 74) 3/3; (3 Mar 74) 4/2; (21 Mar 74) 3/3; (14 Apr 74) 4/4.

TANS'UR, William, 1700-1783.

_____. Singing book, to be sold.
     (6 Jan 74) 3/2; (13 Jan 74) 4/1.

_____. Williams and Tansurs psalmody. "Which at present bear the bell amongst the accomplished and most melodious chanters of our Israel, are to be had of James Rivington." To be sold.
     BUC I, p.26: *The American harmony: or, royal melody complete in two volumes.* Newbury-port: Daniel Bayley, 1771.
     (21 Apr 74) 3/2.

TARTINI, Giuseppe, 1692-1770.

_____. Two solos for violin, to be sold.
     RISM T267: *Two solos for the violin.* London: Longman, Lukey & Co., ca.1775.
     (14 Oct 73) 1/4; (11 Nov 73) Supplement, 1/1.

_____. Two solos for violin and German flute, to be sold.
     RISM T267: See entry above.
     (22 Nov 77) 1/3-4.

Taste, a comedy. Songs between the acts. *SEE Chrononhotonthologos.*

TAYLOR, Raynor, 1747-1825.

_____. Lesson and rondeau for keyboard, to be sold.
RISM T362: *A favorite lesson and rondeau for the harpsichord or pianoforte, with accompaniments for a violin and violoncello.* London: Longman, Lukey & Broderip.
(22 Nov 77) 1/3-4.

Te Deum laudamus. *SEE* Church-music.

The temple of Cloacina. SEE HOPKINSON, Francis.

The temple of Minerva. SEE HOPKINSON, Francis.

Tenor fiddles. *SEE* Fiddle, tenor.

Tenor violins. *SEE* Violin, tenor.

Tetley, W. Birchall.

_____. Dancing instructor. "Late apprentice to Monsieur Gerarde of London, he teaches on the usual terms the minuet, cottillion, allemande, English country dances, single, double and treble hornpipes, &c &c as they are now danced in London and Paris, which last place he has lately visited . . . ."
(3 Nov 74) 3/4; (10 Nov 74) 4/4.
_____. Dancing master and portrait painter. ". . . served a regular apprenticeship under Mons. Gherarde of London: . . . was an assistant under Mons. Gardel, dancing master to the present king, when Dauphin of France . . . his school is now opened at the corner of Beaver-street, where grown persons are taught privately with the utmost expedition . . . ."
(12 Jan 75) 3/4; (19 Jan 75) 4/2.

THACKRAY, Thomas, fl.1770-1780. (THACKERAY)

_____. 40 airs, adapted for one or two guitars, to be sold.
RISM T641: *A collection of forty four airs . . . for one or two guittars.* London: John Johnston, 1772.
(22 Nov 77) 1/3-4.
_____. 44 airs and divertiments for guitar, to be sold.
RISM T641: See entry above.
RISM T639: *Twelve divertimenti for two guittars or a guittar & violin . . . Opera 3d.* London: Longman, Lukey & Co.
(14 Oct 73) 1/4; (11 Nov 73) Supplement, 1/1.
_____. Six lessons for guittar, to be sold.
RISM T636: *Six lessons for the guittar.* York: Thomas Haxby for the author, ca.1770.
RISM T638: *Six lessons for the guittar . . . Opera seconda.* London: Printed for the author, ca.1772.
(22 Nov 77) 1/3-4.

_____. Twelve divertisements for guitar, to be sold.
RISM T640: *12 divertissements pour deux guittars avec l'accompagnement d'un violon ou guittar 2me* . . . n.p.: n.p.
(20-23 Oct 79) 3/3; (3-10 Nov 79) 4/2; (17-20 Nov 79) 4/2; (24 Nov 79) 3/2; (27 Nov - 1 Dec 79) 4/2; (22 Dec 79 - 12 Jan 80) 4/3; (15 Jan 80) 2/4; (26 Jan 80) 3/3; (5 Feb 80) 3/4.

"There's gin and there's bran-dy, and heigh doodle-dandy." Song lyric printed.
(2 Dec 73) 3/1.

There's nae luck about the house. *SEE* Scotch songs.

"There's Pop-li-cola, that lags of a tory." Song lyric printed.
(25 Nov 73) 2/4.

"They tremble at an equal press." Song lyric printed.
(8 Dec 74) 3/3.

"The third day of June in the year sixty-seven." Song lyric printed.
(1 Sep 81) 3/2-3

"Tho' I'm slim, and am young". *SEE* SHIELD, William. Oxfordshire Nancy bewitch'd.

"Tho' the fate of battle on to-morrow wait." *SEE* ARNOLD, Samuel.

Thomas and Sally. *SEE* ARNE, Thomas Augustine.

Thompson, Robert, teacher of vocal music. Advertisement for singing school, Robert Thompson "having given ample proofs of his capacity in various parts of Nova-Scotia, New-England and the province of New-York . . . ."
(6 Oct 74) 2/4.

Thro' the wood laddie. *SEE* Scotch songs.

THUMOTH, Burk, fl.1739-1750.

_____. Six solos for violin and German flute, to be sold.
RISM T762: *Six solos for a German flute, violin or harpsichord* . . . *the three last by Sig. Canaby.* London: J. Tyther, 1746.
(22 Nov 77) 1/3-4.

"Thus, having buried the daemon of enmity." To the tune of If you can caper as well as you modulate. Song lyric printed.
(2 Jan 79) 3/2.

'Tis not yet day. *SEE* "What though last year be past and gone."

"To drive the kine one summer's morn." Song lyric printed.
(16 Aug 80) 3/1.

To thee, O gentle sleep. *SEE Tamerlane.*

The tobacco box. *SEE* ARNOLD, Samuel. "Tho' the fate of battle on tomorrow wait."

TOESCHI, Carlo Giuseppi, 1731-1788. (TOESCHES)

_____. Works by, to be sold.
 (28 Aug 79) 2/2; (1 Sep 79) 2/4.
_____. Quartetto for flauto, to be performed.
 RISM T892: *Sei quartetti per flauto, violino, alto e violoncello, intitolati, il Dialogo musicale . . . Oeuvre Ve.* Paris: Venier, ca.1770.
 (27 Apr 82) 3/3.
 For fuller reference, *SEE* Concert (27 Apr 82).
_____. Sinfonie, to be performed.
 (27 Apr 82) 3/3.
 For fuller reference, *SEE* Concert (27 Apr 82).

Too civil by half. SEE HOOK, James.

The touchstone. SEE DIBDIN, Charles.

TRAVERS, John, ca.1703-1758.

_____. "Bright author." Favourite song to be sung in the theatre by Mrs. Hyde.
 RISM T1124: *Bright author of my present flame. Sung by Mr. Lowe, etc.* London, ca.1750.
 (27 Sep 83) 3/4.

"The trembling muse her grateful lays." Song lyric printed.
 (6 Jun 78) 3/3.

Trick upon trick. SEE HOOK, James.

Trios, to be sold.
 (29 Dec 81 - 23 Feb 82) 1/1; (27 Feb 82) 4/3; (6-16 Mar 82) 1/2; (20 Mar 82) 4/2.

Trios. *SEE ALSO* BARBELLA, Emanuele; CAMPIONI, Carlo Antonio; CANALETTI, Giovanni Battista; CHIESA, Melchior; GIORDANI, Tommaso; HAYDN, Franz Joseph; HUMBLE, Maximilian; LIDEL, Andreas; MAGHERINI; MYSLIVECEK, Josef; PUGNANI, Giulio Gaetano Gerolamo; RICCI, Francesco Pasquale; SODERINI; WEISS, Carl; ZAPPA, Francesco.

"Troddle, troddle, 'tis got in my noodle." Song lyric printed.
 (23 Dec 73) 1/3.

Trumpet. Instruments, to be sold.

_____. Trumpets. For the field or concert, very elegant and finely chas'd.
(28 Aug 79) 2/2; (1 Sep 79) 2/4.

_____. Trumpet. Made in Europe.
(18 Dec 79) 4/1; (22 Dec 79) 4/1; (29 Dec 79) 2/3.

_____. Trumpets.
(23 Dec 80) 3/4; (27 Dec 80 - 3 Jan 81) 4/3; (6 Jan 81) 2/2; (26 Sep 81) 4/1; (28 Sep 81) 4/2; (6-31 Oct 81) 4/2; (11 Sep 82) 3/4; (14-21 Sep 82) 1/2; (19 Oct 82) 2/4; (23 Oct 82) 1/1.

Trumpet. Music, to be sold.

_____. Trumpet. Works for.
(28 Aug 79) 2/2; (1 Sep 79) 2/4.

Trumpeter, mentioned as messenger.
(21 Jul 75) 3/2.

Trumpeters. 13 trumpeters surrendered at Yorktown to General Washington by the British.
(26 Dec 81) 1/4.

Trumpets. Instruments surrendered by British at Yorktown.
(26 Dec 81) 2/2.

Trunks. A number of excellent travelling trunks for musical instruments, to be sold.
(28 Aug 79) 2/2; (1 Sep 79) 2/4.

Tunes for lyrics printed in the newspaper:

Abbot of Canterbury, or Wilkes's wriggle. *SEE* "On Calvert's plains new faction reigns."

Away to the copse. *SEE* A medley for the light infantry. "Behold with what ardor to action they press."

Black sloven. *SEE* "For battle prepar'd in their country's just cause."

Blubber Hall. *SEE* "Some muse assist me to relate."

By the gayly circling glass. *SEE* A medley for the light infantry. "Listen to that swelling noise!"

The cut-purse. *SEE* "The old English cause knocks at every man's door."

Derry down. *SEE* "Our farce is now finish'd"; "Rouse, Britons! at length."

Doodle-doo. *SEE* "The Frenchmen came upon the coast."

The free mason's song. *SEE* "Come let us rejoice."

Hark! hark! the joy-inspiring horn. *SEE* "Hark! hark! the bugle's lofty sound."

Hearts of oak. *SEE* "Come cheer up, my lads, let us haste to the main"; "Here's a bumper brave boys."

Hey! my kitten, my kitten. *SEE* "What did my phlogy, my phlogy."

Hosier's ghost. *SEE* A medley for the light infantry. "Mark yon wretch submissive bending."

How much superior beauty awes. *SEE* "As tyrant power and slavish fear."

If you can caper as well as you can modulate. *SEE* "Thus, having buried the daemon of enmity."

Kitty fell. *SEE* "Some muse assist me to relate."

Lilies of France. *SEE* "Come, each death-doing dog who dare venture his neck."

Lumps of pudding. *SEE* A medley for the light infantry. "We've shewn them full oft' of what stuff we are made."

Nottingham Ale. *SEE* "When faction, in league with the treacherous Gaul."

O mother dear Jerusalem. *SEE* "Come let us run at once they cry."

Over the hills and far away. *SEE* A medley for the light infantry. "Soldier whilst the flowing bowl."

The roast beef of old England. *SEE* "On this day our countrymen, ages before ye."

Rule Britannia. *SEE* chorus to "As bending o'er the azure tide"; "When Britain, by divine command"; "When rival nations first descried."

Smile Britannia. *SEE* "All hail! Britannia hail!"

'Tis not yet day. *SEE* "What though last year be past and gone."

The tobacco box. *SEE* ARNOLD, Samuel. "Tho' the fate of battle on to-morrow wait."

Vicar of Bray. *SEE* "When royal George rul'd o'er this land."

The watry god. *SEE* "As bending o'er the azure tide"; "King Hancock sat in regal state."

Would you have a young virgin of fifteen years. *SEE* "Would you know what a whig is, and always was."

Yankee doodle. *SEE* "From Lewis, Monsieur Gerard came"; "It was on Mr. Peroy's land."

Tuning forks, to be sold.
> (30 Sep 73) 3/4; (7 Oct 73) 4/3; (14 Oct 73) Supplement, 1/3; (14 Oct 73) 1/4; (11 Nov 73) Supplement, 1/1.

Tuning hammers for harpsichord and spinnet, to be sold.
> (14 Oct 73) 1/4; (11 Nov 73) Supplement, 1/1.

Tutors, new. To be sold.
> (28 Aug 79) 2/2; (1 Sep 79) 2/4.

Tutors. *SEE ALSO* Bagpipe; Bassoon; Clarinet; English, or common, flute; Fiddle; Fife; Flute; French horn; German flute; Guitar; Harpsichord; Hautboy; Piano; Sticcado pastorale; Violin; Violoncello.

"'Twas on the twenty fourth of May." Song lyric printed.
> (26 Jun 79) 1/2-4.

Twelve new songs and a cantata for the guitar, to be sold.
> (14 Oct 73) 1/4; (11 Nov 73) Supplement, 1/1.

Twenty-four country dances for the violin, to be sold.
(14 Oct 73) 1/4; (11 Nov 73) Supplement, 1/1.

Twenty-four Italian and Spanish minuets for violin, to be sold.
(14 Oct 73) 1/4; (11 Nov 73) Supplement, 1/1.

"Upon my word it's very hard." Song lyric printed.
(22 Dec 74) 2/2.

Urania. *SEE* LYON, James.

"Vain is beauty's gawdy flowers." *SEE* Hallam, Miss.

VALENTINE. *SEE* BALENTINE.

VANHALL. *SEE* WANHAL, Jan Baptiste.

VAN MALDERE. *SEE* MALDERE, Pierre van.

VENTO, Mattia, 1735-1776.

_____. Works by, to be sold.
(28 Aug 79) 2/2; (1 Sep 79) 2/4.
_____. Sonatas for two German flutes or violins, to be sold.
RISM V1153: *Six sonatas for two violins and a bass.* London: Peter Welcker, ca.1765.
(20-23 Oct 79) 3/3; (3-10 Nov 79) 4/2; (17-20 Nov 79) 4/2; (24 Nov 79) 3/2; (27 Nov - 1 Dec 79) 4/2; (22 Dec 79 - 12 Jan 80) 4/3; (15 Jan 80) 2/4; (26 Jan 80) 3/3; (5 Feb 80) 3/4.

VERNON, Joseph, ca.1739-1782.

_____. *The Irish widow*, a farce, with the songs in character, to be performed.
BUC II p.1039: *A widow bewitch'd with her passion. Epilogue to The Irish widow. Sung by Mrs. Barry. (The Irish fair, a favorite comic dance, etc.)* London: J. Johnston, 1772.
(13 Feb 82) 3/2; (16 Feb 82) 2/4.
_____. *The witches or, the birth, vagaries, and death of Harlequin*, to be performed in the theatre.
BUC II, p.1039: *The new songs in the pantomime of the witches, the celebrated epilogue in the comedy of Twelfth night, a song in the Two gentlemen of Verona and two favorite ballads sung by Mr. Vernon at Vaux Hall . . . . To which are added the new comic tunes, in The witches and a favourite French air sung in . . . Twelfth night, by Mrs. Abington. All properly adapted for the harpsichord, violin, German flute or guittar.* London: John Johnston, 1772.
(12 Jul 83) 3/2.

Vicar of Bray. *SEE* "When royal George rul'd o'er this land."

Viola. *SEE* Fiddle, tenor; Violin, tenor.

Violin. Instruments, to be sold.

_____. Violin. To be sold by Christie and Duncan.
    (24 Oct 78) 3/4.
_____. Violins. From 3£ 4s. to 14£.
    (14 Oct 73) 1/4; (11 Nov 73) Supplement, 1/1.
_____. Violins. Of low prices.
    (14 Oct 73) 1/4; (11 Nov 73) Supplement, 1/1.
_____. Violins. To be sold by George Deblois, sen. and jun.
    (18 Jul 78) 4/4; (22 Jul 78) 1/3.
_____. Violins. From three guineas to twelve.
    (3 May 80) 3/3-4; (27 May 80) 3/3; (17 Jun 80) 4/2; (8 Jul 80)
    3/4.
_____. Violins. Of the most exquisite tones of considerable prices, if not
    approved, to be exchanged for such as may please the purchaser.
    (23 Dec 80) 3/4; (27 Dec 80 - 3 Jan 81) 4/3; (6 Jan 81) 2/2.
_____. Violins, four, to be sold, property of a gentleman going to Europe.
    (11 Dec 82) 2/4.
_____. Violins.
    (4 Oct 77) 4/2; (25 Oct 77) 4/4; (28 Aug 79) 2/2; (1 Sep 79) 2/4;
    (26 Sep 81) 4/1; (29 Sep 81) 4/2; (6-31 Oct 81) 4/2; (27 Oct 81)
    3/4; (3-7 Nov 81) 4/4; (10-21 Nov 81) 4/2; (24 Nov 81) 4/4; (5
    Dec 81 - 5 Jan 82) 4/4; (9 Jan 82) 3/3; (16 Jan 82) 1/2; (19 Jan
    82) 4/4; (23 Jan - 27 Mar 82) 4/2; (13 Apr 82) 3/4; (24 Apr - 1
    May 82) 1/3; (4-29 May 82) 1/1; (1 Jun 82) 1/3; (5 Jun 82) 1/2; (8
    Jun 82) 1/1; (12-22 Jun 82) 4/1; (26 Jun - 13 Jul 82) 4/4; (17 Jul
    82) 1/1; (20-31 Jul 82) 4/1; (3-17 Aug 82) 4/3; (21 Aug - 4 Sep
    82) 4/1.

Violin. Accessories, to be sold.

_____. Bows.
    (27 Oct 81) 3/4; (3-7 Nov 81) 4/4; (10-21 Nov 81) 4/2; (24 Nov
    81) 4/4; (5 Dec 81 - 5 Jan 82) 4/4; (9 Jan 82) 3/3; (16 Jan 82)
    1/2; (19 Jan 82) 4/4; (23 Jan - 27 Mar 82) 4/2; (13 Apr 82) 3/4;
    (24 Apr - 1 May 82) 1/3; (4-29 May 82) 1/1; (1 Jun 82) 1/3; (5
    Jun 82) 1/2; (8 Jun 82) 1/1; (12-22 Jun 82) 4/1; (26 Jun - 13 Jul
    82) 4/4; (17 Jul 82) 1/1; (20-31 Jul 82) 4/1; (3-17 Aug 82) 4/3; (21
    Aug - 4 Sep 82) 4/1.
_____. Bows and bridges, to be sold by Valentine Nutter.
    (23 Dec 80) 2/4; (30 Dec 80) 3/3.
_____. Bows, Giardini sort.
    (14 Oct 73) 1/4; (11 Nov 73) Supplement, 1/1.
_____. Giardini screw-bows.
    (28 Aug 79) 2/2; (1 Sep 79) 2/4.
_____. Bridges.
    (4 Oct 77) 4/2; (25 Oct 77) 4/4; (18 Jul 78) 4/4; (22 Jul 78) 1/3;
    (28 Aug 79) 2/2; (1 Sep 79) 2/4; (23 Dec 80) 2/4; (30 Dec 80) 3/3.
_____. Cases. A beautiful and great variety.
    (28 Aug 79) 2/2; (1 Sep 79) 2/4.

_____. Cases.
    (14 Oct 73) 1/4; (11 Nov 73) Supplement 1/1; (4 Oct 77) 4/2; (25 Oct 77) 4/4.

_____. Mutes to be sold by Benjamin Davies.
    (2 Sep 74) 3/4.

_____. Mutes.
    (14 Oct 73) 1/4; (11 Nov 73) Supplement, 1/1; (4 Oct 77) 4/2; (25 Oct 77) 4/4.

_____. Peggs and bridges.
    (28 Aug 79) 2/2; (1 Sep 79) 2/4.

_____. Strings, the best Italian.
    (14 Oct 73) 1/4; (11 Nov 73) Supplement, 1/1.

_____. Strings, Italian, by the groce or dozen, to be sold by Valentine Nutter.
    (23 Dec 80) 2/4; (30 Dec 80) 3/3.

_____. Strings, to be sold by Peter Goelet.
    (20 Dec 77) 2/3.

_____. Strings and bridges, to be sold by George Deblois, sen. & jun.
    (18 Jul 78) 4/4; (22 Jul 78) 1/3.

Violin. Music, to be sold.

_____. Violin music.
    (14 Oct 73) 1/4; (11 Nov 73) Supplement, 1/1.

_____. Violin music, to be sold by Valentine Nutter.
    (23 Dec 80) 2/4; (30 Dec 80) 3/3.

Violin music. *SEE ALSO* ALEXANDER, B; ASPELMAYER, Franz; AVOLIO, J.; BACH, Carl Philipp Emanuel; BACH, Johann Christian; BATES, William; BLANC; BOCCHERINI, Luigi; CAMPIONI, Carlo Antonio; CAPPELLETTI, Anthonio; CIRRI, Giovanni Battista; Country dances; DAVIS, Thomas; *Essex Orpheus*; FISCHER, Johann Christian; FISHER, John Abraham; FLORIO, Pietro Grassi; GALEOTTI, Salvatore *or* Stefano; GARTH, John; GEMINIANI, Francesco; GERARD, James; GIARDINI, Felice; GIORDANI, Tommaso; GRASSI, Florio; GRONEMAN, Johann Albert; GUERINI, Francesco; HASSE, Johann Adolph; HOLYOAK; HUMBLE, Maximilian; JUST, Johann August; KAMMEL, Anton; KERNTL, C.F.; KLOEFFLER, Johann Friedrich; LIDARTI, Christiano Giuseppe; MALDERE, Pierre van; MANCINELLI, Domenico; MILLER, Edward; Minuets; NARDINI, Pietro; NOFERI, Giovanni Battista; NOTTORNE; NUSSEN, Frederick; PESCH, Carl August; PLA, José; RAMBACH, F. Xaver Max; REINARDS, William; RODIL, Antonio; SABBATINI, Luigi Antonio; SAMMARTINI, Giovanni Battista; SCHWINDL, Friedrich; SIRMEN, Maddalena Laura; STAMITZ, Carl Philipp *or* Johann Wenzel Anton; TACET, Joseph; TARTINI, Giuseppe; THUMOTH, Burk; VENTO, Mattia; WENDLING, Johann Baptist.

Violin solo, to be played in the theatre.
    (9 July 83) 3/4.

Violin. Teachers.

_____. Violin, to be taught by Martin Foy.
    (18 Sep 79) 3/3; (25 Sep 79) 3/4; (2 Oct 79) 2/2; (6 Oct 79) 4/4.
_____. Violin, taught by William Charles Hulett.
    (12 Jan 75) 3/4; (19 Jan 75) 4/2.
_____. Violin, taught by Harman Zedtwitz.
    (29 Apr 73) 3/3; (6 May 73) 4/3; (13 May 73) 4/3.

Violin. Tutors, to be sold.

_____. Violin tutors.
    (14 Oct 73) 1/4; (11 Nov 73) Supplement, 1/1; (21 Jul 75) 3/4; (25
    Jul 78) 3/1; (7 Jun 83) 3/3; (11-14 Jun 83) 1/1.
_____. The pocket companion for the violin.
    (19 Aug 78) 2/3; (12 Sep 78) 1/1.
_____. New instructions for the violin.
    (19 Aug 78) 2/3; (12 Sep 78) 1/1.
_____. A pocket book for the violin.
    (7 Aug 79) Supplement, 1/2; (11 Aug 79) 4/3.
_____. New instruction for playing on the violin.
    (8 Sep 79) 2/4; (2 Oct 79) 2/3; (9 Oct 79) 3/4.

Violin tutors. *SEE ALSO* GEMINIANI, Francesco.

Violin. *SEE ALSO* Fiddle.

Violin, tenor. Instruments, to be sold.

_____. Violins, Tenor.
    (28 Aug 79) 2/2; (1 Sep 79) 2/4; (23 Dec 80) 3/4; (27 Dec 80 - 3
    Jan 81) 4/3; (6 Jan 81) 2/2.

Violin, tenor. Accessories, to be sold.

_____. Bows, Giardini's screw.
    (28 Aug 79) 2/2; (1 Sep 79) 2/4.
_____. Bridges.
    (28 Aug 79) 2/2; (1 Sep 79) 2/4.
_____. Peggs.
    (28 Aug 79) 2/2; (1 Sep 79) 2/4.
_____. Sets of strings.
    (23 Dec 80) 3/4; (27 Dec 80 - 3 Jan 81) 4/3; (6 Jan 81) 2/2.

Violin, tenor. *SEE ALSO* Fiddle, tenor.

Violoncello. Instruments, to be sold.

_____. Violoncellos (some with spare bows).
    (10 Jun 73) 3/2; (17 Jun 73) 4/2; (14 Oct 73) 1/4; (11 Nov 73)
    Supplement, 1/1; (22 Nov 77) 1/3-4; (25 Jul 78) 3/1; (23 Dec 78)

3/4; (26 Dec 78) 3/4; (30 Dec 78 - 9 Jan 79) 1/1; (3 May 80)
3/3-4; (27 May 80) 3/3; (17 Jun 80) 4/2; (8 Jul 80) 3/4; (7 Jun 83)
3/3; (11-14 Jun 83) 1/1.

_____. Violoncellos or bass viols.
(9 Feb 75) 2/4.

Violoncello.   Accessories, to be sold.

_____. Bridges.
(28 Aug 79) 2/2; (1 Sep 79) 2/4; (29 Sep 79) 2/3; (2-9 Oct 79)
3/4;, (13 Oct 79) Supplement, 1/1; (3 Nov 79) Supplement, 2/1;
(10-17 Nov 79) 4/4; (20-24 Nov 79) 1/4.

_____. Peggs.
(28 Aug 79) 2/2; (1 Sep 79) 2/4.

_____. Strings.
(30 Sept 73) 3/4. (7 Oct 73) 4/3; (14 Oct 73) Supplement, 1/3; (14
Oct 73) 1/4; (11 Nov 73) Supplement 1/1; (21 Apr 74) 3/4; (5 May
74) 3/2; (9 Feb 75) 2/4; (4 Oct 77) 4/2; (25 Oct 77) 4/4; (22 Nov
77) 1/3-4. (29 Se 79) 2/3; (2-9 Oct 79) 3/4; (13 Oct 79)
Supplement, 1/1; (3 Nov 79) Supplement, 2/1; (10-17 Nov 79) 4/4;
(20-24 Nov 79) 1/4; (3 May 80) 3/3-4; (27 May 80) 3/3; (17 Jun
80) 4/2; (8 Jul 80) 3/4; (22 Dec 80) 3/4; (27 Dec 80 - 3 Jan 81)
4/3; (6 Jan 81) 2/2.

_____. Sets of strings.
(28 Aug 79) 2/2; (1 Sep 79) 2/4.

Violoncello.   For rent.

_____. Violoncello, to be hired for public and private concerts, assemblies.
(29 Dec 77) 4/1; (6-20 Dec 77) 4/2.

Violoncello.   Music, to be sold.

_____. Violoncello.   Works for.
(28 Aug 79) 2/2; (1 Sep 79) 2/4.

Violoncello music.   *SEE ALSO* AGAZZI, Gaetano;   BISCHOFF, I.C.;
BOCCHERINI, Luigi;   CIRRI, Giovanni Battista;   GIORDANI,
Tommaso.

Violoncello.   Tutors, to be sold.

_____. Violoncello tutors or instructors.
(4 Oct 77) 4/2; (25 Oct 77) 4/4.

Viols, bass.   *SEE* Violoncello.

Vocal music.   To be sold.

_____. Catches, glees . . . with a million of single songs, the words set to
musick for the flute, fiddle, guittar, harpsichord, &c.

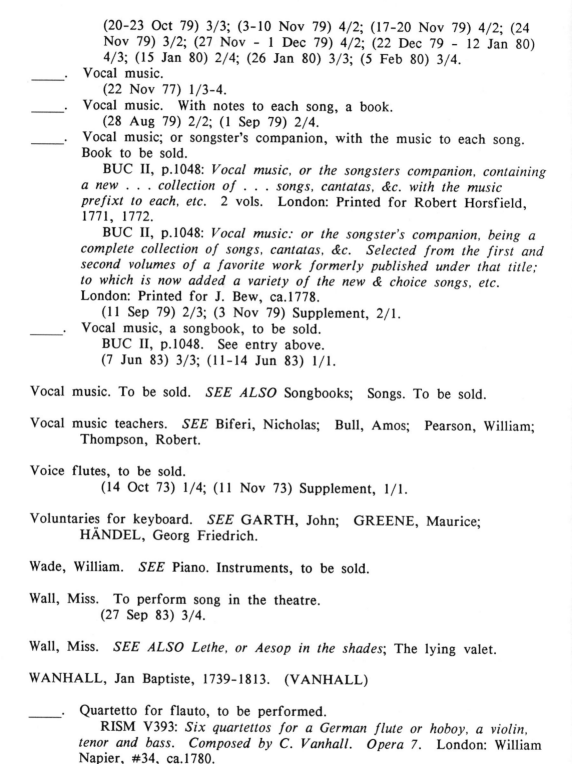

(20-23 Oct 79) 3/3; (3-10 Nov 79) 4/2; (17-20 Nov 79) 4/2; (24 Nov 79) 3/2; (27 Nov - 1 Dec 79) 4/2; (22 Dec 79 - 12 Jan 80) 4/3; (15 Jan 80) 2/4; (26 Jan 80) 3/3; (5 Feb 80) 3/4.

_____. Vocal music.
(22 Nov 77) 1/3-4.

_____. Vocal music. With notes to each song, a book.
(28 Aug 79) 2/2; (1 Sep 79) 2/4.

_____. Vocal music; or songster's companion, with the music to each song. Book to be sold.
BUC II, p.1048: *Vocal music, or the songsters companion, containing a new . . . collection of . . . songs, cantatas, &c. with the music prefixt to each, etc.* 2 vols. London: Printed for Robert Horsfield, 1771, 1772.
BUC II, p.1048: *Vocal music: or the songster's companion, being a complete collection of songs, cantatas, &c. Selected from the first and second volumes of a favorite work formerly published under that title; to which is now added a variety of the new & choice songs, etc.* London: Printed for J. Bew, ca.1778.
(11 Sep 79) 2/3; (3 Nov 79) Supplement, 2/1.

_____. Vocal music, a songbook, to be sold.
BUC II, p.1048. See entry above.
(7 Jun 83) 3/3; (11-14 Jun 83) 1/1.

Vocal music. To be sold. *SEE ALSO* Songbooks; Songs. To be sold.

Vocal music teachers. *SEE* Biferi, Nicholas; Bull, Amos; Pearson, William; Thompson, Robert.

Voice flutes, to be sold.
(14 Oct 73) 1/4; (11 Nov 73) Supplement, 1/1.

Voluntaries for keyboard. *SEE* GARTH, John; GREENE, Maurice; HÄNDEL, Georg Friedrich.

Wade, William. *SEE* Piano. Instruments, to be sold.

Wall, Miss. To perform song in the theatre.
(27 Sep 83) 3/4.

Wall, Miss. *SEE ALSO Lethe, or Aesop in the shades*; The lying valet.

WANHALL, Jan Baptiste, 1739-1813. (VANHALL)

_____. Quartetto for flauto, to be performed.
RISM V393: *Six quartettos for a German flute or hoboy, a violin, tenor and bass. Composed by C. Vanhall. Opera 7.* London: William Napier, #34, ca.1780.
(27 Apr 82) 3/3.
For fuller reference, *SEE* Concert (27 Apr 82).

The Wapping landlady; or, Jack in distress. SEE Pantomime dance.

WARREN, Edmund Thomas, ca.1730-1794.

_____. Works by, to be sold.
(28 Aug 79) 2/2; (1 Sep 79) 2/4.

The watry god. *SEE* "As bending o'er the azure tide"; "King Hancock sat in regal state."

Watts's hymns, to be sold by Valentine Nutter.
(22 Mar 80) 3/4.

The way to keep him. Misses [sic] Hallam singing a song as the character, Widow Belmore.
BUC II, p.1058: *Attend, all ye fair. A song, sung by Miss Macklin in the Way to keep him.* London, ca.1760.
(22 Apr 73) 3/2.

The way to keep him. SEE ALSO ARNE, Thomas Augustine.

The wedding ring. SEE DIBDIN, Charles.

WEIDEMAN, Charles Frederick, d.1782.

_____. Music, to be sold.
(4 Oct 77) 4/2; (25 Oct 77) 4/4.

WEISS, Carl, ca.1735-1795.

_____. Works by, to be sold.
(28 Aug 79) 2/2; (1 Sep 79) 2/4.
_____. Trios, to be sold.
RISM W611: *Six trios for a German flute a violin & violoncello, etc.* London: Welcker, 1772.
(20-23 Oct 79) 3/3; (3-10 Nov 79) 4/2; (17-20 Nov 79) 4/2; (24 Nov 79) 3/2; (27 Nov - 1 Dec 79) 4/2; (22 Dec 79 - 12 Jan 80) 4/3; (15 Jan 80) 2/4; (26 Jan 80) 3/3; (5 Feb 80) 3/4.

Welsh harp. Instruments, to be sold.

_____. The Welsh harp, discoursing most exquisite harmony, to be sold.
(28 Aug 79) 2/2; (1 Sep 79) 2/4.
_____. Welsh harp, a very fine.
(29 Sep 79) 2/3; (2-9 Oct 79) 3/4; (13 Oct 79) Supplement, 1/1; (3 Nov 79) Supplement, 2/1; (10-17 Nov 79) 4/4; (20-24 Nov 79) 1/4.
_____. Welsh harps.
(23 Dec 80) 3/4; (27 Dec 80 - 3 Jan 81) 4/3; (6 Jan 81) 2/2.

Welsh harp. *SEE ALSO* Harp.

WENDLING, Johann Baptist, 1723-1797.

_____. Six sonatas for violin and German flute, Opera 1, to be sold.
RISM W753: *Six sonatas for two German flutes or violins, with a thoro' bass . . . Opera prima.* London: Longman, Lukey & Co., ca.1775.
(22 Nov 77) 1/3-4.

_____. Sonatas for two German flutes or violins, Opera Prima, to be sold.
RISM W753: See entry above.
(20-23 Oct 79) 3/3; (3-10 Nov 79) 4/2; (17-20 Nov 79) 4/2; (24 Nov 79) 3/2; (27 Nov - 1 Dec 79) 4/2; (22 Dec 79 - 12 Jan 80) 4/3; (15 Jan 80) 2/4; (26 Jan 80) 3/3; (5 Feb 80) 3/4.

"We've shewn them full oft' of what stuff we are made." *SEE* A medley for the light infantry.

"What a hubbub is here, my dear father, of late." Song lyric printed.
(4 Aug 74) 4/1.

"What did my phlogy, my phlogy." Doctor Lucas. To the tune of Hey! my kitten, my kitten. Song lyric printed.
(17 Feb 74) 1/1.

"What though last year be past and gone." To the tune 'Tis not yet day.
Song lyric printed.
(2 Jan 79) 3/1.

"When ancient Rome, the empress of the world." Song lyric printed.
(12 Feb 83) 2/4.

"When at first this land I prest." Song lyric printed.
(12 Feb 80) 2/1.

"When Britain, by divine command." To the tune of Rule Britannia. Song lyric printed.
(1 Jan 80) 3/3.

"When Britain on her sea-girt shore." *SEE* ARNE, Thomas Augustine.

"When faction, in league with the treacherous Gaul." To the tune of Nottingham ale. Song lyric printed.
(16 Feb 80) 3/2; (16 Sep 80) 3/3-4.

"When Hawke, the British Neptune, reign'd." Song lyric printed.
(12 Feb 83) 2/4.

"When rival nations first descried." To the tune of Rule Britannia. Song lyric printed.
(11 Mar 80) 3/2-3.

"When royal George rul'd o'er this land." To the tune of The Vicar of
    Bray. Song lyric printed.
        (30 Jun 79) 3/3.

"Which of my sons, proclaim'd war's god." Song lyric printed.
        (12 Feb 83) 2/4.

"Whilst all with duteous zeal contend." Song lyric printed.
        (7 Apr 74) 2/2.

Whistling. Advertised as skill of runaway slave named Jess.
        (8 Nov 83) 3/4.

Whiston and Ditton. *SEE* HOPKINSON, Francis. "Strain hard! Strain hard!"

White Conduit House.

_____. "Ranelagh Gardens, formerly called the White Conduit House, is now
    opened, in the most superb and elegant taste, by John M'Kenzie . . . a
    band of music to attend every Saturday evening . . . ."
        (19 Jul 80) 3/3.
_____. A concert of musick to be performed on Sept. 10, 1780.
        (9 Sep 80) 2/4.
_____. "This evening will be a band of music for the entertainment of the
    ladies and gentlemen who are pleased to favour the subscriber with
    their company. The best attendance will be given by their humble
    servant, John M'Kenzie."
        (16 Sep 80) 2/4.

"Who dares--tho' ev'n of patriot name." Song lyric printed.
        (2 Nov 82) 3/1.

Wilkes's wriggle. *SEE* "On Calvert's plains new faction reigns."

WILLIAMS, Aaron, 1731-1776.

_____. Williams and Tansurs psalmody. "Which at present bear the bell
    amongst the accomplished and most melodious chanters of our Israel,
    are to be had of James Rivington." To be sold.
      BUC I, p.26: *The American harmony: or, royal melody complete in
    two volumes*. Newbury-port: Daniel Bayley, 1771.
        (21 Apr 74) 3/2.

The witches. *SEE* VERNON, Joseph.

"With flames they threaten to destroy." Song lyric printed.
        (9 Feb 80) 2/1.

The wooden walls of England. *SEE* ARNE, Thomas Augustine. "When Britain
    on her sea-girt shore."

Wools, Mr. [Stephen Wools?, d.1799] (Woolls)

_____. Singing in the theatre.
  (22 Apr 73) 3/2; (8 Jul 73) 3/1; (22 Jul 73) 3/2.
_____. Singing a Mason's anthem at the end of a farce.
  (17 Jun 73) 3/3.

Wools, Mr. *SEE ALSO The Earl of Essex*; The entered apprentice's song.

"The world can bear witness, that nothing cou'd ruffle." Song lyric printed.
  (1 Jan 80) 2/3.

Would you have a young virgin of fifteen years. *SEE* "Would you know what a whig is, and always was."

"Would you know what a whig is, and always was." To the tune of Would you have a young virgin of fifteen years. Song lyric printed.
  (26 Jan 75) 2/3.

Yankee Doodle. *SEE* "From Lewis, Monsieur Gerard came"; "It was on Mr. Peroy's land."

Yankee Doodle's expedition to Rhode-Island. *SEE* "From Lewis, Monsieur Gerard came."

"Ye Devonshire lads, and ye lasses." Song lyric printed.
  (15 Jan 80) 2/3.

"Your boy, my good master, is happy to find." Song lyric printed.
  (2 Jan 79) 3/3.

ZAPPA, Francesco, fl.1763-1788.

_____. Trios Op. 4, to be sold.
  RISM Z87: *Six trios à deux violons avec la basse . . . Oeuvre IV.*
 London: Welcker, ca.1770.
  (20-23 Oct 79) 3/3; (3-10 Nov 79) 4/2; (17-20 Nov 79) 4/2; (24 Nov 79) 3/2; (27 Nov - 1 Dec 79) 4/2; (22 Dec 79 - 12 Jan 80) 4/3; (15 Jan 80) 2/4; (26 Jan 80) 3/3; (5 Feb 80) 3/4.

ZAPPER.

_____. Works by, to be sold.
  (28 Aug 79) 2/2; (1 Sep 79) 2/4.

Zara. Between the play and interlude will be a song.
  (22 Mar 80) 2/4; (25 Mar 80) 3/3.

Zedtwitz, Harman.

_____. Teacher of the violin; pupil "of several of the most eminent masters now in London and Germany."
   (29 Apr 73) 3/3; (6 May 73) 4/3; (13 May 73) 4/3.
_____. Advertisement for concert of vocal and instrumental music for the benefit of Mr. Zedtwitz. Mr. Zedtwitz, first violin and conductor.
   (6 May 73) 3/3.
   For fuller reference, *SEE* Concert (6 May 73).
_____. Selling tickets for concert and ball, Jan. 4, 1774.
   (23 Dec 73) 3/4; (30 Dec 73) 4/1.
_____. Involved in public concert to be held on April 28.
   (14 Apr 74) 3/3; (21 Apr 74) 3/2; (28 Apr 74) 2/2.
   For fuller reference, *SEE* Concert (14 Apr 74).
_____. To perform in concert April 4.
   (30 Mar 75) 2/3.

BIBLIOGRAPHY

Anderson, Gillian B. "Eighteenth-century evaluations of William Billings: A reappraisal." *Quarterly journal of the Library of Congress* 35/1 (January 1978): 48-58.

_____. *Freedom's voice in poetry and song.* Part I: *An inventory of political and patriotic lyrics in colonial American newspapers, 1773-1783*; Part II: *Songbook.* Wilmington, DE: Scholarly Resources, 1977.

_____. "'The Temple of Minerva' and Francis Hopkinson: A reappraisal of America's first poet-composer." *Proceedings of the American Philosophical Society* 120/3 (June 1976): 166-77.

Boorstin, Daniel J. *The Americans: The colonial experience.* New York: Random House, 1958.

Crary, Catherine Snell. "The Tory and the spy: The double life of James Rivington." *William and Mary Quarterly*, 3rd series, 16 (January 1959): 61-72.

Cripe, Helen. *Thomas Jefferson and music.* Charlottesville: University Press of Virginia, 1974.

Gottesman, Rita Sussman. *The arts and crafts in New York, 1726-1799.* 2 vols. New York: New York Historical Society, 1938, 1954.

Hewlett, Leroy. "James Rivington: Loyalist printer, publisher, and bookseller of the American Revolution, 1724-1802." PhD dissertation, University of Michigan, 1958.

Hopkinson, Francis. *America Independent, or, The Temple of Minerva.* Ed. by Gillian B. Anderson. Washington, DC: C.T. Wagner, 1977

Jones, Howard Mumford. *O strange new world: American culture, the formative years.* New York: Viking Press, 1964.

Johnson, David. *Music and society in lowland Scotland in the eighteenth century.* London: Oxford University Press, 1972.

Longman and Broderip. *Catalogue of music.* London, 1779?. DLC call number ML145.L75 1779.

Longman, J. and Co. *Catalogue of vocal and instrumental music, printed and sold by J. Longman & Co.* London, 1769. DLC call number ML145.A2L.

Longman, Lukey and Co. *No. 26 Cheapside, London. Music . . . The following new music may be had at the above place, and at most music and book sellers throughout England, Scotland, Ireland and America.* London [1772]. DLC call number ML145.A2L76.

Marcuse, Sibyl. *Musical instruments: A comprehensive dictionary.* New York: W.W. Norton & Co., 1975.

Messiter, Arthur H. *A history of the choir and music of Trinity Church, New York, from its organization to the year 1897.* New York: Edwin S. Gorham, 1906.

Oleson, Alesandra, *et al. The pursuit of knowledge in the early American Republic: American scientific and learned societies from the colonial times to the Civil War.* Baltimore: Johns Hopkins University Press, 1976.

Peyser, Ethel. *The house that music built: Carnegie Hall.* New York: Robert M. McBride & Co., 1936.

Philadelphia, PA. University of Pennsylvania. [Typescript of Inventory of Francis Hopkinson's music library presented to the University of Pennsylvania by Edward Hopkinson, Jr., on 27 December 1948.]

Raddin, George G., Jr. "The music of New York City, 1797-1804." *The New York Historical Society quarterly* 38/4 (October 1954): 478-99.

Randall, Elizabeth. *A catalogue of vocal and instrumental music, printed for and sold by Elizabeth Randall.* London [1782?]. DLC call number ML145.A2R25.

Redway, Virginia Larkin. *Music directory of early New York City.* New York: New York Public Library, 1941.

Rivington, James. *Rivington's New York gazette.* New York: James Rivington, 1773-1783. [The five titles listed immediately below are available in microform from the Readex Microprint Corporation in its series *Early American newspapers*, and are found in most major libraries.]

> *Rivington's New-York gazetteer; or The Connecticut, New-Jersey, Hudson's-River, and Quebec weekly advertiser.* No. 1 (22 April 1773)-- No. 136 (23 November 1775).
>
> *Rivington's New-York gazette; or The Connecticut, Hudson's River, New-Jersey, and Quebec weekly advertiser.* No. 137 (4 October 1777)-- No. 138 (11 October 1777).
>
> *Rivington's New-York loyal gazette.* No. 139 (18 October 1777)--No. 146 (6 December 1777).
>
> *Royal gazette.* No. 147 (13 December 1777)--No. 746 (19 November 1783).
>
> *Rivington's New-York gazette, and universal advertiser.* No. 747 (22 November 1783)--No. 758 (31 December 1783).

Sadie, Stanley. "Concert life in eighteenth-century England." *Proceedings of the Royal Musical Association* 85 (1958-59): 17-30.

Saloman, Ora Frishberg. "Victor Pelissier, composer in federal New York and Philadelphia." *Pennsylvania magazine of history and biography* 102 (1978): 93-102.

Scott, Kenneth. *Rivington's New York newspaper: Excerpts from a Loyalist press, 1773-1783.* New York: New York Historical Society, 1973.

Shanet, Howard. *Philharmonic: A history of New York's orchestra.* New York: Doubleday & Co., 1975.

Silverman, Kenneth. *A cultural history of the American Revolution: Painting, music, literature, and the theatre in the colonies and the United States from the Treaty of Paris to the inauguration of George Washington, 1763-1789.* New York: Thomas Y. Crowell Co., 1976.

Smith, Henry Nash. *Virgin land: The American West as symbol and myth.* New York: Vintage Books, 1950.

Sonneck, Oscar. *Early concert life in America, 1731-1800.* Leipzig: Breitkopf & Härtel, 1907.

Taylor, George Rogers. *The Turner Thesis concerning the role of the frontier in American history.* Rev. ed. Boston: D.C. Heath and Co., 1956.

Temperley, Nicholas and Charles Manns. *Fuging tunes in the eighteenth century.* Detroit studies in music bibliography, 49. Detroit: Information Coordinators, 1983.

Thompson, Samuel, Ann, and Peter. *A catalogue of music, printed and sold by Samuel, Ann, and Peter Thompson.* London [1781]. DLC call number ML145.A2T46.

_____. *A catalogue of music, printed and sold by Samuel, Ann, and Peter Thompson.* London, n.d. DLC call number ML145.A2T462.

Tilmouth, Michael. "The beginning of provincial concert life." *Music in eighteenth-century England: Essays in memory of Charles Cudworth.* Ed. by Christopher Hogwood and Richard Luckett. Cambridge: Cambridge University Press, 1983. pp.1-17.

Walsh, T.J. *Opera in Dublin, 1705-1797: The social scene.* Dublin: Allen Figgis, 1973.

Webster's third new international dictionary of the English language unabridged. Springfield, MA: G.&C. Merriam Co., 1961.

Welcker, John. *A catalogue of vocal & instrumental music.* London, n.d. DLC call number ML145.A2W45

Welcker, Peter. *A catalogue of vocal & instrumental music.* London [1772?]. DLC call number ML145.A2W4.

Winthrop, John. "A model of Christian charity." *The American Puritans: Their prose and poetry.* Ed. by Perry Miller. Garden City, NY: Doubleday Anchor Books, 1956. pp.78-84.